New Light on
the Earliest Gospel

SEVEN MARKAN STUDIES

New Light on the Earliest Gospel

SEVEN MARKAN STUDIES

By T. A. Burkill

CORNELL UNIVERSITY PRESS
ITHACA AND LONDON

International Standard Book Number 0-8014-0706-0
Library of Congress Catalog Card Number 74-37777

PRINTED IN THE UNITED STATES OF AMERICA
BY KINGSPORT PRESS, INC.

*Libraians: Library of Congress cataloging information
appears on the last page of the book.*

for

BELLA CARISSIMA

Preface

In *Mysterious Revelation* I aimed at elucidating the doctrinal position of the person responsible for the redaction of the gospel attributed to St. Mark, and it is my hope that in the present volume I may have succeeded in shedding further light on the evangelist's way of thinking. While I am not unaware that since 1963, when the earlier book was published, the two-document solution of the synoptic problem has been, and is still being, called into question in some quarters (see Chapter 4, below, note 6), I still maintain that St. Mark is the earliest of the four canonical gospels, written (perhaps at Rome) soon after the fall of Jerusalem in A.D. 70.

Although most of the material collected in the book is now published for the first time, four of the studies have appeared elsewhere, and for permission to reproduce them in modified form I am indebted to the editors and publishers of various books and periodicals: *Die Zeitschrift für die neutestamentliche Wissenschaft*, ed. W. Eltester (W. de Gruyter & Co., Berlin), LII (1961), 189–213, for Chapter 1; LVII (1966), 23–37, for Chapter 4; *The Classical Tradition: Literary and Historical Studies in Honor of Harry Caplan*, ed. L. Wallach (Cornell University Press, Ithaca, N.Y., 1966), pp. 329–344, for Chapter 3; *Novum Testamentum*, eds. W. C. van Unnik, J. W. Doeve, A. F. J. Klijn (E. J. Brill, Leiden), IX (1967), 161–177, and *Studia Evangelica*, IV, ed. F. L. Cross (Akademie-Verlag, Berlin, 1968), 166–170, for Chapter 5. I have also to thank The Abingdon Press, Nashville, Tennessee, for allowing me, in Chapter 6, to make use of my contribution "Ecclesiasticus" to *The Interpreter's Dictionary of the Bible*, II (1962), 13ff.

T. A. B.

University of Rhodesia
Salisbury, Rhodesia
March 1972

Contents

Abbreviations

Ev.T.	*Evangelische Theologie.*
H.J.	*Hibbert Journal.*
H.T.R.	*Harvard Theological Review.*
J.B.L.	*Journal of Biblical Literature.*
J.T.S.	*Journal of Theological Studies.*
M.R.	*Mysterious Revelation: An Examination of the Philosophy of St. Mark's Gospel* (Ithaca, N.Y., 1963), by T. A. Burkill.
Nov.T.	*Novum Testamentum.*
N.T.S.	*New Testament Studies.*
R.H.R.	*Revue de l'histoire des religions.*
R.Q.	*Revue de Qumran.*
S.-B.	H. L. Strack and P. Billerbeck, *Kommentar zum Neuen Testament aus Talmud und Midrasch,* 6 vols. (Munich, 1922–61).
S.T.	*Studia Theologica.*
T.L.Z.	*Theologische Literaturzeitung.*
T.W.N.T.	*Theologisches Wörterbuch zum Neuen Testament.*
T.Z.	*Theologische Zeitschrift.*
Vig.C.	*Vigiliae Christianae.*
V.T.	*Vetus Testamentum.*
Z.N.T.W.	*Zeitschrift für die neutestamentliche Wissenschaft.*
Z.T.K.	*Zeitschrift für Theologie und Kirche.*

New Light on
the Earliest Gospel

SEVEN MARKAN STUDIES

The Hidden Son of Man
in St. Mark's Gospel

This chapter is divided into three sections and attempts: (1) to outline the evangelist's doctrine regarding the messianic secret; (2) to identify secrecy motifs in the pre-Markan traditions; (3) to detect what may lie behind the traditions in the teaching of Jesus himself, by way of a critique of Erik Sjöberg's significant work *Der verborgene Menschensohn in den Evangelien*.

1. Markan Doctrine. St. Mark's thought is informed and sustained by a theology of salvation and the treatment of his subject—a religious one, the Messiahship or Christhood[1] of Jesus, the content of the apostolic gospel—would seem to resolve itself into the exposition of two central themes, namely, the secret fact of the messianic status of Jesus and the mysteri-

---

[1] Perhaps the term "Christhood" is preferable here, for, as 14:62 shows, the evangelist, doubtless following the interpretation which prevailed in the Hellenistic churches (cf. I Thess. 4:17), understood the messianic status of Jesus in terms of the transcendent eschatology of the apocalyptic Son of Man, whereas among Aramaic-speaking Palestinian Jews "Messiah" in eschatological parlance would ordinarily refer to the divinely promised King or Anointed One, destined to restore Israel's political independence in the present world. However, the term "Messiahship" has the advantage of bringing out the Jewish provenance of the church's original christology. Cf. n. 27, below.

ous meaning of that fact. Broadly, the first of these themes dominates the earlier part of the work, and the second dominates the later part. For prior to his account of Peter's confession (8:29), the evangelist is mainly concerned to represent the words and deeds of Jesus as esoteric manifestations of the secret fact of the Messiahship; and, after his account of the confession, the evangelist is mainly concerned to show how the fact of the Messiahship mysteriously meant that Jesus had to endure the shame of the crucifixion in the fulfillment of his redemptive mission in the world. It is not to be assumed, however, that the exposition of the two themes is characterized by perfect logical coherence. St. Mark was perhaps the first writer who sought to supply the church's increasing need for a comprehensive account of the career of Jesus in terms of the apostolic faith, and, in view of the difficulty of the undertaking, it is not surprising to find that the various parts of his gospel hang together somewhat loosely; conflicting motives evidently compete for dominance in his mind as he writes, and this considerably weakens the formative power of his thought to weld the multifarious materials at his disposal so as to present a wholly consistent pattern of ideas.

The subject matter of the work is clearly indicated at the outset—Jesus, Messiah (1:1), subsequently identified with the unique Son of God (1:11) and the eschatological Son of Man (2:10; cf. 8:38); here comes to light the religious conviction which lay at the heart of the apostolic message of salvation. But the plain fact was that Jesus had not been received as the promised Messiah by the people among whom he had lived and worked, and so what had happened in the past was calculated to militate against the living faith of the present. A philosophical problem was thus created, a problem which the church sought to solve by maintaining that the rejection and the crucifixion of the Messiah were really provided for in God's sovereign purpose—Jesus was not welcomed as Messiah and, in the early Christian view, it was divinely intended that he should not have been so welcomed. The divine intention could be discovered in the Old Testament, the church sharing the belief that those scriptures contained the disclosed will of God, whose plan for human redemption was being worked out in the complicated happenings of history. It was in fulfillment of canonical prophecy (cf. Luke 24:25f.) and it was by the determinate counsel and foreknowledge of God (cf. Acts 2:23) that Jesus died in shame and humiliation (cf. I Cor. 15:3).

So we notice that in his passion narrative St. Mark is at pains to demonstrate that the events recounted all occurred according to the will of God, and he employs two main methods in this connection.[2] In the first place, the scriptures are appealed to,[3] and this is done in various ways; thus in 14:27 there is a (not quite accurate) quotation of Zech. 13:7, which is ex-

---

[2] Cf. *M.R.*, 222ff.

[3] St. Mark regards the necessity of the passion as equivalent to its accordance with the scriptures; cf. Mark 8:31 where the *dei* ("must") corresponds to the *gegraptai* ("it is written") in Mark 9:12. It is not impossible that the scriptures were sometimes appealed to in a general way before a definite passage could be adduced. Perhaps, too, in certain scriptural passages, such as Pss. 22; 31; 69; Isa. 53, the passion was found depicted in advance; and if, as seems likely, passages of this kind were frequently read in early Christian circles, some of the motifs present there may have found their way into the passion narrative in the process of its formation at the hands of the tradents. But creative influence operated in the opposite direction, at least in one case: the *titulus* on the cross (Mark 15:26) prompted Christians to alter the wording of Ps. 96:10 (LXX 95:10); cf. P. Winter, *On the Trial of Jesus* (Berlin, 1961), pp. 108f.

pressly introduced as a scriptural citation; in 15:34 the opening words of the twenty-second psalm are ascribed to Jesus,
but without any explicit reference to the fact that they are
scriptural; in 14:21 there is a general appeal to the scriptures,
but no particular passage is adduced; and in 14:61a (cf.
15:5a), although scripture is neither quoted nor mentioned,
the motif is reminiscent of Isa. 53:7. In the second place, the
precise foreknowledge of Jesus is stressed; thus in 14:8 he
speaks of his coming burial; in 14:18 he predicts that one of
the twelve will betray him; and in 14:27-31 he announces
that all his disciples will be caused to stumble, that he will
proceed into Galilee after his resurrection and that Peter will
disown him three times before the cock crows twice. Such
foreknowledge does not merely illustrate Jesus' powers of
supernatural prognostication; it also suggests that his earthly
destiny has been determined in advance as a provision of a
presiding purpose.[4]

All this goes to show that it was a matter of special urgency
to demonstrate that the passion was a fulfillment of the divine
will; the doctrine of the crucified Messiah was a stumbling
block to Jews and foolishness to Gentiles (cf. I Cor. 1:23).
Men asked how the shamefulness of the betrayal, the disgrace
of the rejection and the horror of the crucifixion could be
compatible with the transcendent dignity of the heavenly
Son of Man; and the exponents of the apostolic faith replied
by maintaining that a right appreciation of the prophecies of
the Old Testament made clear that Jesus' ignominious death
was an integral part of his divine mission for man's redemp-

---

[4] Cf. the predictions in Mark 8:31; 9:31; 10:33f. On the other hand,
according to Mark 13:32, Jesus does not know the exact hour of the
parousia; this limitation to his represented prescience would serve to
give point to the ethical demand for vigilance (Mark 13:33-37).

tion. No doubt those to whom post-resurrection christophanies had actually been vouchsafed would feel that their personal experience of the risen Lord was in itself a sufficient guarantee of the validity of their belief in the Messiahship of Jesus; but as soon as they sought to justify the mode of interpretation which they gave to their religious experience, they would naturally resort to the scriptures in which, as was assumed, God's purpose was made known to his servants of old.[5]

But of course St. Mark holds that the whole career of Jesus, and not merely its shameful end, was worked out according to the revealed will of God, and here we may observe that the opening words of his gospel are immediately followed by a citation of biblical prophecies (1:2f.). Thus the reader is at once presented with a clue to the evangelist's orientation. Jesus had not been received as the Messiah by the people, and it was divinely intended that he should not have been so received. Hence the proof from prophecy, and hence further the representation of Jesus as a clairvoyant and as a thaumaturge and teacher who deliberately conceals the truth from the public by enjoining the demons to silence (1:34; 3:11f.) and by addressing the multitude in the cryptology of parables (4:11f.). St. Mark's conception of the hidden Son of Man is thus a form of divine predestinarianism no less than the notion that Jesus fulfilled scriptural prophecies. At Caesarea Philippi, however, the messianic secret is revealed to the disciples

[5] Cf. I Cor. 15:3ff. where the appeal to scripture in verse 4 ("Christ . . . was raised on the third day in accordance with the scriptures") reinforces the direct appeal to personal experience in verse 8 ("Last of all . . . he [the risen Christ] appeared also to me"). Winter (*op. cit.*, pp. 4f.) has observed that in Luke 16:29–31 Moses and the prophets are resorted to in an attempt to weaken the criticism that the argument from the christophanies had not persuaded the people generally.

(8:27ff.). In a moment of inspiration and in the presence of his fellow disciples, Peter declares that Jesus is the Messiah. The Messiahship is therefore made known to a privileged group of human beings, and the members of the group—as was the case with the demons previously—are at once enjoined to guard the secrecy of their knowledge (8:30). Now perceiving the words and acts of their master as words and acts of the Messiah, they are in a position to receive special instruction in the deep significance of the secret. But they soon show themselves to be quite incapable of assimilating such instruction. They see and yet are blind; the essential meaning of the Messiahship—its fateful implications for the Son of Man himself and its ethical implications for all who would be his followers—is a heavenly mystery which persistently eludes their grasp (8:33; 9:10; 9:32; 9:34; 10:24; 10:37). Apparently, it is not until Jesus has been raised from the dead that they can come to understand the mysterious meaning of the secret; for St. Mark seems to have held that the resurrection meant the end of the predetermined period of service and suffering in obscurity and the beginning of the predetermined period of enlightenment in which the gospel is openly proclaimed to the world with understanding and confidence (9:9). Thus Peter's confession is of importance in the evangelist's scheme because it can serve as a basis for further instruction which, besides preparing the reader for what he takes to be a right understanding of the passion narrative as a delineation of the mysterious meaning of the Messiahship in its historical realization, enables the disciples to receive the saving truth of the gospel from the Son of Man himself. For, although they cannot understand the divine word (cf. 8:32a) when it is communicated to them, they can retain it as authentic tradition and can thus equip themselves for their future role as apostles and pillars of the expanding church.

In St. Mark's interpretation, then, the career of Jesus, despite its outward show of tragic frustration, is really a continuous fulfillment of God's revealed plan of salvation. The failure of the people generally to recognize the fact of the Messiahship and the failure of the disciples to comprehend its meaning are alike integral to the divine scheme. But it is important to observe that the two instances of failure do not come about in the same way. For while the fact of the Messiahship is concealed from the public by the injunctions to silence and by the teaching in parables, it is discovered by Peter at Caesarea Philippi, whereupon its fateful significance is expounded to the Twelve and something of its inherent glory is made manifest to the privileged few on the occasion of the transfiguration (9:2ff.). The veil is withdrawn in the presence of the elect, the nucleus of the church to be, and the heavenly voice addresses them and gives supernatural confirmation to the truth, but they cannot comprehend the essential content of the mystery laid open. The light is too unseasonal. Their spiritual sight is dim, and so it must remain until, thanks to the resurrection faith, the period of obscurity gives way to the period of enlightenment in which the mystery of the gospel can be publicly proclaimed in the wake of the parousia of the exalted Son of Man at the termination of the present cosmic order (13:26).

It would appear, therefore, that St. Mark is facing the same kind of problem as that with which St. Paul deals in Rom. 9–11, but whereas the evangelist takes the view that the public are prevented from knowing the mystery of the Kingdom through the cryptology of parabolic teaching (Mark 4:11f.) and through the injunctions to silence (Mark 3:11), the apostle argues that God actually dulls the faculties of the Jewish people. As we read in Rom. 11:5–8:

Even so at the present time also there is a remnant, elected by grace. But if it is by grace, it is no longer on the basis of works; otherwise grace would be grace no more. What then? Israel did not obtain what it sought. The elect obtained it, but the rest were hardened, as it is written:

> 'God gave them a spirit of insensibility,
> Eyes that they should not see
> And ears that they should not hear
> Down to this very day.' (Cf. Isa. 29:10; Deut. 29:4)

Thus, in spite of their differences in standpoint, both thinkers agree that the failure of men to apprehend the saving truth of the Messiahship of Jesus, or, to use Loisy's words, "l'échec de l'évangile auprès des juifs"[6] was, in the last resort, neither a freak of chance nor even a consequence of human perversity, but a provision of God's determinate counsel and inscrutable will. Indeed, in view of the disciples' complete incapacity to comprehend the inner significance of the secret vouchsafed in Mark 8:29, the evangelist could have aptly applied to them the notion of a divinely conditioned spirit of insensibility which St. Paul derives from Isa. 29:10 and applies to Israel generally. But in the case of the disciples, who correspond to the Pauline "remnant, elected by grace," the stupefying affliction from which they suffer is of relatively brief duration.

There is a reminiscence of St. Mark's mode of interpretation, specifically with regard to the function he ascribes to parabolic teaching, in John 16:25, though here the word *paroimia* ("similitude" or "figure") is used, and it is the

---

[6] See *Les évangiles synoptiques* (Paris, 1907), I, 741.

disciples, not the general public, from whom the mysterious truth is in some sense hidden. Since the concern is with the elect, the concealment cannot continue indefinitely, and we are duly informed that the Spirit of Truth is destined to lead the disciples into all the truth.[7] Thus the fourth evangelist, like his predecessors, resorts to a form of supernatural predeterminism in his endeavors to account for the inadequacy of human response to the gospel. This is further illustrated in John 12:37ff., where unbelief is explained by a citation of Isa. 6:10, the passage quoted by St. Mark in somewhat different form in 4:12:

> He [that is, God] has blinded their eyes and hardened
> their heart,
> Lest they should see with their eyes and perceive
> with their heart,
> And turn for me to heal them.

The same mode of doctrine is found in such passages as John 1:12f. and 3:3ff., where the acceptance of the saving truth in Jesus is made a consequence of a new birth in the individual, effected by the action of God's will or spirit (6:65), whose operations are no more governed by "the will of the flesh" or "the will of man" (1:13) than the movements of the wind (3:8).

In certain other passages, however, the fourth evangelist strikes a dualistic note, and the conception is variously set forth as an opposition between life and death (5:21), light and darkness (3:19), flesh and spirit (3:6), the celestial and the terrestrial (3:12), truth and evil (3:20f.). What belongs

[7] On the other hand, in St. Mark's gospel it is Jesus who offers private elucidations of the parables (4:34), although the elucidations are not understood until the period of obscurity has passed, when what is secret comes to light (4:22; 9:9).

to darkness cannot apprehend the light (1:5). The world
knew not the true light that was coming into the world (1:9–
11). It is the spirit that gives life, the flesh being of no avail
(6:63). Unlike his Jewish auditors, Jesus is not of this world
(8:23). He who walks in the darkness does not know where
he goes (12:36), and cannot receive the Spirit of Truth
(14:17). Hence the need for spiritual regeneration under
divine agency, that men of this world may be enabled to apprehend the Kingdom of God (3:3). The dualism is not an
absolute one, and yet St. John offers no explanation of the
degeneracy of the world. All things were originally created
by God through the instrumentality of the Logos (1:3,10),
but in the meantime corrupting forces, apparently representing something more than a mere tendency to lapse into
primordial chaos, have vitiated cosmic existence. Although
the true light may still enlighten every man (1:9), the con-
genital light has become so feeble that men require the divine
quickening of their faculties in the new birth to bring them
to a perception of the truth (3:3). The world is now under
the control of an evil ruler (12:31; 14:30), who has no truth
in him, and it is because "the Jews" are offspring of the devil,
the father of falsities (8:44), that they do not hear the words
of God (8:47).

Accordingly, a predeterministic doctrine, expressed in a
variety of ways, figures in the fourth gospel as it does in the
second. But whereas St. Mark basically adopts the position
that the Son of Man is hidden from the people, the fourth
evangelist's usual view is that the Messiahship is openly revealed to the world (1:14; 1:18), yet men generally, as if
blinded by the light, cannot see its transcendent glory; and so
it may be said that Jesus came into the world to give sight to
the blind and to blind those who see—as in the case of the

man born blind (9:1ff.) and as in the case of the Pharisees
who do not respond with belief (9:35ff.).

Despite his predestinarianism, however, the author of the
fourth gospel betrays no doubts regarding the reality of personal responsibility. Those who do not see the truth refuse to
do so (John 5:40), and some will rise to the resurrection of
life, others to the resurrection of judgment (5:29). Now that
Jesus has come into the world and spoken to men, those who
oppose him and his followers have no excuse for their sin
(15:22), and their hatred of him who represents God (14:9)
and the truth (14:6) has no cause other than a voluntary act
of their evil will (15:25). St. Mark, too, can shift his position
in this connection, as well as with regard to the conception
of the hiddenness of the Son of Man—two matters which,
as we shall see, are not unrelated in the evangelist's thought.
Apparently he is not completely satisfied with the doctrine
that the humiliation of the Messiah is the appointed means to
his future triumph, and he goes some way toward closing the
gap, as it were, between the notion of the Messiah's suffering
in obscurity and that of his glorious supremacy, or toward
overcoming the bipolarity of what seems to be his primary
philosophical position. So in Mark 9:2ff. the veil of the flesh
temporarily becomes translucent, and three disciples are permitted to behold their master as he really is and in the form
in which he will be made manifest to the world when he comes
again finally to establish the Kingdom of God with great
power and glory.

Thus there is a counter-tendency at work which militates
against the bipolarity of the evangelist's basic point of view, a
counter-tendency more pronounced in some passages than
in others, and in these St. Mark is tempted to overstep the
limits prescribed by his doctrine of the secret and to delineate

the incarnate life openly in terms of the apostolic faith. Hence certain passages suggest that the true nature of Jesus is reaching out for some definite form of articulate expression which it cannot yet properly receive;[8] in 11:1ff. and 14:3ff., for example, the Markan belief in the reality of the Messiahship — is apparently pressing for overt recognition, thereby putting great strain on the requirement of secrecy. And, notably, in the account of the nocturnal trial the pressure exerted by the evangelist's conviction subjects his doctrine of the secret to a strain it cannot withstand, the result being that in 14:62 there is actually a disclosure of the Son of Man outside the circle of the initiated, so that we are here presented with what is, from one point of view, the most striking example in the whole work of St. Mark's inclination to move away from the conception of the incarnate life as a period of obscurity towards the kind of philosophy discerned in the fourth gospel, where the Son of Man is not hidden and where the passion is the hour of the Messiah's glorification or exaltation (John 12:23, 32; 13:1). In the momentous declaration of Mark 14:62, however, the urge to set forth the earthly ministry directly in terms of the apostolic faith seems to be reinforced by the motive to ascribe responsibility to the Jews as represented by their leaders. For, although St. Mark holds that the passion was provided for in God's overruling purpose, he nonetheless wishes to show that the crucifixion took place through the unwarranted hostility of Jesus' own people and hence that the burden of guilt for the crime is to be borne by a nation whose divine privileges only serve to make their conduct the more reprehensible.[9] The presence of such a motive naturally

[8] Cf. *M.R.*, pp. 188ff.
[9] Cf. our paper "L'antisémitisme dans l'évangile selon Saint Marc" in *R.H.R.*, CLIV (1958), 10ff.

makes for a certain inconsistency in the evangelist's treatment of his materials. As we should expect, insofar as he is concerned to stress the culpability of the Jews he tends to contravene the requirement of secrecy by allowing what he assumes to be the true character of Jesus to come out into the light of day; consequently, Jesus does not always address the public in the cryptology of parables, as he is said to do in Mark 4:34,[10] and he does not always seek to perform his miracles in private, as he does, for instance, in Mark 5:40. On the contrary, in certain passages the Son of Man is to a greater or less extent exposed to public view, and so it could be argued that the Jewish opponents of Jesus were in an inexcusable position since they had rejected Jesus not in ignorance but with a cognizance of his real status.

Thus, although St. Mark sought to delineate the earthly life of Jesus, his whole method of treatment was radically different from what would today be normally expected of a biographer. The gospel was written for the edification of believers, not for the furtherance of the cause of historical research. This important point seems to have received its first systematic demonstration in W. Wrede's *Messiasgeheimnis in den Evangelien*,[11] a work which, together with J. Wellhausen's pregnant studies on the synoptic gospels[12] may be said to have laid the foundations of the subsequent researches of the form-critical school. Wrede maintained that the element of secrecy in the gospel follows directly from doctrinal considerations on the part of the evangelist; and he went on to argue, doubtless with excessive confidence, that those considerations ultimately derived from an endeavor to conceal

[10] Cf. *M.R.*, pp. 96ff.   [11] Göttingen, 1901.
[12] Especially *Das Evangelium Marci* (Berlin, 1903/1909) and *Einleitung in die drei ersten Evangelien* (Berlin, 1905/1911).

the circumstance that apostolic belief was a consequence of the post-resurrection christophanies: Jesus made no claim to messianic dignity, and St. Mark tried to reconcile this fact with his Christian belief by supposing that Jesus intentionally withheld the truth from the multitude. But whatever our views on this piece of speculation may be, it can scarcely be doubted that Wrede rightly insisted on the dominance of doctrinal motives in the mind of the evangelist. It may well be that the evidence used by Wrede is not all of a piece and calls for more than one type of explanation. But, as H. J. Cadbury points out,[13] Wrede by no means neglected the aspect of contradiction in the gospel, though the probability is that he over-simplified matters by referring merely to two opposite motives which failed to cross in the evangelist's mind, namely, a desire to show that the Messiahship was deliberately hidden and a natural inclination to give direct expression to his Christian conviction; other motives, some of which had come to be "submerged" (to use Cadbury's terminology) were apparently involved in several instances. In other words, the items of tradition which the evangelist chose to include in his work probably contained features which, while not identical with his own theory of the secret, were nevertheless correspondent to it, and may indeed have actually prompted the formation of his own type of predestinarianism. If it is true that St. Mark adapted the traditions to his own point of view, it is no less true that the traditions themselves were pre-adapted in a certain measure to the evangelist's mode of representation. The question of the nature and extent of such pre-adaptation may now be examined.

---

[13] See his paper "Mixed Motives in the Gospels" in *Proceedings of the American Philosophical Society*, XCV (1951), 117ff.

2. Pre-Markan Secrecy Motifs. It would appear, then, that
St. Mark's notion of the hidden Son of Man follows from a
lively belief in the operative effectiveness of the divine will in
human affairs, and the probability is that a belief of this sort,
being deeply rooted in biblical theology, was present in the
earliest strata of the gospel traditions. We have already noticed
how St. Paul cites Isa. 29:10 and Deut. 29:4 in his attempt to
interpret the rejection of Jesus, arguing that God actually
dulled the faculties of the Jewish people (Rom. 11:5–8). If
Jesus had died according to the scriptures (I Cor. 15:3), the
events leading up to the crucifixion would also have occurred
in accordance with the revealed will of God. The earliest
extant passion narrative exemplifies a concern to demonstrate
this doctrine in its frequent allusions to scripture, and there
is no need to suppose that St. Mark was responsible for these
in their entirety. The shameful events recounted were apprehended as phases in the realization of God's purpose. What
Jesus did and the consequences of his actions must have been
the outcome of an overruling plan which could be discerned
by the seeing eye and the hearing ear. Moreover, Jesus' own
will was held to be at one with God's, so that, in apostolic
teaching, his life up to his death on a cross could be construed
in terms of obedience (cf. Phil. 2:8). Jesus' decisions were
"godly" in a metaphysical and not merely in an ethical sense,
a notion evinced in those parts of the passion narrative (*e.g.*
Mark 14:18–21) where Jesus speaks as if what is to happen
to him issues from his will: he appears as the arbiter of his
fate and the determiner of his destiny, even in its most terrible
and ignominious aspects. Thus it is only a short step from
predeterministic motifs already present in the tradition to St.
Mark's representation of the hidden Son of Man. Consequences
of his activities, even unfavorable consequences, failure as well

as success, rejection as well as acceptance, are brought within the ambit of his deliberate design.

With respect to the injunctions to silence,[14] St. Mark's theory comes to clear expression in 1:34 ("And he would not permit the demons to speak because they knew him") and again in 3:12 ("And the unclean spirits whenever they beheld him used to fall down before him and would cry, saying, 'You are the Son of God.' But he would strictly enjoin them that they should not make him manifest"), passages which evidently occur in editorial sections composed by the evangelist himself. Accordingly, in the first main section of the gospel (1:14–8:26) a contrast is drawn between the supernatural knowledge of the demons and the ignorance of the people whose normal response to Jesus is merely one of bewildered amazement at his words and works (e.g. 1:27), a contrast which in some degree falls away with Peter's confession reported in 8:29. On the other hand, in 1:23ff., where the first injunction occurs, the evangelist is probably not creating new narrative, but for the most part transmitting traditional material derived from a story already in circulation. The principal elements in the passage are characteristic features of a typical exorcism story which St. Mark apparently reproduces in abbreviated form and with its introduction and conclusion adapted to the requirements of its context in the gospel. But in this case the address of the demon (1:24; cf. 5:7) and the injunction to silence (1:25) have a meaning within the framework of the story itself and quite independently of the evangelist's philosophy of the messianic secret. And an investigation of the motifs of stories of this type suggests that the injunction in its original significance would have nothing directly to do

[14] Cf. our discussion in *T.Z.*, XII (1956), 585ff., and in *M.R.*, pp. 62ff.

with the idea of concealing a mystery; the verb *phimoun* (literally "to muzzle") seems to have been commonly employed in incantations as a technical term for binding a demon and thus subduing it to the will of the exorcist. Jesus utters an authoritative word and the demon can do nothing more than make futile (if violent) agitations and force an inarticulate cry prior to taking its abrupt departure as a fugitive thief dispossessed of his spoils (cf. 9:26), thereby showing the utter ineffectiveness of its powers of defense. For a study of the parallels in similar stories (both Jewish and Hellenistic) suggests that the demon's address in Mark 1:24 would be originally intended as an instrument of apotropaic power. The unclean spirit sensing the menace of impending disaster raises its voice to defend itself against its opponent by resorting to an apotropaic formula with scriptural allusions. The demon knows the divine status of Jesus, and by giving full expression to its knowledge it seeks to ward off the threatened offensive of its dangerous opponent. In St. Mark's interpretation, however, the formula becomes a confession or mode of supernatural witness to the Messiahship, to be compared with the pronouncements of the heavenly voice at the baptism (1:11) and at the transfiguration (9:7), while the formula for binding the demon (1:25) becomes a command to secrecy for the purpose of preventing the publication of the hidden truth concerning Jesus.

Besides the injunctions to silence imposed upon the demons, there are in the first main section of the gospel four passages, namely, Mark 1:44; 5:43; 7:36; 8:26, where human beings are enjoined to keep silence, in each instance concerning a miracle which Jesus has performed. The injunctions in 5:43; 7:36 and 8:26 are to be distinguished from the secrecy which belongs to the miraculous processes described in the stories to

which the injunctions are attached. This latter feature may
well have been present in the three stories as St. Mark received
them, for the same motif is exemplified in popular wonder
stories of widely separated cultures, and would be due to a
feeling that divine action should be concealed from the profane eyes of the public. On the other hand, in each of the three
instances the almost stereotyped injunction to silence may not
have constituted an original part of the story (which has already reached a satisfactory conclusion in the demonstration
of the success of the miracle) and could be a supplementary
conclusion appended by the evangelist himself. The injunction is disobeyed in 7:36 so that the miraculous deeds of Jesus
are proclaimed, seemingly against his will. One might compare Mark 1:45 (if the first word of the verse refers to the
patient), 5:20[15] and, particularly, 7:24 ("And he went into a
house and desired no one to know it, and he could not be
concealed"). The meaning intended is scarcely that Jesus was
actually frustrated, but rather that his real nature was such
that he could not escape winning a great reputation as a
performer of miraculous works. Though it is not reported
that the injunctions of 5:43 and 8:26 were disobeyed, it
would have been impossible to carry them out, for the little
girl and the blind man could hardly have spent the rest of
their days in hiding. But St. Mark does not consider the matter
in this aspect, any more than he considers the difficulty which,
from a historical or biographical point of view, is raised by
the audibility of the demon's address in 1:24. In the evangelist's interpretation, the deeds of Jesus are not the deeds of an
ordinary thaumaturge but of the Messiah himself; and since
the miracles were not construed in this sense by the general

[15] Cf. our note "Concerning Mark 5:7 and 5:18–20" in S.T., XI
(1957), 159ff., and in M.R., pp. 86ff.

public that witnessed them, the evangelist argues that it was part of the divine scheme that they should not have been properly understood. Hence Jesus is represented as taking precautions to prevent his miraculous deeds from disclosing his unique status and enjoins silence upon those who witness them; nevertheless, the uniqueness of his status must needs manifest itself if only in the form of a miracle worker's widespread fame. Accordingly, while it would be an exaggeration to say that we have here *merely* a literary device and that the injunctions to silence are given so that they can be overstepped,[16] the mode of representation in such passages as 7:36f. does aptly bring out the point that the truth revealed to the readers of the gospel was not meant to be known to Jesus' contemporaries, and yet was powerful enough to shine through his activities and arouse considerable excitement among the people.

But while St. Mark may have thought on these lines in connection with the passages under consideration, there is the possibility that other motives were involved and that injunctions to silence in 5:43; 7:36; 8:26 (if not the report of the disobedience in 7:36f.) were present in the tradition before St. Mark undertook his work, and that they were meant to defend Jesus against the calumny of those who declared that he was in league with Beelzebul, the prince of the demons (Mark 3:22ff.; Matt. 12:24ff. / Luke 11:15ff.). Jesus was not a charlatan of the stamp of Lucian's Alexander. Such is the kind of exegesis for which Anton Fridrichsen forcibly argues:

When he was represented as a magician on a grand scale, it was replied from the Christian side that all self-advertisement was alien

---

[16] Cf. H. J. Ebeling, *Das Messiasgeheimnis und die Botschaft des Markus-Evangelisten* (Berlin, 1939), pp. 178f., 192f., 221ff.

to him . . . instead of having his glory published abroad by those whom he had healed, he cast them aside and ordered them to keep quiet—here we have the opposite extreme to the practices of the ordinary thaumaturge.[17]

It should be noticed, however, that in Mark 3:22ff., while it is denied that Jesus is in any sort of alliance with the prince of the demons, there is no mention of the common character- istics of miracle workers, such as their predilection for self- advertisement; and that in the parallel in Matt. 12:15ff., the reticence of Jesus is simply given a scriptural warrant by a citation (in v. 19) of Isa. 42:2 ("He shall not strive nor cry aloud; neither shall any one hear his voice in the streets.") Nevertheless, in spite of the indirect nature of the evidence, it is not impossible that St. Mark was to some extent influenced by a desire to bring out a contrast between Jesus and the ordinary thaumaturge. Moreover, a similar desire could have been operative in the circles in which the traditions con- cerned were handed down, and may also have affected the pre-Markan understanding of the confessions of the demons. As Fridrichsen puts it:

How could one speak of the alliance with and the assistance of Beelzebul when the spirits themselves call Jesus the Holy One of God?[18]

Accordingly, prior to the composition of the gospel, the apotropaic significance behind Mark 1:24 and 5:7 could have been supplemented by an apologetic concern, the refutation of the Beelzebul charge by the witness of the demons them- selves. If this is so, the tradition already contained a motif

[17] See *Le problème du miracle dans le christianisme primitif* (Stras- bourg, 1925), p. 81.
[18] *Ibid.*, p. 79.

which approaches the evangelist's conception of the hidden Son of Man, and entails a contrast between human ignorance and supernatural (demonic as well as divine) knowledge of the true status of Jesus. Attention ought also to be drawn to the possibility of the effect of a pre-Markan anxiety to show that Jesus was innocent of all seditious messianic activity: although his doings greatly impressed the public, so far from seeking to arouse excitement among the people he did his utmost to check it.[19] Hence it is not impossible that the injunctions to silence in 5:43; 7:36; 8:26, no less than that in 1:25, were present in the stories as St. Mark received them, though in his interpretation they would in all likelihood be primarily understood in the sense already indicated.

Regarding the injunction to silence in Mark 1:44, it may be argued that the evangelist actually interpolated verse 43 and the words "See that you say nothing to anyone" of verse 44, into the text of the story of the cleansing of the leper as he received it.[20] On the other hand, one would have thought that the doctrine of the secret itself would have hardly required the employment of such forceful language as that used in verse 43; and it is noteworthy that the words "he cast him out" seem to express an affective violence which accords well with the emotional tone already given to the story by the *orgistheis*—"moved with anger" (the D reading)—in verse 41. So perhaps verse 43 was included in the pre-Markan form of the story. For when orders are given in a mood of angry irritation, they usually contain a negative command, that is, a prohibition of the action (whether actual or possible) which

---

[19] Cf. R. H. Lightfoot, *The Gospel Message of St. Mark* (Oxford, 1950), pp. 37, 46.
[20] Cf. R. Bultmann, *Die Geschichte der synoptischen Tradition* (Göttingen, 1931), p. 227; English ed., p. 212.

occasions the speaker's irritation. Accordingly, we should assume that, with the exception of verse 45, St. Mark is transmitting the text of the story substantially in the form in which he found it, and hence that verse 43 and the interdiction of verse 44 have a significance independently of the evangelist's own doctrine of the secret.

Seeing that no spectators are mentioned in the story, one could suggest that the original motif behind verses 43f. was that the nature of the cure is a holy thing which must on no account be profaned by being disclosed to the public. But this story does not refer to any mysterious technique (such as that described in Mark 7:32ff. or 8:22ff.) and no special prescription (such as that of Mark 9:29) is given. An alternative possibility is that Jesus does not advertise his miraculous power. But neither this nor the preceding suggestion seems to afford a satisfactory explanation of the emotional agitation evinced in verse 43 which, in all probability, has a cause similar to that of the *orgistheis* in verse 41. Jesus is displeased with the leper because he has not complied with the provisions of the Mosaic law; and the continued displeasure of verse 43 is perhaps occasioned by the thought that the man will further contravene the law by associating with healthy people and informing them of the cure before he is officially pronounced clean by the competent authority. Hence Jesus is represented as brusquely casting the man forth and forbidding him to have any social intercourse prior to the pronouncement of the priest's verdict. The legal procedure would then be "a testimony to them" in the double sense that it affords official proof of the reality of the cleansing and witnesses to Jesus' respect for the law. Such a motif, in addition to that of the secret, may have been in the evangelist's own mind when he decided to include the story in his work and place it in its present position; for in Mark 2:1ff. he illustrates the conflict of Jesus with certain Jewish authorities, and he may wish to make it plain to his readers at the outset that the differences are really not due to any disrespect for the Mosaic law on the part of Jesus, but to the evil nature of his opponents—the official custodians of the Torah (cf. Mark 7:10–13; 12:28–34).

St. Mark's doctrine that Jesus' practice of teaching in parables was intended to conceal the truth from the public is set forth in 4:1ff. The opening verse of the section was probably composed by the evangelist to provide an appropriate setting for the teaching in the general framework of the gospel; it seems to refer back to 3:9 where Jesus requests that a small boat be held in readiness so that he can put out to sea should the crush of the thronging crowd become too great, and this verse occurs in a pericope (3:7–12) apparently written by St. Mark as a summary account of the nature and effects of Jesus' activities in Galilee. The immediate introduction to the parable of the sower in verse 2 may have already existed in the evangelist's source; it should then be compared with the words "and he said" which in verses 26 and 30 introduce the parables of the seed growing secretly and of the mustard seed respectively. It is possible that the explanation of the parable of the sower (vv. 13–20) was also included in the source, for verse 13 presupposes that the disciples have asked for the meaning of this particular parable whereas in verse 10 they inquire about the significance of parabolic teaching in general and receive the required reply in verses 11f. With its emphasis on the things which prevent the word from coming to its proper fruition, the explanation makes the parable more obviously an exhortation to be on one's guard against certain temptations. On the assumption that this explanation was found in the source, the evangelist probably modified the original question by substituting the plural "the parables" for the singular "the parable" in verse 10; he may also have added the words "when he was alone" and was perhaps responsible for appending "with the twelve" to "they that were about him." If this is so, the source, with its particular question and with its distinction between the parable and the explanation, would afford the evangelist with an opportunity for putting forward his generalizing doctrine concerning the significance of Jesus' parabolic teaching. This he does by adapting verse 10 in the manner described and by inserting verses 11f., 21–25, and 33f., which convey the meaning that the truth lying in the form of parables is truth concealed from the public and revealed privately to the disciples.

In St. Mark's view, then, over and above the secret meanings concealed in the particular parables, there is the fundamental secret which is common to them all since, as it seems, it concerns the Person who composed the parables. Admittedly, the evangelist affords no formal explanation of what precisely he understands by the mystery of the Kingdom of God. He assumes that his meaning is clear as, indeed, it is when the passage is considered in the light of the doctrine of the work as a whole. He is referring to the truth disclosed by the heavenly voice at the baptism—the truth hitherto unrecognized by mortals, but known to the demons—that Jesus is the Messiah, the Son of God and the hidden Son of Man; and the passage may be said to point forward to 8:27ff. where Peter, as the representative of the elect, confesses that his master is the Messiah and where the disciples are at once forbidden to divulge this newly acquired knowledge. It appears, therefore, that St. Mark in 4:11 is not thinking of the Kingdom of God in any abstract sense, whether as a future or as a present reality, but of the Kingdom as it is embodied in the person of

Jesus the Messiah. In other words, the reference is to the saving message of the apostolic preaching or the essential content of the church's gospel; the phrase "the Kingdom of God" has similar significance in Acts 1 : 3, for example, where "speaking the things concerning the Kingdom of God" means "preaching the gospel" (cf. Acts 8 : 12; 19 : 8). "Those who are outside" are accordingly those who cannot accept the good news of the Messiahship which the apostolic preachers proclaim to the world. They are outside in the sense of being uniniated into the Christian mystery of salvation. The multitude, being addressed in parables, are prevented from knowing the divine mystery, the secret which, according to Col. 2 : 2f., is none other than "Messiah in whom are hidden all the treasures of wisdom and knowledge" (cf. Col. 1 : 25ff.). They are strangers to the gospel and, in consequence, are excluded from the blessings enjoyed in the fellowship of the Christian communities.

St. Mark's conception is therefore opposed to the common supposition that the parable, as a concrete representation of its subject matter, is designed as a means of facilitating comprehension. That he should come to think of the nature of parabolic discourse in this way, though surprising to us at first sight, would be a natural consequence of his doctrine of the messianic secret. The true impact of Jesus' teaching, as well as of his mighty acts, was concealed from the multitude, and since the teaching preserved in the tradition was to a large extent in parabolic form, it would be easy to come to assume that this form must have been chosen for the set purpose of hiding the truth. Moreover, it is evident that the parables were handed down and circulated in the churches isolated from their original contexts, with the result that the question of their precise significance would not infrequently become a debatable matter. For a parable would normally be spoken in response to a particular situation, which would exercise control over the meaning and limit the application. But with the loss of such contextual control much greater scope would be afforded for the contemplation of alternative possibilities in the way of interpretation, and adapted meanings would be supplied under the pressure of prevailing needs and purposes. Standards of interpretation would establish themselves pragmatically; and perhaps under the influence of primitive notions associated with epiphanies and greatly emphasized in the mystery religions, it would be felt that the right standards could be known only by the initiated few. Thus the notion that the truth (or some of it), being reserved for the elect, is hidden from the public (a notion which became tremendously important during the second century in the church's struggle with Gnosticism) could have already been present in the tradition before St. Mark wrote.[21]

3. *Behind the Traditions.* Accordingly, in his work on the hidden Son of Man, Erik Sjöberg rightly insists that St. Mark's doctrine of the secret is not imposed upon an alien tradition; ideas corresponding to it pre-existed in the materials with which the evangelist deals.[22] On the other hand, despite its erudition and its accumulation of much valuable information, Sjöberg's study is characterized by certain inadequacies, which perhaps arise partly from a failure to recognize the rich

[21] Morton Smith sees this motive particularly in Mark 4:34: "In Mark 4:11f. the concern is to explain the rejection by the Jews, in 4:34 to discredit outside teachers and justify the disciples' claim to a monopoly of true, secret doctrine" (*H.T.R.*, XLVIII [1955], 31).

[22] See his treatise *Der verborgene Menschensohn in den Evangelien* (Lund, 1955); page references to this work are given parenthetically in the text.

variety of motives entailed in the gospel traditions, and partly from an overeagerness to demonstrate that the ultimate historical basis of the evangelist's doctrine was Jesus' own belief that he was the Son of Man, temporarily concealed on earth but destined shortly to be revealed in glory as the plenipotentiary of God to judge the world (cf. pp. 39f., 148f.).

1. In the first chapter of his work (pp. 1–40) Sjöberg maintains that St. Mark's mode of representation was bound up with apostolic belief generally. The gospel was an apocalyptic proclamation and, as in Jewish apocalyptic literature, divine mysteries were announced. It is pointed out, for example, that according to DS Hab. 7:1ff., even the prophets did not know the eschatological import of their pronouncements; the secret meanings of their words were revealed to the Teacher of Righteousness (p. 9). So St. Paul in 1 Cor. 4:1 can refer to himself and his associates as "stewards or dispensers of the secrets of God" (p. 19); in Eph. 5:31f. he can apply the relation between man and wife as indicated in Gen. 2:24 to the relation between Christ and the church, understanding the result of his exegesis as "a great mystery" (p. 16); in 1 Cor. 2:6ff. he can represent the gospel as a primordial secret, divinely imparted to the exponents of the new faith and not understood by the "immature" or "unspiritual" (p. 23). These and other parallels which Sjöberg adduces are pertinent to the subject under consideration, although much of his associated discussion seems to revolve around the commonplace that revelation necessarily involves an element of secrecy; what is revealed must have been somehow concealed prior to the act of revelation. Moreover, the marshalling of parallels is no substitute for a careful investigation of the kind of thinking which lies behind the primitive Christian conception of the gospel as a divine mystery. For

St. Paul, no less than for the earliest evangelist, the conception is, as we have seen, connected with a predeterministic principle, and can hardly be elucidated without reference to that principle. The gospel of the crucified Messiah was a mystery, and its mysteriousness could be considered in various aspects: (*a*) The work of the Messiah realized a divine intention, conceived before creation, a secret primevally known to God alone; (*b*) God communicated his will to Moses and the prophets, but the imparted mystery remained a mystery to readers of the scriptures; (*c*) Jesus of Nazareth was the Messiah, but men did not understand what was happening before their eyes; (*d*) in the light of the Messiah's resurrection the apostles gladly announced the revealed truth far and wide, and yet many, especially Jewish hearers, were offended. Thus mysteriousness persisted, and this persistent mysteriousness followed directly from the primordial secret itself. In other words, the continuing human failures to appropriate the saving content of divine revelation were taken to be integral to God's sovereign purpose.

2. In his second chapter (pp. 41–98) Sjöberg, instead of offering an exposition of the philosophy behind the apostolic doctrine, searches out from the mass of rabbinical literature a few examples of the notion of a secret or concealed Messiah. He notices that while in Jewish apocalyptic works the idea of a Messiah, hidden in heaven prior to his eschatological appearance, plays an important part, particularly in connection with the Son of Man, the notion of a pre-existent Messiah is virtually absent from talmudic writings. On the other hand, as Justin's *Dialogue with Trypho* may show, certain rabbis played with the possibility that the Messiah had come into the world, was temporarily concealed and awaited his public manifestation; there are also one or two illustrations of the

thought that the Messiah, during the period of his earthly hiddenness, must suffer for the people (cf. Isa. 53:4f.). However, the scattered pieces of rabbinical evidence to which Sjöberg calls attention, all belong to the second century or later, and they are far too meager and elusive to warrant his contention (p. 40) that they clarify the necessary presuppositions for the primitive Christian contrast between the Messiah as hidden and the Messiah as revealed.

3. So far as the third chapter is concerned (pp. 99–213), while one may agree that possibilities in the way of secrecy motifs in the pre-Markan traditions have not been sufficiently explored in the form-critical school, there is much in Sjöberg's exposition that is open to objection.

It is argued (p. 106) that, in view of the open confession in Mark 14:62 at the nocturnal trial, the injunction to silence in Mark 9:9, which makes the period of concealment terminate at the time when the Son of Man is raised from the dead, must be taken to refer specifically to the transfiguration experience, not to the messianic secret as such—for the evangelist could not have been inconsistent on so important a theme. Here we have an illustration of the inadequacy of Sjöberg's analysis and of his failure to appreciate the complexity of the motivation entailed in and behind St. Mark's work. As we have seen, such complexity accounts for the frequent inconsistencies in the evangelist's representation. Sjöberg's failing in this connection is rather surprising, as he makes a favorable allusion (p. 112, n. 1) to Fridrichsen's perspicacious study *Le problème du miracle*, in which certain valuable suggestions are made in regard to the significance of the injunctions to silence in the formation of the traditions. It is also surprising to discover later (pp. 131f.) that Sjöberg, as though he had forgotten what he had previously stated, argues that even after the confession of Mark 14:62 the Messiahship remains a mystery —the members of the sanhedrin are "outsiders" who, unlike the disciples and pilgrim crowds in Mark 11:1 ff., fail to grasp the truth and regard the messianic claim as blasphemous. Moreover, this contrast, quite apart from the question of the exegesis of Mark 14:62, is based on a misunderstanding. For, as careful examination shows, the people in Mark 11:1ff. do *not* acclaim Jesus as Messiah.[23]

Sjöberg asserts (p. 114, n. 1) that Wrede, when stressing the theological character of St. Mark's doctrine, overlooked the possibility that Jesus himself might have been theological too. But in applying the epithet "theological" to St. Mark's presentation, Wrede merely wished to indicate the non-biographical nature of the evangelist's aims—not to deny that Jesus' teaching was theological.

Opposing Ebeling's thesis, Sjöberg emphasizes (pp. 120ff.) that St. Mark's notion of secrecy is not a literary convention imposed upon a tradition alien to it, but a motif integral to Jewish apocalyptic—a religious motif which must have been ultimately rooted in the teaching of Jesus himself (p. 123, n. 1). But does not this assume what needs to be proved? Moreover, Sjöberg's argument does not appear to be altogether consistent. For example, he asserts (p. 122) that Rudolf Otto found the key to an understanding of the motif in the apocalyptic Son of Man, and yet when he considers the crucial passage in I Enoch 71, on which Otto set great store, he finds Otto's exegesis erroneous. According to Sjöberg (p. 96, n. 2; cf. p. 125, n. 1), Enoch becomes the Son of Man only *after* his exaltation, so that (contrary to Otto's opinion) while on earth he cannot be the incarnate and concealed Son of Man.

---

[23] Cf. Z.N.T.W., LI (1960), 34ff., and M.R., pp. 193ff.

Thus the importance of the Jewish apocalyptic conception for Sjöberg's thesis would seem to fade away.

Despite his view that St. Mark's gospel is a consistent and intelligible unity (pp. 106, 132), Sjöberg is forced to admit (p. 132, n. 2) that there are certain discordant elements, such as the public appeal to "the Son of David" in 10:47f. and the public mention of the Son of Man in 2:10 and 2:28. He evidently finds difficulty with passages of this sort, and his suggestion that they were accidentally taken over from the tradition, would seem considerably to weaken his general contention´that the concept of the hidden Son of Man is an apocalyptic presupposition of the materials St. Mark used.

In his discussion of the miracle stories (pp. 150ff.) Sjöberg finds the fact of messianic hiddenness in the pre-Markan tradition, but not the notion that Jesus willed to be hidden. The explanation in terms of volition is due to the evangelist, and so it is held that in certain cases, for example, 5:43; 7:36; 8:26, the injunctions to silence are due to St. Mark. Sjöberg sees that in 1:23ff. the injunction would be the exorcist's reply to the demon's defensive confession, though he goes on to argue that already in the tradition the demon's address in verse 24 could be meaningful only if it gave expression to a knowledge not accessible to ordinary mortals. But what are the grounds for such a contention? Why, in the circles under consideration, should not the naming of the relevant name be apotropaically effective, independently of the question whether certain human beings had knowledge of the person named? In any case, the confession fails as a defense. It is true that most of the miracle stories reproduced by St. Mark indicate that the people, though impressed by Jesus as a wonder worker, do not recognize him as Messiah. But this by no means implies that all such stories circulated in the apostolic communities with the alleged apocalyptic presupposition that the Messiahship was hidden during Jesus' life on earth. Sjöberg could not overlook Mark 10:46ff., in which the title "Son of David" may well have belonged to the pre-Markan form of the story (p. 159, n. 5; cf. pp. 162f.), and this alone is enough to show that, according to some of the current Novellen, certain witnesses did respond with a faith that anticipated that of the church. The probability is that the spectators in the miracle stories usually make what is, from the standpoint of apostolic belief, a limited response to the things they see, partly because of the unforgettable reminiscence firmly embedded in the passion narrative (the core of the gospel traditions) that Jesus was not accepted by his people, and partly because of the church's experience that the power to work miracles was no compelling means of inducing people to embrace the gospel.

Respecting the parables (pp. 165ff.), Sjöberg rightly holds that the evangelist was responsible for Mark 4:11f., but it is scarcely satisfactory to argue (p. 192) that the parables specifically came to have a puzzling content in the tradition because it was believed that they contained the messianic secret. For why should the parables have been singled out in this way from Jesus' other forms of utterance? And are there any good grounds for supposing that the pre-Markan tradents held that the explanation of the parable of the sower, for example, was an exposure of the messianic secret enclosed in the parable itself (4:1ff.)?

In his consideration of the fourth gospel (pp. 202ff.), Sjöberg argues that the mode of representation therein is so radically different from what we find in the earliest gospel that it must have risen not from the *willed* hiddenness characteristic of St. Mark's doctrine, but from the *factual* hiddenness exemplified in the pre-Markan traditions (p. 211).

Such an assessment, however, overlooks that in both gospels the haunting mystery of the Son of Man is referred to the sovereign will or purpose of God, and that in Mark 8:29ff. the revelation of the secret to the disciples is analogous to the kind of representation we find in the fourth gospel. Though disclosed, the secret remains a mystery to the disciples as it does to "the world" or to "the Jews" in the Johannine presentation. Furthermore, there are definite approaches to the point of view of the fourth gospel with respect to the public in such passages as Mark 12:12, and 14:62; and Sjöberg surely errs in asserting (p. 212) that the portrayal of Jesus as making public pretensions to Messiahship is original to the fourth evangelist and his circle.

4. In his final chapter (pp. 214–246) Sjöberg considers whether the secrecy motifs existent in the traditions, motifs of which the Markan theory is a *Zuspitzung*, can be said to go back to Jesus himself. He comes to an affirmative answer: although he occasionally hinted at his real status, Jesus actually moved among men with an unexpressed messianic claim, awaiting the glorious revelation of himself as Son of Man after a period of suffering (p. 246). Once again, however, the arguments are unconvincing.

According to Sjöberg (p. 218), the Jewish parallels show that if Jesus had considered himself to be the Messiah he must, seeing that the final judgement had not yet come, have thought of his true nature as concealed for the time being. But, as we have seen, the few parallels cited in the second chapter of his work are late and of doubtful provenance; and, on Sjöberg's own showing, I Enoch 71 cannot be quoted in support of his view. Moreover, did not Bar-Kokhba work on Jewish presuppositions, and did not he make a public claim to Messiahship?

Sjöberg argues (p. 238) that the Messiah's hiddenness is a

dominant theme in the tradition and would be quite inexplicable if Jesus had openly claimed to be the Messiah. But perhaps the notion is not quite so dominant as Sjöberg supposes; and in so far as it is present in the multifarious traditions it could be based largely on the firm reminiscence that Jesus was not recognized and welcomed as Messiah by his contemporaries. Furthermore, Sjöberg presents no systematic elucidation of such passages as Mark 14:62; 15:26, which state or imply that Jesus did make open messianic pretensions.[24]

Toward the end of his treatise (pp. 243ff.) Sjöberg apparently wearies of patient argument and resorts to dogmatic pronouncement. The hesitancies of the earlier pages give way to a confidence of statement which the evidence supplies no warrant for. Perhaps most scholars would agree that behind the gospel traditions was a historical Jesus with a deep sense of vocation who worked and spoke in the name of God (p. 243). But to act in the name of God is one thing—to be something more than a mere Messiah *designatus* is quite another. Also, it is not explained why there could be no realized eschatology for a Messiah *designatus*, or why Jesus must have been Messiah, though concealed as such, to have spoken of the breaking-in of the Kingdom (p. 243; cf. pp. 233f.). And in any case, can we be sure that realized eschatology belongs to the earliest strata of the tradition?

Sjöberg (pp. 244f.) supposes that Jesus went beyond current expectation apropos of the Son of Man by not thinking of his mission merely in terms of judgment. As hidden Son of Man on earth he called for repentance and proclaimed forgiveness through his words and works; the season of grace would end with his eschatological appearance to judge the

[24] Cf. *Vig.C.*, XII (1958), 1ff. and *M.R.*, pp. 28off., where some relevant suggestions are made.

world in righteousness. According to Sjöberg, such passages as Mark 8:33 and 10:45 serve to indicate that Jesus took up and applied to himself in his capacity as hidden Son of Man the role of the Suffering Servant of Deutero-Isaiah. But can it be quite excluded that Mark 8:33 is a piece of anti-Petrine polemic? And can we be so certain that Mark 10:45 is based on Isa. 53?[25] Also, if the figure of the Suffering Servant played so crucial a part in the thought of Jesus, why are echoes of Isa. 53 all but absent from the earliest surviving form of the passion narrative?

Sjöberg (pp. 234ff.) seems too easily to infer from such sayings as Mark 8:38 that Jesus must have contemplated his own glorification to fulfill the eschatological role of the Son of Man. But the *logion* is so framed that it by no means excludes the possibility that the speaker distinguished himself as "I" from the Son of Man.[26] Jesus could have thought of an ethical correspondence between his own work and the final judging action of the Son of Man; and perhaps such correspondence was transformed into a relation of substantial identity after the resurrection christophanies. But extreme caution is necessary in this connection. In an important paper, P. Vielhauer has shown that in the synoptic records the eschatological sayings concerning the coming of the Kingdom are not intimately bound up with those concerning the final appearance of the Son of Man; and after a careful analysis he is led to the conclusion that Jesus envisaged an imminent and unmediated intervention of God's sovereign rule, the interpretation in terms of the Son of Man being a more concrete repre-

---

[25] See C. K. Barrett's contribution to the T. W. Manson memorial volume, *New Testament Essays*, ed. A. J. B. Higgins (Manchester, 1959), pp. 1ff.
[26] Cf. J. Wellhausen, *Das Evangelium Marci*, p. 73.

sentation which originated in the apostolic communities.[27] A somewhat similar view comes to expression in P. Winter's

[27] "Gottesreich und Menschensohn in der Verkündigung Jesu" in *Festschrift für Günther Dehn* (Neukirchen, 1957), pp. 51ff., reprinted in the collection of Vielhauer's essays *Aufsätze zum Neuen Testament* (Munich, 1965), pp. 55ff., a volume that also contains two papers "Jesus und der Menschensohn" (pp. 92ff.) and "Ein weg zur neutestamentliche Christologie?" (pp. 141ff.), in which Vielhauer seeks further to clarify and defend his position. A number of scholars, while agreeing that Jesus did not identify himself with the coming Son of Man, argue that he did sometimes speak of the last judgment in terms of the Son of Man apocalyptic, and they would uphold the historical authenticity of such dominical sayings as those preserved in Luke 11:30; 17:24, 26f. (so Tödt, Jüngel and Hahn, among others). However, much recent German discussion of the problem presupposes that the expression "Son of Man" was not used in Palestinian-Galilean Aramaic as a circumlocution for "I," and G. Vermes brings forward evidence to the contrary in his contribution ("The Use of *Bar Nash/ Bar Nasha* in Jewish Aramaic") to the third edition of M. Black's *An Aramaic Approach to the Gospels and Acts* (Oxford, 1967), pp. 310ff. Hence perhaps Jesus did in fact sometimes modestly refer to himself (in the circumstances of his earthly ministry) as the Son of Man, in which case a saying like that preserved in Luke 9:58 ("Foxes have holes . . . but the Son of Man has nowhere to lay his head") might well be authentic; and instances of this circumlocutional usage in the tradition could have facilitated a post-resurrection transformation of an eschatology of the Kingdom into a more concrete eschatology of the Son of Man, a transformation that would have its scriptural roots in Dan. 7:13. Cf. H. B. Sharman, *Son of Man and Kingdom of God* (New York, 1943), where Vielhauer's view finds anticipation, and N. Perrin, *Rediscovering the Teaching of Jesus* (London, 1967), where it is argued that the concept of the coming Son of Man derived from an early Christian interpretation of the passion (see esp. pp. 203ff.). In his *Jesus and the Son of Man* (London, 1964), A. J. B. Higgins offers a valuable critical study of the Son of Man sayings, although some scholars discern a discrepancy between the conclusions Higgins wishes finally to reach and the actual consequences of his analysis; see, for example, W. C. Robinson's review in *J.B.L.*, LXXXIV (1965), 46of.

contention[28] that in the gospels three stages of development in eschatological belief can be distinguished: (*a*) Jesus awaited and prayed for the coming of the Kingdom of God; (*b*) after the resurrection this basic expectation was transformed into the expectation that Jesus the Messiah would return as the glorified Son of Man; (*c*) with the delay in the arrival of the parousia, it came to be held that the Kingdom had already dawned in the Messiah's earthly activities.

In any case, whether or not Jesus actually spoke in terms of the Son of Man apocalyptic, the preceding discussions would seem to indicate that behind the gospel traditions was a Jesus who proclaimed the nearness of the end of the current order of existence, and who assumed that his own words and works stood in a vital relation to the prospective judgment of the world. Presumably, the final divine intervention would be construed as a triumphant vindication of his present mission with its exhortations, warnings and promises, and, unlike that mission, so far from being restricted to a small imperial province, would be effected on a cosmic scale. It would happen for all to see, a compelling demonstration of God's ultimate power, so that what was now hidden would then be made manifest, and what was now secret would then come to light (cf. Mark 4:22). If such a presumption is soundly based, besides a contrasting notion of hiddenness, a strong predestinarian conviction must also have been fundamentally in-

[28] See *T.L.Z.*, LXXXV (1960), cols. 745f. Cf. E. Grässer, *Das Problem der Parousieverzögerung in den synoptischen Evangelien und in der Apostelgeschichte* (Berlin, 1957); also, the article "Sequence and Dates of the Extra-biblical Dead Sea Scroll Texts and 'Damascus' Fragments" in *V.T.*, III (1953), 176f., where I. Rabinowitz distinguishes four typical phases in episodes of eschatological excitement deriving from scriptural prophecy.

volved in the teaching of Jesus—no less than in the case of his great prophetic predecessors; as the earth produces fruit of itself, quite independently of the art and device of man (cf. Mark 4:28), so God's purpose is being realized in history and presses forward to its inevitable eschatological consummation.

Accordingly, while the evidence scarcely authenticates the view that Jesus actually thought of himself as the hidden Son of Man, Sjöberg is on firm ground when he maintains that St. Mark's doctrine of the messianic mystery is not imposed *ab extra* upon an utterly alien tradition. Various secrecy motifs were already present in the materials he uses, and the notion of hiddenness, associated with a form of divine predestinarianism, may well have been exemplified, after the manner outlined, in the teaching of Jesus himself.

2

Should Wedding Guests Fast?
A Consideration of Mark 2:18–20

Since it is the disciples (not Jesus) who are attacked
for not fasting, the presumption is that the pericope
reflects a controversy in an early Christian *milieu*. And
form-critical investigations suggest that three phases
in the life-history of the paradigm may be distinguished: (1) a possible traditional saying of Jesus
which commended feasting or rejoicing as opposed to
fasting on some particular occasion (v. 19a); (2) a
utilization of the saying in a conflict story that was
meant to justify the nonobservance of fasts on the part
of some sections of the apostolic church that had been
criticized by followers of the Baptist (and certain
Pharisees?) for their irregularity (vv. 18–19a); (3) an
adaptation of the paradigm by the addition of verses
19b–20 to a Christian situation in which the practice
of fasting had established itself, resulting in the formation of the story as it now stands (vv. 18–20). It appears that commentators generally have not recognized the importance in this connection of the christological Bridegroom as a presence and as an absence.

Since it is the disciples (not Jesus himself) who are criticized for not fasting, the presumption is that Mark 2:18–20
reflects a controversy which took place in an early Christian

milieu. Presumably, certain Baptists and Pharisees disapproved of certain members of the primitive church for not fasting as they themselves fasted.[1]

In verse 18 the reference could be to some particular fast; the passage reads: "And the disciples of John and the disciples of the Pharisees were fasting; and they come and say to him, 'Why do the disciples of John and the disciples of the Pharisees fast, but your disciples do not fast?' " But the rhetorical question in verse 19a suggests that the followers of Jesus concerned had definitely renounced the custom of fasting; the text runs: "And Jesus said to them, 'Are the sons of the bride-chamber able to fast while the bridegroom is with them?' " Evidently the relevant apostolic groups felt that they were living at a time when the practice of fasting was no longer appropriate; that is, they believed that the messianic age had come. Despite his crucifixion the Messiah-Bridegroom was still with them, since, in a mystico-sacramental sense, did not his body continue to exist as the focal point of their fellowship at the eucharistic table (cf. Mark 14:22; I Cor. 11:24)? Whether or not Jesus himself actually uttered such a question as that given in verse 19a, it seems clear that some non-fasting Christians used it to express a form of realized eschatology; and if Jesus ever did make an utterance of that kind, the likelihood is that it would have had a different sort of significance, for his eschatology appears to have been futuristic.[2]

The qualification in verses 19b–20 seems to be a later addition; the verses read: "So long as they have the bridegroom

---

[1] Cf. P. Winter, *On the Trial of Jesus* (Berlin, 1961), pp. 118f., and F. W. Beare, "The Sabbath was made for Man?" in *J.B.L.*, LXXIX (1960), 130ff.

[2] See E. Grässer, *Das Problem der Parusieverzögerung* (Berlin, 1957), pp. 16f., 74f.

with them they cannot fast, but the days will come when the bridegroom shall be taken away from them, and then they will fast in that day." These words set a time-limit to non-fasting and adapt the paradigm to a state of affairs in which the observance of fasts had come to prevail in certain sections of the apostolic church. Also, with this addition the mystical significance of verse 19a is allowed to fall away, and Jesus is made to offer a ruling which sanctions the Christian practice of fasting. A new and contrary point is made.

Thus three phases in the historical development of the paradigm may be distinguished:

Phase 1 (v. 19a)—a possible traditional saying of Jesus which commended feasting or rejoicing as opposed to fasting.

Phase 2 (vv. 18–19a)—a utilization of the traditional saying in a controversy story meant to justify the non-observance of fasts on the part of certain members of the apostolic church who had been criticized by Baptists and Pharisees for their irregularity.

Phase 3 (vv. 18–20)—an adaptation of the paradigm by the addition of verses 19b–20 to a Christian situation in which the practice of fasting had established itself.

In Phase 3 the mystical meaning given to verse 19a in Phase 2 is discounted, and the implications are, in the first place, that the disciples (and Jesus) refrained from fasting before the crucifixion, and, in the second place, that they took up fasting immediately after the occurrence of that dreadful event. We are thus provided with an interesting example of early Christian indifference to historical accuracy, for the second implication is evidently a false generalization and the first implication may be false; at all events it would be rash to assume that the disciples (and Jesus) never fasted prior to the crucifixion.

The rhetorical question in verse 19a may have been a cur-

rent proverbial saying ascribed to Jesus by certain members
of the apostolic communities, but it could have been original
to him. The synoptic tradition contains indications that Jesus
opposed gloomy expressions of piety. Thus in Matt. 6:16 we
read: "And when you fast be not as the hypocrites of a dismal
countenance, for they disfigure their faces that their fasting
may be seen of men." But this is to be interpreted as a condemnation of ostentation in the practice of pious formalities
rather than as a commendation of the spirit of rejoicing such
as is commonly expected to be displayed at wedding recep-
tions. More relevant would be Luke 7:33f. (par. Matt.
11:18f.), where Jesus is reported as saying: "For John the
Baptist has come eating no bread and drinking no wine; and
you say, 'He has a demon.' The Son of Man has come eating
and drinking; and you say, 'Behold a gluttonous man and a
winebibber, a friend of publicans and sinners!' " So it is arguable that Jesus opposed asceticism or at least exaggerated
forms of asceticism, and that the rhetorical question of Phase 1
was uttered by him on some occasion when, as he felt, feasting
and rejoicing should have taken precedence over some legal
or customary demand for fasting. Without possessing any
messianic significance the question (v. 19a), as Jesus might
have put it, would have been in line with his apparent tendency to subordinate ritual observance to moral and deeply
personal considerations (cf. Mark 7:1ff.; 12:28ff.). Moreover,
it is also arguable that some eschatological motivation was entailed, namely, the feeling that the repentant should rejoice
because of the drawing near of the Kingdom of God. But in
view of such passages as Matt. 6:16, which we have already
cited, it would be rash to conclude that Jesus advocated a complete abolition of fasting for his followers and that he himself
never fasted.

It is not impossible that the eschatological motive suggested was in fact the starting point from which certain disciples came to refrain altogether from fasting after the Easter faith had emerged. Jesus' subordination of the ritualistic to the ethical and his notion that the repentant would soon be enjoying the blessings of the consummated Kingdom could thus have provided the historical bases for Phase 2. And the practice of refraining from fasting would find reinforcement in the distinctive apostolic belief that the crucified Jesus was the promised Messiah. For it could be argued that, with the advent of the Messiah in the person of Jesus, the Mosaic law and all its attendant customary observances, such as were multiplying in Pharisaic circles, were no longer in force: the age of fulfillment had come, and, as a living presence, Jesus continued to preside over a new dispensation under which the Torah had been superseded (cf. Gal. 3:24ff.). So some apostolic groups were led to eliminate fasting, as well as sabbath keeping and circumcision, from their practical piety. But, unlike sabbath observance and circumcision, fasting was not permanently left behind by the main stream of early Christianity.[3] Certain Pharisaic elements apparently came to fast twice a week, and some influential sections of the early church adopted a similar practice, although the latter chose two different days of the week for their times of abstinence.[4] And Phase 3 of our paradigm's supposed life history clearly presupposes that fasting had become an established practice in the Christian *milieu* in which the final adaptation was made and, of course, in the circles for which St. Mark's gospel was written. The bride-

---

[3] Cf. F. W. Beare's observations, *op. cit.*, p. 136.
[4] Cf. Luke 18:12; *Didachē* 8:1; *Apost. Constitutions* 7:23:1; also, T. W. Manson in *The Sayings of Jesus* (London, 1949), p. 311; G. F. Moore, *Judaism* (Cambridge, Mass., 1927/1930), II, 260.

groom of verse 19a is still identified with Jesus as the Messiah, but the lively realized eschatology characteristic of Phase 2 has been discarded. Jesus is the Messiah-Bridegroom but, within the intentional scope of the paradigm as it now stands, he is no longer *with* the Christian groups concerned, doubtless because he had been put to death on a cross and exalted to sit at God's right hand (cf. Mark 14:62). In other words, verse 19a is taken literally, not mystically, by those responsible for the third and final form of the story.

As for the identification of the Messiah with the eschatological Bridegroom, it is not attested in the Old Testament or—apart from the Qumran material[5]—in the extant literature of the intertestamental period.[6] And this strengthens the presumption that, although the question of verse 19a could have been an actual utterance of Jesus, the use to which the question is put in Phase 2 bespeaks a post-resurrection situation, the speaker being tacitly equated with the messianic Bridegroom who is continuously operative among his chosen. The

[5] Scholars of the so-called myth-ritual school would derive the idea of the messianic Bridegroom from the alleged annual ceremony of enthronement in the pre-exilic period. Thus in his *Aspects of Syncretism in Israelite Religion* (Lund, 1963), p. 85, n. 1., G. W. Ahlström writes, "We must point out in this connexion that the concept of 'bridegroom' as a Messianic epithet may be derived, through the recognition of a *hieros gamos* ritual, from the sacral kingship of the pre-exilic period; the sacral king, himself a saviour-king in his liturgical function, played the part of the 'bridegroom' in the sacred marriage. Brownlee's view, that 'bridegroom' was a late Jewish Messianic epithet, of which there is evidence in Q Isa, in which the bridegroom functions as priest, is thus correct, 'Messianic Motifs in Qumran and the New Testament,' *N.T.S.*, III (1956–57), pp. 12–30, 205. It should however be clear from the above argument that the phenomenon can be traced still further back in time."

[6] Cf. G. Kittel, ed., *T.W.N.T.*, IV, 1097f.

apostolic doctrine that the Messiah was the eschatological Bridegroom could have arisen partly from the concept of the church as the New Israel (cf. Gal. 6:15f.) and partly from the Old Testament representations of Yahweh as the husband of his people, and of Israel as Yahweh's betrothed (Hos. 1:1ff.; Ezek. 16:7ff.; Isa. 62:5). Thus Christ the Lord would be to the New Israel what Yahweh the Lord had been to the Israel according to the flesh (cf. Rom. 2:28f.), and it is quite in accordance with this correspondence that spokesmen of the early church should think of the risen Jesus in terms of the marital relation (cf. John 3:29; II Cor. 11:2; Eph. 5:21-33; Rev. 19:7, and so on). The same idea of the messianic Bridegroom is involved in Phase 2 and in Phase 3 of our paradigm, the former also reflecting a lively sense of the Lord's continuing presence (cf. Matt. 28:20).

The thought of the messianic Bridegroom was not unnaturally associated with that of an eschatological marriage banquet, a figure sometimes used respecting the coming age of fulfillment in rabbinical literature.[7] Both the idea of an eschatological wedding feast and the hybrid notion of a Messiah-Bridegroom are to be found in the parable of the wise and foolish virgins in Matt. 25:1-13, and such a combination of images is particularly interesting because in Mark 14:25 there is the suggestion that eucharistic commemorations of the last supper anticipated the messianic banquet to be enjoyed by the elect in the consummated Kingdom of God. Furthermore, confidence in the Christ's continuing presence with his people seems to be entailed in the eucharistic identification of the sacred bread with the body of the sacrificed Jesus, and, as already observed, the same kind of confidence would be as-

---

[7] See S.-B., IV, 517.

sumed in the supposed second form of Mark 2:18–20 (Phase 2).

The pronouncement "This is my body" (Mark 14:22; I Cor. 11:24) seems to signify that every celebration of the eucharist testified to a perpetuation of the risen Lord's incarnate life. During the period of the earthly ministry the fellowship of the disciples had its rallying point or tangible center in the bodily presence of the Master and, subsequently, the corporate life of the church had its tangible center in the bread of the holy table.[8] The eucharistic bread served as an agency of integration in the society of the elect, and therefore its function corresponded to that of the Messiah himself in his incarnate form. Such an analogy, as it seems, comes to expression in the formula "This is my body," where, indeed, it is pressed to the point of identification, the bread being actually assimilated to the corporeal life of its distributor at the last supper. On the other hand, if the Apostle Paul, for example, could think of the crucified Messiah as a living Lord whose presence was realized at the eucharist, he could also think of him as an absence, and this even when dealing with the eucharistic rite (I Cor. 11:26b; cf. Phil. 1:23). The same idea of an absent Christ is found not only in Phase 3 of our paradigm's supposed evolution, but also in passages like Mark 14:7, where we read: "For you always have the poor with you . . . but you do not always have me." Thus the shift in attitude which characterizes the transition from Phase 2 to Phase 3 is not so peculiar as *prima facie* it might appear to be. In the thought of the apostolic church the Messiah-Bridegroom could be, pending the parousia, an absence, and at the same time he

---

[8] Cf. *M.R.*, pp. 271f.

could be a mysteriously continuing presence apprehended by faith.[9]

A further question needs to be raised: Did "the Pharisees" and "the disciples of the Pharisees" figure in the original form of Phase 2? Doubts are prompted by the consideration that there obtained an increasing tendency in the course of the development of the synoptic tradition to regard the Pharisees as the principal opponents of Jesus.[10] Hence the mention of the Pharisees in verse 18 may have been an addition made with the emergence of Phase 3. That is, Phase 2 may have first concerned a criticism made on the part of certain followers of John the Baptist; the Pharisees were associated with them at a later date, possibly by the person responsible for the adaptation which resulted in Phase 3 of the suggested development.[11]

[9] Could it be that the christological title "Son of Man" virtually fell into disuse in the Hellenistic church partly because of its implication that, prior to the parousia, the Christ was absent from his people? (Cf. above, Chapter 1, sec. 3).

[10] Cf. below, Chapter 3 and esp. Chapter 7 (re Markan antipathies).

[11] It might be noted here that H Merkel's ascription of literal historicity to Mark 2:18–20 is bound up with an unproven preconception that Jesus de facto stood in fundamental opposition to the Mosaic law; see his article "Jesus und die Pharisäer" in N.T.S., XIV (1967–68), 194ff., esp. 202f.

3

The Syrophoenician Woman: The Context of Mark 7:24–31

Mark 6:31–8:26, in which the story of the Syrophoenician woman occupies a central position, owes its form and much of its content to the doctrinal design of the evangelist. In the sequences 6:31–7:37 and 8:1–26 St. Mark is not reproducing two parallel cycles of a supposed basic common tradition with scattered adaptations of his own, as he reproduces a traditional series of controversy stories in 2:1–3:6, but is more or less freely creating his own arrangement of certain materials at his disposal; and in some instances, notably, the feeding of the four thousand (8:1–10) and the conversation about bread (8:14–21), he actually composes the constituent pericopes.

Commentators have frequently suggested that in Mark 6:31–7:37 and 8:1–26 the evangelist may be reproducing two parallel cycles of the same tradition, for apart from 6:45–52 (the report of Jesus' walking on the sea) the main items of the first of the two sequences have corresponding items in the second: 6:31–44 (the feeding of the five thousand) is analogous to 8:1–9 (the feeding of the four thousand); 6:53–56 (the crossing to Gennesaret) to 8:10 (the crossing to Dalmanutha);[1] 7:1–23 (a conflict with the Pharisees about

[1] The name "Dalmanutha" occurs only here. J. Finegan (*Light from the Ancient Past* [Princeton, 1946], p. 225) suggests that "Magdal

| 48

purity regulations) to 8:11-12 (a conflict with the Pharisees about a sign from heaven); 7:24-30 (a conversation with a Syrophoenician woman concerning bread) to 8:13-21 (a conversation with the disciples about bread); and 7:31-37 (the healing of a deaf-mute) to 8:22-26 (the healing of a blind man). When, however, these correspondences are closely examined, it becomes clear that they really afford little warrant for the hypothesis that the evangelist is here making use of two varying accounts of the same events. The walking on the sea has no parallel in 8:1-26, and the other pericopes, with the exception of the two miraculous feedings, while evincing certain similarities, are so disparate as to make it most unlikely that they derive from a common ancestry.

Thus the repudiation of the regulations for ceremonial cleanness (7:1-23) has little in common with the refusal to give a sign from heaven (8:11f.); that it is members of the Pharisaic sect who are opposed in each case is in no way remarkable, for St. Mark inclines to introduce the Pharisees as the agreed enemies of the Lord. Also, while the notion of the sacramental bread is probably entailed both in the story of the Syrophoenician woman (7:24ff.) and in the conversation in the boat (8:13ff.), no Gentile figures as the center of interest in the second of these two pericopes. Again, while the healing of the deaf-mute (7:31ff.) and the restoration of sight to the blind man (8:22ff.) belong to the same category of miracle story, it would be unwise to assume that they are varying accounts of the same thing. Moreover, with regard to the miracles of the loaves, the feeding of the four thousand

---

Nuna" or "Nunaita" ("Magdal of Fish") may lie behind both "Dalmanutha" and the "Magada" of the Matthean parallel (15:39), and this conjecture seems to be as satisfactory as any; cf. S. E. Johnson, *A Commentary on the Gospel According to St. Mark* (New York, 1960), p. 141.

(8:1ff.) has all the appearance of being an abbreviation of the feeding of the five thousand (7:31ff.). Perhaps, as Dibelius argues, the evangelist, finding that different numbers concerning the miracle were in circulation, composed a second form of the story to include both numbers.[2] Accordingly, it would seem that in 6:31–7:37 and 8:1–26 St. Mark is not simply reproducing two parallel cycles of a hypothetical basic common tradition with scattered adaptations of his own, as he apparently reproduces a received series of conflict stories in 2:1–3:6,[3] but is more or less freely designing his own arrangement of certain materials at his disposal; and in some instances, notably, the conversation about bread (8:14ff.) as well as the feeding of the four thousand (8:1ff.), he seems to be actually creating the constituent pericopes. If this is so, the similarities to which attention has been drawn must be largely due to the evangelist's continuing preoccupation with the same doctrinal motifs, motifs that to a greater or less extent find exemplification elsewhere in the gospel.

St. Mark is *inter alia* concerned to emphasize a contrast between the success of Jesus among the people generally and the hostility he encountered among the religious leaders. Already in 1:45 Jesus has quickly won so great a reputation that he can no longer openly walk in urban areas; he resorts to sparsely inhabited rural places, and even there people come to him from every quarter. But this brief indication of Jesus' popularity with the multitude is immediately followed by a series of conflict stories (2:1–3:6); opposition comes from "some of the scribes" (2:6),[4] from "the scribes of the Phari-

---

[2] M. Dibelius, *From Tradition to Gospel* (London, 1934), p. 78, n. 1.
[3] See *M.R.*, p. 123, n. 15.
[4] Perhaps the scribes here are simply men learned in the Mosaic law, whereas in Mark 14:1, and elsewhere in the passion narrative, the

sees" (2:16), from "the disciples of John and the Pharisees" (2:18), from "the Pharisees" (2:24), and from "the Pharisees" who conspire with the "Herodians" against Jesus as to how they might destroy him (3:6).[5] Also, in 3:7–12 Jesus wins much public favor; a great multitude from Galilee follows him, as well as a great multitude from Judea, Jerusalem, Idumea, Transjordania, Tyre and Sidon. So he is forced to ask his disciples to have a boat ready for him, lest he should be crushed by the crowds. But once again an indication of Jesus' attraction for the public at large is followed, after a brief account of the calling of the twelve (3:13–19), by a section devoted to the theme of opposition (3:20ff.); "the scribes who come down from Jerusalem" openly assert that Jesus is possessed by none other than Beelzebul, the prince of the demons (3:22).

The same kind of contrast is to be found in 6:31–8:26. In 6:31ff. Jesus seeks refuge from the thronging multitude; he takes to the boat, but the people pursue him on foot, reaching his destination ahead of him, so that when he disembarks a great multitude awaits him. After miraculously feeding the people he walks on the water and lands at Gennesaret (6:53), where he is immediately recognized; his presence is made known and they begin to bring sick people to him wherever

---

"scribes" are probably thought of in their capacity as members of the Jewish politico-religious administration. Of course (nepotism apart) all the scribes who were state officials would have had a legal training, but it would be rash to assume that every expert in the pentateuchal legislation (the basic law of state and society in Jewry) held an official position in the civil service. St. Mark may tend to think of the scribes as being of the Pharisaic persuasion, but this in fact by no means was necessarily the case. Cf. below, Chapter 5, n. 7, and Chapter 7 (re Markan antipathies).

[5] Regarding this coalition, see *M.R.*, p. 138, n. 38.

he might go, and all those who touch him are healed. But in 7:1ff. the evangelist hastens to point out that "the Pharisees" and "some of the scribes who have come from Jerusalem" take Jesus to task for allowing his disciples to eat with defiled hands, whereupon Jesus moves into the counterattack, citing the scriptures (Isa. 29:13) against his opponents and contending that their tradition makes void the word of God. Also, in 8:1ff. a great multitude gathers and, after the second miracle of the loaves, Jesus gets into the boat with his disciples and proceeds to the region of Dalmanutha. But in 8:11ff. St. Mark once again turns to the motif of opposition: "the Pharisees" come and wrangle with Jesus, putting him to the test by making a peremptory demand for a sign from heaven. This is promptly refused. Jesus sighs or groans in his spirit and after declaring that no sign shall be given to "this generation," he leaves them, gets into the boat and makes for another shore.

Perhaps the groan or sigh of Jesus is meant to signify the exasperation of a divine being who finds himself amid the ignorance and weakness of mortal men (cf. the anger in the D reading of Mark 1:40 and the despairing questionings of Mark 9:19); and perhaps the evangelist sees in the demand for a sign an indication of Pharisaic preoccupation with externals in the conduct of the religious life. Just as they fail to see that nothing from outside can defile a man (7:1ff.), so they seek an immediate visible demonstration of the validity of the gospel, failing to realize that the cosmic signs or cataclysms inaugurating the glorious manifestation of the Son of Man do not belong to the first but to the second Christian generation. After the greatest of all tribulations in world history the sun will be darkened and the moon will cease to give its light, the stars will fall from heaven and the celestial powers will be shaken (13:14ff.). Although the end is not yet (13:7), nevertheless some of Jesus' contemporaries will still be alive (9:1), and "this generation"—that is, presumably, the generation of St. Mark's readers (cf. 13:14)—will not pass away before all things come to their consummation (13:30).

But the favorable reactions of the multitude are contrasted not merely with hostility from the Pharisaic side; the evangelist is also concerned to show that there was some measure of opposition to Jesus in influential political circles. As we have seen, in 3:6 "the Pharisees" take counsel with "the Herodians" against Jesus for the purpose of devising ways and means of having him eliminated, and in 8:15 the disciples are cautioned to beware of "the leaven [or evil influence] of Herod" and that of "the Pharisees." The same kind of alliance is mentioned again in 12:13, where "the Pharisees and some of the Herodians" seek to entrap Jesus as he talks to the people. The first of the two warnings in 8:15 may be meant to refer back to 6:14-29, the report of the death of John the Baptist at the order of Herod Antipas, the tetrarch of Galilee and Perea.[6] Herod thinks that Jesus is really John the Baptist come to life again. Although he had feared John as a just and holy man, yet "for the sake of Herodias," his "unlawful" wife, Herod ruled that he should be arrested and incarcerated, and eventually Herodias seized an opportunity to force him to have the prisoner decapitated. Thus a woman is the evil genius behind the dreadful affair, and perhaps her character in this regard was to some extent shaped by the role assigned to Jezebel in the scriptural tales about Elijah (I Kings 16:29ff.).

[6] Cf. *M.R.*, pp. 182ff. Antipas was in office from 4 B.C. (the date of the death of his father Herod the Great) to 39 A.D. (when he was banished to Gaul by the emperor Caligula). He is called "king" in Mark 6:14 (cf. Matt. 14:9), but he is correctly designated in Matt. 14:1; Luke 3:19.

However this may be, St. Mark makes it clear that Herod acts with great reluctance when he orders the execution of the Baptist, Herodias' function being similar to that ascribed by the evangelist to the chief priests in the account of the condemnation of Jesus. Pilate does not wish to have the Messiah put to death, but his hand is forced by the multitude that has itself been stirred up against the prisoner by the priestly aristocracy.[7]

That the evangelist sees the death of the Baptist in relation to the crucifixion seems to find confirmation in the conversation of 9:11–13, where the doctrinal suggestion is made that John—not Jesus, as some suppose (6:15)—appears on the scene of history as the promised Elijah redivivus who must suffer violent death as part of the divine scheme for human salvation. The Baptist's shameful death does not preclude him from fulfilling the eschatological role of Elijah, any more than the passion precludes Jesus from being the promised Messiah. On the contrary, the fact that John is "delivered up" (1:14) only goes to strengthen the belief that he is the Messiah's divinely appointed forerunner, for the Messiah himself is also "delivered up" (9:31; 10:33), and as the earthly fate of the latter is in accordance with the declared will of God, so is the earthly fate of the former. But there is a topographical difference, for, unlike the Elijah-forerunner, the Son of Man must be "delivered up" and condemned to death at Jerusalem (10:33).

There seems to be no justification for the notion that, in St.

[7] See Mark 15:6ff. If St. Mark's story of the death of John represents a tradition that was originally handed down among the Baptist's followers (which may well be the case), the motif of Herod's reluctance could have been introduced from a desire to show that the Baptist movement was politically innocuous.

Mark's view, the movements of Jesus in 6:31ff. were conditioned by his fear of the possibility that Herod might take action against him similar to that which he had already taken against the Baptist. Basically the evangelist holds that the eventual withdrawal from Galilee and the journey to Jerusalem were determined by the sovereign purpose of God revealed in the scriptures. It is true that, despite his fundamental predestinarianism, St. Mark can on occasion explain on a mundane level and think in terms of proximate volitional causation, as when he inclines to ascribe responsibility for the Messiah's death to the Jewish authorities. But so far as the hostility of Herod and his supporters (or members of his administration) is concerned, the evangelist nowhere gives any indication that such political opposition shaped the course of the Messiah's earthly career.[8] In 8:15 the disciples are warned against the leaven of the Pharisees as well as against the leaven of Herod, and this can hardly be meant to suggest that Jesus himself was afraid of the Pharisees. In St. Mark's presentation Jesus no more avoids public activity in the territory of Herod than he avoids direct encounter with the Pharisees. As in the sections of the gospel prior to 6:31, so subsequently he openly teaches and heals in Galilee (6:34-44; 6:53-56; 7:31-37; 8:1-9), and before he finally reaches Jerusalem he teaches the gathered multitudes in Judea and in Transjordania—that is, we may legitimately infer, in Perea, a region which, like Galilee, was part of the tetrarchy of Herod Antipas (10:1). Also, he continues to engage in polemical verbal exchanges with exponents of Pharisaism (7:1-23; 8:1-13; 10:2-9, etc.).

In 13:1ff. the four disciples, to whom the admonitions of the apocalyptic discourse are privately addressed, clearly

---

[8] Cf. *M.R.*, pp. 117ff., 201ff., 224ff., 294.

represent the Christian community or communities for which the evangelist writes, and in the parenthesis of 13:14 an exhortation is explicitly directed to readers of the gospel.[9] A similar situation doubtless obtains in 8:14–21. Disregarding the requirements of credible historical description and contravening the demands of his own theory of the messianic secret,[10] St. Mark suggests that the disciples ought to see what he himself sees and what, as he feels, his readers need to be reminded of, namely, that Jesus, as the bread of life, is the one true loaf with the disciples in the boat, and that "the Pharisees" and "Herod" are alike dangerous opponents of the gospel. Evidently, during the years around the time of the outbreak of the great Jewish revolt against Rome (A.D. 66) both leading Pharisees and officials of the Herodian administration had used their power to curb the eschatological ardor of the Christian communities in Palestine and elsewhere, recognizing that it could be but a short step from such a mode of religious enthusiasm to the militant revolutionary activity of the Zealotic movement.[11]

Hence the Herod of Mark 8:15, like the Herod whose agents in 3:6 and 12:13 conspire with Pharisees against Jesus, cannot be Herod Antipas, the tetrarch who ordered the decapitation of John the Baptist and who in A.D. 39 was banished to Gaul by the emperor Caligula.[12] He must be, anach-

---

[9] In this respect 13:14 is unique in St. Mark's gospel.

[10] Cf. *M.R.*, 103ff., and 69ff., 155f., 202f. In Mark 8:14–21 Jesus rebukes the disciples by asking them several questions they cannot answer, and the same method of reproving is resorted to in 4:13, 40.

[11] For a similar view, see P. Winter, *On the Trial of Jesus* (Berlin, 1961), pp. 127ff.

[12] According to Josephus, *Ant.* 18:5:2, Antipas arrested John, not because (as in Mark 6:17ff.) the latter asserted the illegality of the marriage with Herodias, but because the tetrarch feared him as a

ronistically, Herod Agrippa II who, thanks to the emperor Claudius became king of Chalcis in A.D. 50 and was endowed with the right to nominate candidates for the office of high priest in Jerusalem—or at any rate to advise the procurators in the appointment of such dignitaries.[13] He retained his tiny kingdom in the Antilebanon after the fall of Jerusalem (A.D. 70), remaining *persona grata* with the successors of Claudius and continuing faithfully to serve the interest of the imperium until his death in A.D. 100. Throughout a troubled half-century he exercised a moderating influence upon the Jewish inhabitants of the eastern regions, and in the latter part of his reign he worked to prevent an alliance of the Jewish communities in Mesopotamia, Syria and elsewhere with the Parthians, who were dangerously hostile to Rome.

The primitive Christian sectaries largely shared with most other Jewish elements, including the Pharisees, a pronounced antipathy against Herod the Great (40–4 B.C.) and his offspring. The aversion seems to have remained fairly constant and comes to clear expression in such a passage as Matt. 2:1ff. where Herod the Great, appearing in the role of villain of the piece, may well be meant to stand for the type of all the Herods. There was not the same constancy of feeling with regard to the Pharisees, and the synoptic tradition betrays a

---

possible revolutionary leader. Also, according to *Ant.* 18:5:4, Salome the daughter of Herodias, not Herodias herself (as in Mark 6:17), was the wife of Philip, the tetrarch of Gaulanitis and Trachonitis.

[13] This view, which is strongly defended by P. Winter, differs from that of E. Lohmeyer, *Das Evangelium des Markus* (Göttingen, 1951), p. 67, who argues that the coalition of Mark 3:6 and 12:13 has its historical basis in the pro-Pharisaic policy of Herod Agrippa I (41–44 A.D.), the father of Herod Agrippa II. In our exegesis the Herod of Mark 8:15, like the Pharisees, was not dead but very much alive when St. Mark was writing (cf. the bread of life, the one loaf of 8:14).

definite tendency to become increasingly anti-Pharisaic. But intense though it was, the resultant animadversion was by no means sufficient to obliterate all traces of a period when Pharisees, or certain representatives of Pharisaism, were recognized as standing in a close relationship with Jesus and with exponents of the doctrine of his Messiahship. Thus in Mark 12:28-34, although the evangelist refrains from identifying the assenting scribe's sectarian affiliation, the summary of the Torah proposed by Jesus is definitely in line with a significant trend in Pharisaism as we know it from the talmudic evidence.[14]

Again, in Luke 13:31-33 the memory is apparently preserved of a time when upholders of Pharisaism were on the

[14] Cf. S. E. Johnson, *op. cit.*, pp. 202ff. We should point out here that in Matt. 22:34-40, the parallel to Mark 12:28-34, the scribe (who becomes a *nomikos*—"lawyer") is expressly identified as a Pharisee, and *prima facie* this may seem to constitute evidence against the view that the tradition tends to become increasingly anti-Pharisaic. But such is not really the case, as the following considerations show: (a) the scribe in Mark 12:28 is favorably disposed to Jesus, whereas the lawyer of Matt. 22:34f. is definitely hostile; (b) in Mark 12:28 the scribe poses his question after perceiving that Jesus can deal competently with enquiries, but in Matt. 22:34f. the lawyer volunteers his question after hearing that Jesus has dumbfounded the Sadducees; (c) while the implied motive of St. Mark's scribe seems to be a genuine wish to learn, the lawyer of Matt. 22:35 explicitly seeks to upset Jesus by putting him to the test, and implicitly he doubtless means to put on a better performance than his Saducean rivals; (d) but if this is so, the lawyer is foiled (as were the Sadducees earlier) and he ventures no response to Jesus' answer, whereas in Mark 12:32f. the scribe tells Jesus that he is right, rehearses the gist of the reply given, and supplements it with a derogatory remark about the sacrificial cultus (cf. Matt. 12:7); (e) the absence of any comment on the answer given in Matt. 22:37-40 contrasts strikingly with Mark 12:34, where Jesus, having noted the scribe's wisdom, declares that he is not far from the Kingdom of God.—Regarding St. Matthew's tendency to identify scribes with Pharisees, see below, Chapter 7, n. 69.

side of Christianity in opposition to Herodian rule: certain Pharisees advise Jesus to take flight, alleging that Herod seeks to kill him. So far as the warning itself is concerned, the evangelist does not take it seriously. Replying to the warning, Jesus, after referring contemptuously to the tetrarch as "that fox," asserts cryptically that he must go on with his healing work for a day or two and that it is impossible for a prophet to perish away from Jerusalem. No more than in St. Mark's gospel does a fear of Herod affect the course of the Messiah's career, and it is noteworthy that in Luke 23:6–12, the report of the Herodian trial, there is no mention of any intention on Antipas' part to have Jesus put to death; he hopes to see a sign performed by Jesus, and when the prisoner fails to answer the questions put to him he is treated with contempt and sent back to the procurator. Of course it is by no means incredible that Antipas did in fact take repressive measures against Jesus or against the earliest Christian groups operating in his territory. Nevertheless, the tradition of Luke 13:31 that Herod wished to kill Jesus needs to be considered in relation to that maintained in Matt. 2:13–18, according to which Herod the king sought to destroy the Messiah in his infancy. Both are ascribable to the anti-Herodian sentiment present in the apostolic communities *ab initio* and kept alive in the later decades of the first century by the policy of Herod Agrippa II. And in the case of Luke 13:31 the animadversion in question may have combined with a feeling that the person responsible for the execution of the divinely appointed forerunner must also have sought to eliminate the Messiah himself.[15]

---

[15] It is remarkable that the part played by the Pharisees in Luke 13:31 is played by an angel of the Lord in Matt. 2:13.

Doubtless, in St. Mark's literary scheme, subsequent to
6:30, Jesus changes his location with considerable frequency.
In 6:31ff. the Master and his disciples retreat by boat to a
lonely spot only to find that they have been anticipated by a
great throng; in 6:45ff., though intending to go to Bethsaida,
they land at Gennesaret (6:53); in 7:24 Jesus crosses the
border to visit the region of Tyre; in 7:31 he returns through
Sidon to the Sea of Galilee in the midst of the borders of the
Decapolis; in 8:10 Jesus and the disciples travel by boat to the
district of Dalmanutha; in 8:13 they embark and land at
Bethsaida (8:22); in 8:27 they proceed to the villages of
Caesarea Philippi; in 9:30 they pass through Galilee, not wish-
ing anyone to know it;[16] in 10:1 they (see 10:10) go to the
region of Judea and Transjordania; in 10:32 they are on the
road, going up to Jerusalem; in 10:46 they come to Jericho;
and in 11:1 they are near the Mount of Olives, and are about
to enter Jerusalem.

On the other hand, striking though they are, the itineraries
of 6:31–8:26 are not wholly without precedent in the earlier
sections of St. Mark's work. Already in 1:21–39 the Lord is
represented as being unfailingly active and continually on the
move; in verses 21–28 he teaches and exorcises an unclean
spirit in the synagogue at Capernaum, his fame spreading

[16] This does not mean that because of government opposition he is
now working clandestinely as the head of an underground movement.
The evangelist supplies the reason for the secrecy in the following
verse: Jesus is privately instructing the disciples concerning the
mysterious meaning of the Messiahship, a fact which Peter has acknowledged on behalf of the disciples at Caesarea Philippi (cf. 4:11f.,
34; 7:17; 10:10f.). Johnson, *op. cit.*, p. 163, asserts that Mark 9:30
signifies the end of the Galilean ministry. But it should be noticed
that it does not signify the end of Jesus' public activity in the territory of Herod Antipas since the region beyond Jordan in 10:1 is
probably Perea.

throughout Galilee; in verses 29–31 he enters the house of Simon and Andrew and cures Simon's mother-in-law of a fever; in verses 32–34 the whole town gathers at the door of the house in the evening and he heals many who suffer from various maladies; and in verses 35–39 he arises the next morning, a great while before dawn, in order to pray in a lonely place and, on being discovered by Peter and others, he declares that they should proceed to neighboring towns so that he may preach there also, and that it was for this purpose that he came forth. The general impression of the strain and pressure of the ministry is fortified by the frequent use of the adverb "immediately," which occurs no less than nine times in 1:12–43. Also, the journey into Gentile territory in 7:24 has a precedent in 4:35ff., where Jesus crosses the sea to the country of the Gerasenes and performs a marvellous exorcism among people who raise pigs. Admittedly, the transitions from place to place are more extensive in 6:31ff. than in the earlier sections of the gospel. But this is probably deliberate. In view of the impending announcement that the Son of Man must suffer many things and be delivered up at Jerusalem (8:31; 9:31; 10:33f.), there are many places in which the gospel needs to be proclaimed (cf. 1:38)—much still remains to be done, and there is now but little time in which to do it.

But if in the body of St. Mark's work the favorable response of the general public is set in contrast with the malevolence of the Pharisees and the Herodians, it is also set in contrast with the enmity of his own kith and kin and with the faithlessness of his compatriots. In 3:7ff. a description of Jesus' popularity among the great multitudes (vv. 7–12) and a report of the appointment of the twelve (vv. 13–19) are followed by an account of the hostility of his relatives (vv. 20–21, 31–35), which is divided by the Beelzebul controversy

(vv. 22–30). By this intercalation the evangelist probably means to suggest a significant parallel between the kinsfolk of Jesus, who declare that he is beside himself (v. 21) and apparently seek to prevent him from continuing his work (vv. 21, 31) and the scribes from Jerusalem who attribute his miraculous power to the inspiration of Beelzebul, the prince of the demons (v. 22). The Messiah is born of Israel, and yet he is rejected by the competent authorities of Israel. Nevertheless, the blindness and hostility of Jesus' own people serve to bring out the true nature of the Messiah's relatives; they are those who belong to the community in which the will of God is done. The mother and the brothers of Jesus stand outside (v. 31), whereas the multitude are seated in the house with the Lord (vv. 20a, 32) and symbolize the genuine family of the Messiah (v. 34). Thus the evangelist presents a concrete prefigurement of the integrated fellowship of Hellenistic Christianity, which (as he implies) transcends all racial distinctions.[17]

Again, in Mark 5:21ff. Jesus crosses the water, returning to the western shore of the sea; a great multitude collects and throngs about him (vv. 21, 25), and he goes on to bring a dead girl back to life so that the bystanders are overcome with amazement (vv. 35ff.). This is immediately followed by the story of Jesus' rejection in his native place (6:1ff.), which affords dramatic illustration of his pronouncement that a prophet is not without honor, save in his own country, among his own kin and in his own house (v. 4). Although he does perform a few cures, he is unable to do any mighty work, and he marvels at the people's lack of faith—despite the pro-

---

[17] Cf. Gal. 3:28; *M.R.*, pp. 137f. There is a further favorable appeal to the multitude in Mark 8:34—though this time it is from the blindness of the disciples as represented by Peter.

nouncement he has just made (vv. 5f.). As we have previously argued,[18] St. Mark takes this story to foreshadow the Messiah's final rejection by his own nation, an act that resulted in the crucifixion and the apostolic mission to the world which is to some extent symbolized in the sending out of the twelve (6:7–13, 30). But there is a further complement to the account of the rejection in the *patris* in addition to the report of the mission of the twelve, and this falls within the section 6:31–8:26: it is the story of the Syrophoenician woman (7:24–31), in which the obtuseness and unbelief of the Messiah's own people has its counterpart in the intelligence and implicit faith of a Gentile mother, who prostrates herself in Jesus' presence and addresses him as "Lord." Although the Jewish people, being God's chosen, have prior claims on the saving grace of the Messiah (v. 27), a Greek woman can nonetheless discern the divine status of Jesus, and the validity of her insight receives signal vindication in the healing of her daughter there and then (vv. 29f.). The old dispensation is already passing away.

Another persistent motif which comes to expression in 6:31–8:26, no less than in other parts of St. Mark's gospel, is the retiringness of Jesus, his tendency to withdraw from the multitude and to seek seclusion. In 1:35–39 Jesus steals away from Simon's house long before dawn; he goes to a lonely place and prays there. On being sought out by Simon and others he asserts that he must proceed to the neighboring towns so that he may preach there also, this being the purpose for which he came forth. Here the evangelist apparently intends the unannounced retreat to have two explanations, namely, a desire for prayer in privacy and a desire to extend

[18] See *M.R.*, pp. 138ff.

the field of the ministry. Privacy is again sought for prayer in
6:45f.,[19] and withdrawal from the multitude for the purpose
of proclaiming the gospel elsewhere seems to be exemplified
in such a passage as 4:35f. (cf. 5:19f.). Furthermore, in 6:31
the need for rest and the desire for leisure in which to eat (cf.
3:20) are mentioned to explain Jesus' proposal for a retreat
to a lonely place, and in 9:30f. the Master does not wish anyone to know where he is because he is engaged in privately
instructing his disciples concerning the mysterious meaning
of his messianic status.[20]

In St. Mark's representation, Jesus' persistent quest for
seclusion is not always successful. In 1:35ff. he is sought out
by his disciples when he is praying in a lonely place; in 1:45,
though he keeps clear of urban areas, people resort to him
from all quarters; in 2:1ff. he is in a house at Capernaum, but
it is crowded with people, both opponents and sympathizers;
in 3:20 he is again in a house, yet a multitude gathers so that
there is no leisure even for eating; in 6:31ff. a lonely place is
sought by boat, but a great throng gets there ahead by hurry-
ing on foot; and in 7:24ff. Jesus enters a house in the region of
Tyre, but he cannot be hidden, for immediately a Syrophoenician woman appears with a request that he should heal
her daughter. On the other hand, according to various passages Jesus secures the seclusion he desires: in 7:17ff., leaving
the multitude, he enters a house and privately explains a parable to his disciples (cf. 4:10ff., 34; 8:31; 9:30–32; 10:32–34;
13:1ff.); in 6:45f. he dismisses the disciples and the multitude,
and goes into the hills to pray (cf. 1:35; 3:13; 14:32ff.); and
in 4:35ff. he leaves the multitude, crosses the sea and performs
a marvelous exorcism in the country of the Gerasenes.

[19] Cf. 14:34f., though here Jesus goes forward, distancing himself,
not from the multitude, but from the three closest disciples.
[20] See above, n. 16.

Thus St. Mark is inclined to think of a house as a place of retreat from the multitude, an inclination that is evinced in 6:31–8:26 as well as in other parts of the gospel (7:17, 24; 9:33; 10:10). The evangelist is also inclined to think of the boat, first mentioned at 3:9, in the same connection. In the passage just mentioned, Jesus tells the disciples to make a boat available for him lest he should be crushed by the multitude. Although *ploiarion*, the diminutive for "boat," is used here, in 4:1 the *to ploion* ("the boat"—adopting the reading of D and certain other authorities) probably refers to the same boat;[21] a very large multitude crowds in upon him, and so he gets into the boat and teaches the people from it, thereby avoiding the thronging of the eager audience. The boat is further used on a number of occasions: for a round trip to the country of the Gerasenes (4:36; 5:21), in a vain quest for leisure at a lonely place (6:32), for a projected voyage to Bethsaida which ends at Gennesaret (6:45, 53), for a trip to Dalmanutha (8:10), and for a voyage to Bethsaida (8:13, 22). After this arrival at Bethsaida the boat does not figure again in St. Mark's narrative, for the announcement of the passion is made at 8:31, and this means that Jesus must journey by land to the south until he reaches Jerusalem (9:30; 10:1, 32; 11:1ff.).

The tendency to depict Jesus as one who seeks seclusion and does not secure it needs to be considered in relation to the injunctions to silence in 1:44. 5:43, 7:36 and 8:26. In these four passages human beings are enjoined to keep quiet, each time concerning a miracle which Jesus has just performed.[22] The first of the injunctions is disobeyed in 1:45 and the third

[21] St. Mark is free in his use of diminutives; see C. H. Turner, *The Gospel According to St. Mark* (London, 1928), p. 37.

[22] These injunctions to silence should be carefully distinguished from those imposed on the demons, 1:25, 34; 3:11f. For a detailed treatment, see *M.R.*, pp. 62ff.

in 7:36. Such disobedience is not to be taken as an actual frustration of the purpose of Jesus, for in the four passages under consideration, St. Mark is not concerned with credible historical description, the commands being (at least in the last three instances) all but impossible of execution.[23] His intention is to make it clear to his readers that Jesus' messianic status necessarily expresses itself, if only in the form of a miracle worker's widespread fame. In the evangelist's view, the mighty deeds of Jesus are the deeds of no ordinary thaumaturge but of the Messiah himself; and since the miracles were not construed in this sense by the public that witnessed them, St. Mark maintains that it was part of the divine plan of salvation that they should not have been properly understood. Hence Jesus (whose will is assumed to be concordant with God's purpose) is represented as deliberately taking precautions to prevent his marvelous works from disclosing his real nature to the people generally, by enjoining silence on the witnesses of his mighty deeds.

The disobedience of the command not to tell anyone receives greater stress in 7:36 than it does in 1:45 (see also 5:20): the more he charges the witnesses that they should tell no one about the miracle, the more they make it public. Thus, the impression is given that the miraculous deeds of Jesus are proclaimed against his will, and the situation is reminiscent of that in 7:24, where Jesus, having entered a house in the region of Tyre, desires no one to know it—and yet he cannot be concealed. As we have already argued, the idea intended is not that Jesus was foiled, but rather that his essential nature being what it was, he could not escape winning great fame as a

___

[23] In the case of the little girl raised to life (5:21-24, 35-43), for example, how could one avoid informing the mourners (v. 38) of the miracle?

performer of miracles. In other words, St. Mark's mode of representation in this connection is intimately bound up with his soteriological philosophy of history which has its focal point in the concept of Jesus as Messiah, the Son of Man and Son of God.[24] Such a philosophy obviously excludes two other possible assessments of Jesus, and the evangelist makes this plain to his readers: Jesus is not a sorcerer in league with Beelzebul or a charlatan given to self-advertisement, nor is he an aspirant to royal dignity who seeks to arouse excitement among the toiling masses or to stir them up to seditious activity.

But it would be a grievous mistake in hermeneutics to assume that Jesus in St. Mark's interpretation is afraid of his enemies. On the contrary, in such passages as 2:1ff., 3:20ff., 7:1ff., and 11:12ff., where Jesus is confronted by his opponents, he takes the initiative and sometimes, as in 7:6–8, 11:17, 12:1–11, he seems deliberately to evoke the wrath of his enemies by making ominous utterances against them. He who is to be accused and condemned at the forthcoming trial before the sanhedrin (14:55ff.) here becomes the accuser and even condemns those who are to be his judges. No nervousness or timidity is shown, and in 14:62 he is so forthright that he divulges the secret of his Messiahship in the presence of all the senators, and declares that they will see the Son of Man sitting at the right hand of Power and coming with the clouds of heaven.

Accordingly, the tendency of Jesus to retreat from the multitude and to seek seclusion is not understood by the evangelist in terms of fear, and the journey to the north in 7:24 is not the forced exile of a refugee who has dealings with a

[24] See Mark 14:62 and P. Winter's article, "The Marcan Account of Jesus' Trial by the Sanhedrin" in *J.T.S.*, n. s., XIV (1963), 94ff., esp. 100.

foreign woman because he is no longer able to serve his own people in Galilee.[25] Not that the Jesus of St. Mark's gospel is incapable of fear. On the contrary, in 14:32ff. he betrays profound anxiety in face of the fate that awaits him, and he comes to conform with the will of God only by surmounting the weakness of his carnal nature through the mediation of an agonized effort of volition. Here, however, to do justice to the evangelist's thought, three points should be borne in mind.[26] In the first place, the Gethsemane story is wholly a record of the divine purpose, since, as St. Mark and his earliest readers believed, the Messiah's anguish is indicated beforehand in the passion psalms (Pss. 22; 31; 69). In the second place, if the *peirasmos* (the dire tribulation which necessarily precedes the final triumph of the elect) were not dreaded, it could scarcely be the eschatological prelude that it is. In the third place, fear in this connection seems ultimately to have its object neither in hostile political and religious authorities nor in the pain and suffering envisaged, but in the possibility that because of the stress human loyalty to God might fail through the weakness of the flesh (14:38). He only who endures to the end shall be saved (13:13), and so the fear in question is a dread of apostasy, a fear occasioned by man's ever-present liability to succumb to the forces of evil.[27]

But if there is little or no basis for the view that in Mark 7:24 Jesus seeks concealment in Syria because he fears that

[25] See Johnson, *op. cit.*, pp. 136f.
[26] See *M.R.*, pp. 238ff., and E. Grässer, *Das Problem der Parousieverzögerung in den synoptischen Evangelien und in der Apostelgeschichte* (Berlin, 1957), pp. 103ff.
[27] The fear evidently involved in the Messiah's anguish in Gethsemane should be distinguished from the kind of fear which St. Mark on certain occasions attributes to the disciples. See *M.R.*, pp. 169, n. 2, 256, n. 7.

Herod intends to take action against him, there is still less for the view that he travels north because, recognizing the failure of his work in Galilee, he feels the need for time and opportunity to reflect on the nature and scope of his ministry.[28] The evangelist nowhere gives any indication that the ministry in Galilee proves unsuccessful. Admittedly, in 6:1ff. Jesus is rejected in his native place, but this only leads to the evangelization of the surrounding villages (v. 6b.), while in 6:7ff. the twelve are sent out two by two, and they preach that men should repent and they perform many miracles. In 6:31 Jesus and his disciples have no leisure in which to eat, and in 6:53ff. he is again thronged by the people.[29] Moreover, St. Mark nowhere hints that Jesus is uncertain about the character or scope of his messianic mission in the world. From the outset of his ministry the Mightier One (1:7) is sure of himself. He knows that the Kingdom of God is at hand (1:15); he can secure the allegiance of men at a moment's notice (1:16ff.); he teaches and commands with such authority that he astonishes the public (1:22ff.); he can forgive sins and prove it by a miraculous demonstration (2:1ff.); he knows that he has come to call not the righteous but the sinful, and that the wedding guests will fast when the Bridegroom is taken away from them (2:15ff., 18ff.). *Ab initio* Jesus is fully aware of his soteriological vocation and of the destiny he must fulfill.

As we have already argued, the significance of Mark 7:24b

----

[28] See V. Taylor, *The Gospel According to St. Mark* (London, 1952), pp. 349, 635f. We use the words "still less" advisedly, for there is always the possibility that the evangelist may have been to some slight extent affected by the notion that just as he and his readers must beware of Herod (Agrippa II), so Jesus had to beware of Herod (Antipas).

[29] Cf. 8:1, though the location here is somewhat uncertain (see 7:31).

is that Jesus, despite his reserve, wins great fame as a worker of miraculous deeds—fame that in this case goes before him into a foreign land. The secret Messiahship must needs reveal itself if only in the form of authoritative utterance and thaumaturgical power. Such a motif finds ample exemplification elsewhere in the gospel, and the same holds of other themes that figure prominently in 6:31—8:26. This section, in which the story of the Syrophoenician woman occupies a central place, is intimately bound up with the doctrinal structure of St. Mark's literary scheme. Doubtless the pace quickens after 6:30, and the Lord's movements become more extensive. But this feature, so far from being a sign of the section's discontinuity with the rest of the gospel, seems to have direct reference to the impending announcement of the passion (8:31): time is running short, and much remains to be done. Thus the situation portrayed reflects that of the Christian communities with which the evangelist is concerned: the gospel has to be preached to all the Gentiles (13:10), and the end of history is not far distant (9:1; 13:30).

4

The Congruence of Mark 7:24–31

The story of the Syrophoenician woman is securely integrated into St. Mark's theologico-literary scheme, being adequately motivated as part of a work intended for members of one or more early Christian communities that resulted from the apostolic mission to the Gentiles. For when 7:24–31 is examined in relation to the evangelist's constructive effort as a whole, it becomes palpable that the content of the pericope is thoroughly congruent with his creative design. The main body of the present consideration of the passage divides into five sections centering respectively around the following principal motifs: (1) defilement, (2) residual superabundance, (3) the bread of life, (4) reciprocal visitation, and (5) Jesus as Lord.

In Mark 7:24ff. Jesus travels to the borders (or region) of Tyre.[1] He enters a house and does not wish anyone to know it (cf. 9:30). But he cannot be concealed, for presumably his fame as a worker of miraculous cures has gone before him even into a foreign land. Immediately a woman, whose daughter is suffering from demon possession, hears about him,

[1] The words "and Sidon" are omitted by D and other authorities; probably they were brought into the text through the influence of Matt. 15:21 and Mark 7:31; cf. Mark 3:8.

and comes and prostrates herself before him. The woman is a Greek, a Syrophoenician by race;[2] and she implores him to rid her daughter of the demon. And he says to her, "Let the children first be fed, for it is not good to take the children's bread and throw it to the dogs." But she replies, "Yes,[3] Lord; yet even the dogs under the table eat of the children's crumbs." And he says to her, "Because of this saying you may go; the demon has left your daughter." And she goes to her house, and finds the child lying on a bed, the demon gone. Then he goes out of the region of Tyre and passes through Sidon to the Sea of Galilee in the midst of the borders (or territory) of the Decapolis.

Like the story of the exorcism in the country of the Gerásenes (5:1ff.), this account of the saving work in the borders of Tyre probably owes its place in the gospel to a desire on the evangelist's part to show that the apostolic mission to the Gentiles found prefigurement in the Messiah's earthly career.

---

[2] The term "Syrophoenicians" was used to distinguish Syrian from Carthaginian or Libyan Phoenicians; see V. Taylor, *The Gospel according to St. Mark* (London, 1952), p. 349. Perhaps *'ărammūthā'* ("Aramean woman") stood in the original Aramaic form of the story, the words, "the woman was a Greek, a Syrophoenician by race," representing an exegetical paraphrase intended to make it clear that the woman was not only a Gentile by birth but also a pagan by upbringing and education. If this is so, then (as G. Vermes of Oxford University has pointed out to me) *'ărammūthā'* was taken to mean what it normally signified and, in addition, what (in Galilean Aramaic) the word *'aramyaithā'* signified, namely, "pagan woman." The reading of "widow" for "Greek" in the Sinaitic Syriac may well have arisen partly through confusing *'ărammūthā'* with *'armaltā'* ("widow"), and partly through the influence of the story of the widow of Zarephath, near Sidon, to whom Elijah was sent (I Kings 17:18–24; cf. Luke 4:26).

[3] The "yes" (v. 28) is omitted in P45, D, Family 13 *etc.*, and it may have crept into the Markan text from the parallel in Matt. 15:27; the word does not occur elsewhere in St. Mark's gospel.

In any case the framework of the story in verses 24 and 31, supplying the topographical details of the northerly excursion, betrays unmistakable signs of having been composed by St. Mark himself. Thus, for the *ekeithen* ("from there"), the *anastas apēlthen* ("having arisen he went away"), and the *ta horia* ("the borders" or "the region") of verse 24a, one might compare 10:1 (doubtless a redactional connecting link), where we have the same usages. A house as a place of concealment (v. 24b) is paralleled in 7:17; the clause "he would not have anyone know it" (v. 24b) in 9:30; the vain quest for seclusion (v. 24c) in 6:31–34; the *euthus* ("immediately") of verse 25a and the *palin* ("again") of verse 31 (cf. 8:1; 10:1) are favorite Markan terms, the former especially so, occurring no less than ten times in 1:10–43; also, *ta horia* ("the borders") reappears (in the genitive plural) in verse 31.

Further parallels could be cited, but these are sufficient to demonstrate that in all likelihood the evangelist is here providing a traditional story with a suitable framework, thereby bringing it into relation with his general literary scheme. And perhaps he comes to associate the itinerary with the region to the north of Galilee because in the story as it came to him the heroine's nationality was identified as Syrophoenician. The continued journey, briefly described in verse 31, follows a devious route. But this does not necessarily mean that St. Mark was deficient in his geographical knowledge, erroneously imagining that Sidon, being to the south, was on the way from Tyre to the Sea of Galilee.[4] For if, as seems probable, he had apostolic missionary itineraries in mind, he would

[4] Cf. C. E. B. Cranfield, *The Gospel according to Saint Mark* (Cambridge, 1959), p. 250; F. W. Beare, *The Earliest Records of Jesus* (Oxford, 1962), p. 133. The reading of P45 and certain other authorities ("And he went forth from the region of Tyre and Sidon and came . . .") might also be taken to presuppose that the evangelist's geography needed correction.

not unnaturally wish to give the impression that Jesus' journey abroad was both circuitous and relatively extensive, an impression that is strengthened by the vague reference to the Sea of Galilee as being in the midst of the borders of the Decapolis.[5]

Some scholars have seen in Matt. 15:21–28 an earlier form of the story than that given in Mark 7:24–31.[6] Also, the story does not appear in the third gospel, and it has been argued that

[5] Thus there is no real need for J. Wellhausen's ingenious conjecture, *Einleitung in die drei ersten Evangelien* (second edition, Berlin, 1911), pp. 38f., that the Aramaic *bētsīdhōn* was wrongly rendered into Greek by *dia sidōnos*, instead of by *eis bēssaidan* (the spelling of Bethsaida in D at 6:45). Wellhausen noted that if his conjecture were accepted, the healing of the deaf-mute (7:32–37), would have the same localization as the restoration of sight to the blind man (8:22–26), 7:31 being rendered: "And having again come out of the region of Tyre, he arrived at Bethsaida on the shores of the sea of Galilee, in the midst of the towns of the Decapolis." Cf. M. Goguel, *L'évangile de Marc et ses rapports avec ceux de Mathieu et de Luc* (Paris, 1909), p. 155, n. 4. As we understand the matter, however, Mark 7:31 does not go back to the Aramaic tradition, being an editorial connecting link supplied by the evangelist.

[6] See B. H. Streeter, *The Four Gospels: A Study of Origins* (London, 1924), p. 260. It should perhaps be expressly stated here that in principle we continue to uphold the two-document hypothesis (St. Matthew and St. Luke used St. Mark's gospel and a sayings collection Q as their principal sources), a theory endorsed in Streeter's influential book (the posteriority of Mark 7:24–31 to Matt. 15:21–28 was of course, in Streeter's view, an exceptional case). However, we are well aware that since 1963 the whole matter of Markan priority has been seriously called into question in certain circles, and that the Society of Biblical Literature now has a continuing seminar on the synoptic problem. Significant in this general connection is W. R. Farmer's attack on the received solution in his scholarly treatise *The Synoptic Problem: A Critical Analysis* (New York, 1964). We briefly examine Farmer's work in *The Christian Century*, LXXXI (1964), 1430. Also, in an article "The Condemnation of Jesus: A Critique of Sherwin-White's Thesis" in *Nov. T.*, XII (1970), 321ff., while not denying that St. Luke may have had access to an early non-Markan passion tradi-

the Syrophoenician woman did not figure in the first edition
of St. Mark's work.[7] On the other hand, St. Luke may have
been offended by the reference to Gentiles as dogs in Mark
7:27, and for this reason decided to omit the story. Moreover,
St. Matthew may have based his account of the incident on
the Markan story, modifying and expanding it by utilizing
certain other traditions, particularly the Q report of the healing of the centurion's servant at Capernaum (Matt. 8:5–10/
Luke 7:1–10), a tradition evidently of the same provenance
as Mark 7:24ff., for in each case a Gentile's servant or offspring is healed by Jesus from a distance in response to an urgent request.

Among the respects in which the Matthean account of the
Syrophoenician woman differs from the Markan are: Jesus is
accompanied by his disciples, the woman is designated a
Canaanite, the saying about the priority of the children
(Mark 7:27a) is omitted, Jesus is addressed as "Son of David"
(as well as "Lord"), the journey may not be into extra-
Galilean territory, the woman's faith is explicitly commended, the disciples assert that Jesus ought not to concern
himself with the woman, and the immediate effectiveness of
the saving pronouncement is indicated. It is sometimes posited
that the Matthean version is the more vivid of the two,[8] but
this is doubtful. In an experiment conducted by the present
writer the two forms of the story were read successively to
twenty people, and sixteen of these felt that the Markan version was the more vivid. In any case, vividness can scarcely
provide a sure criterion in attempts to determine orders of

---

tion (*ibid.*, p. 322), we imply that in general the hypothesis of Markan
priority offers the most satisfactory basis for an understanding of the
crucial matter of the trial of Jesus.
   [7] See W. Bussmann, *Synoptische Studien* (Halle, 1925–31), I, 49ff.
   [8] Cf. F. W. Beare: *op. cit.*, p. 132.

literary dependence, and it should also be borne in mind that
fiction may be more vivid, and more interesting, than the
factual reports of historical transcriptions from life.

The saying in Matt. 15:24 ("I was sent only to the lost
sheep of the house of Israel"), which certainly has an Aramaic ring about it, could have been suggested by the saying
ascribed to Jesus in the Matthean version of the mission
charge ("Do not go anywhere among the Gentiles and enter
no town of the Samaritans, but rather go to the lost sheep of
the house of Israel"—10:5b–6). The introduction of the
logion of 15:24 is obviously connected with the possibility
that St. Matthew means to imply that Jesus does not actually
travel outside Galilean territory in 15:21: the Greek may
signify that Jesus retires *in the direction of* the district of
Tyre and Sidon; and, according to the following verse, the
woman *comes out* from that region. Also, the introduction of
this pronouncement is doubtless associated with the evangelist's decision to omit the saying of Mark 7:27a ("Let the
children first be fed"), which could be taken to signify that
the Messiah himself, within the confines of his earthly life, is
intended to work first among Jews, then among Gentiles. To
guard against such a misunderstanding St. Matthew inserts
the saying of verse 24 and excludes that of Mark 7:27a. The
vineyard of the kingdom will be handed over to others only
when the existing tenants have finally shown their utter un-
worthiness by casting out the owner's son and putting him to
death (Matt. 21:41–43).

Of course both evangelists agree in a general way regarding the order of temporal priority, but St. Matthew is in this
connection the more logical of the two writers, being less inclined to read mystical prefigurements of the church's Gentile mission into the sphere of the Lord's ministry. A certain
reluctance of this kind is discernible in other passages. Two

examples may be cited here. In the first place, in Matt. 8:28–34 Jesus travels to the country of the Gadarenes (Gergesenes or Gerasenes), and apparently it is from the motive of self-defense that he here makes use of his thaumaturgic power—a feature that is not so evident in the Markan parallel (5:1–20). St. Mark's demoniac has become two;[9] they meet Jesus and are so ferocious that no one is able to pass that way; sensing the danger, he at once takes radical action against the demons, the implication being that, if he had failed to do so, they would have promptly taken action against him. Also, when the demons cry out, they betray a recognition that he is tormenting them before the appropriate time; evidently the period for casting out demons from Gentile victims has not yet really come. In the second place, in Matt. 16:13–28, which corresponds to Mark 8:27—9:1 and concerns Peter's confession in the vicinity of Caesarea Philippi, Jesus does not address the multitude at verse 24, as he does in the Markan parallel (8:31).

Furthermore, St. Matthew may detect an incoherence in Mark 7:27f., for according to verse 27a, the children must first be fed, whereas in the woman's response (v. 28), which is accepted as valid, the dogs under the table are fed (though unintentionally) at the same time as the children.[10] Again, in view of his explicit emphasis on the woman's faith, St. Mat-

[9] Cf. Matt. 20:30 where two blind men appear instead of blind Bartimaeus (Mark 10:46).

[10] Cf. M. J. Lagrange's comment: "La femme modifie seulement un peu l'hypothèse. Si les chiens mangent les miettes qui tombent de la table, ils sont donc servis en même temps que les enfants, et non pas à attendre. Naturellement leur part est moins bonne, la femme s'en contente" (*Évangile selon Saint Marc*, Paris, 1920, p. 185). But it remains that the children are the intended object of the service, the consumption of the crumbs by the dogs *under* the table being of the nature of a side-effect. Gentiles still have to wait before they can take their places *at* the table of the Lord.

thew may wish to make the test more severe than it is in the Markan form of the story. It is arguable that she receives some encouragement in Mark 7:27a, the suggestion being that she will receive benefit from the Messiah, but as a Gentile she must wait her turn. Thus St. Matthew has an additional motive for the omission of the saying of Mark 7:27a from his account of the incident. On the obverse side, such an omission would also subserve the evangelist's anti-Semitism: Jesus remained consistently in harmony with his messianic vocation to his own people, ever recognizing that the mission was exclusively a mission to them. Thus the Jewish act of rejecting the Messiah becomes the more reprehensible; and the Lord's compatriots cannot plead the excuse that he in any way neglected them in order to serve pagans.[11]

---

[11] Anti-Semitism is also involved in St. Mark's gospel, but it is stronger in St. Matthew's; see *M.R.*, pp. 224ff.—We ought perhaps to notice here that some scholars think it unwise to use the term "anti-Semitism" in this general regard. Their reasons include: (a) The word is inaccurate and misleading (Arabic is no less semitic than Hebrew); (b) The term came to be employed in connection with a relatively recent racialist theory of Nordic superiority that has no relevance to the ambiance in which Christianity emerged; (c) Partly because of its association with the aberrations of Hitlerism, the word is highly emotive. Despite its dangers, however, we consider our present use of the term advisable, and this on two main grounds. In the first place, such somewhat clumsy alternatives as "anti-Jewish sentiment" or "bitter opposition to Judaism" are only too liable to perpetuate the mistaken idea that the original exponents of the apostolic faith did not regard themselves as defenders of genuine Judaism. In the second place, there still persists widespread reluctance in Christian circles to face up to the fact that the evangelists' engagement in an internecine struggle with the mother religion engendered an *odium theologicum* which over the subsequent centuries has been to some extent responsible for what in present-day parlance would ordinarily be described as "anti-Semitic."—In his remarkably well-documented work *Le secret messianique dans l'évangile de Marc* (Paris, 1968), p. 18, G. Minette

The climax in Matt. 15:28 ("Then Jesus replied to her, 'O Woman, great is your faith! Be it done for you as you wish.' And her daughter was made whole from that hour") could easily be a modification of Mark 7:29f. ("And he said to her, 'For this saying you may go; the demon has left your daughter.' And she went home, and found the child lying on the bed, the demon gone.") in the light of the commendation of the centurion of Capernaum in Matt. 8:10 ("And when Jesus heard him, he was astonished and said to those who followed him, 'Truly, I say to you, I have not found such faith even in Israel' "—cf. Luke 7:9). The cry of the woman in Matt. 15:22 ("Have mercy on me, O Lord, Son of David. . . .") may have been suggested by the form of the appeal in Mark 10:47, where blind Bartimaeus calls out, "Jesus, Son of David, have mercy on me!" (cf. Matt. 20:30). A further feature, absent from the Markan story of the Syrophoenician woman, namely, the brusque demand of the disciples in Matt. 15:23 ("Send her away, for she is shouting after us"), could also be derived from St. Mark's account of the healing of blind Bartimaeus; for in Mark 10:48 many bystanders remonstrate with the hapless man, ordering him to hold his peace, but he cries out all the more, "Son of David, have mercy on me!"[12]

It seems probable, therefore, that the Markan story of the Syrophoenician woman is more primitive than Matt. 15:21–28. St. Matthew based his account of the incident on St.

---

de Tillesse gently reproaches us for attributing inconsistency to the author of our earliest gospel; but in his attempt to demonstrate the essential harmony of St. Mark's thinking, Minette *inter alia* turns a blind eye upon the anti-Semitic tendencies plainly involved in the evangelist's mode of representation; cf. *M.R.*, pp. 15, 117ff., 153, 201ff., 224ff., 294; and below, Chapter 6.

[12] The same motif appears in the story of the blessing of the children; see Mark 10:13f.

Mark's, adapting and elaborating Mark 7:24–31 by making use of certain other traditions. This means that the story figured in the Markan edition used by St. Matthew, a conclusion consonant with what one would expect on internal grounds. For, as is shown in the following pages, when Mark 7:24–31 is examined in relation to St. Mark's constructive effort as a whole, it becomes palpable that the content of the pericope is thoroughly congruent with his theologico-literary scheme; it is integral to the evangelist's creative design. Our examination of the passage may be conveniently divided into sections centering respectively around five principal concepts: (1) defilement, (2) residual superabundance, (3) the bread of life, (4) reciprocal visitation, (5) Jesus as Lord.

1. Defilement. The introduction of the northerly journey at Mark 7:24 is probably motivated by a desire on the evangelist's part to provide an illustration of Jesus' emancipation from the Mosaic regulations regarding ritual cleanness, such as demands for the performance of certain lustrations and the dietary restrictions. Being unhampered by the ancient laws of formal or external purity, the Lord can freely travel into foreign territory, enter a house there and communicate saving grace to a pagan, thereby anticipating the church's mission to the Gentile world.[13] We are thus presented in Mark

---

[13] Of course if St. Mark is here implying that representatives of strict Pharisaism could not make excursions from Palestine and converse with Gentiles, he is giving a false impression; they travelled abroad when necessary (as on embassies), held conversations with non-Jews, and certainly came into contact (if not actual physical contact) with prospective proselytes and semi-proselytes. However, perhaps the evangelist merely wishes to stress the comparative ease with which agents of the apostolic gospel moved among the heathen. As for Acts 10:28, its explicit exclusion of social intercourse suggests that Jewish-Gentile relations had deteriorated still further when St. Luke wrote (90–100 A.D.?); cf. below, Chapter 7, n. 66.

7:24–31 with what is evidently intended as a sequel to the immediately preceding section (7:1–23), where Jesus is depicted as repudiating the doctrine that outside factors can defile the essential life of man.[14] In 7:1ff. the Pharisees, with some of the scribes from Jerusalem, notice that Jesus' disciples eat with defiled or unwashed hands, and the evangelist (apparently forgetting that Jesus himself was Jewish) explains for the benefit of his Gentile readers that the Pharisees and all the Jews refrain from eating unless they first purify themselves. When the Master is approached for an explanation as to why his followers do not conform to the tradition of the elders, he replies by citing Isa. 29:13 ("This people honors me with their lips, but their heart is far from me; in vain they worship me, teaching as doctrines the precepts of men"); forsaking divine commandments, the nation holds fast to a tradition of purely human contrivance. Nothing that comes from outside a man and enters into him can defile him (7–15); for it is from within, out of men's minds, that evil thoughts proceed, and it is only through such thoughts that defilement comes about (7:20–23). In the parenthesis of 7:19c the evangelist points out that in virtue of such pronouncements all foods are made clean—an implication which means that much even of the *written* law is no longer binding.

[14] At this juncture the evangelist is clearly overstating his case, for the doctrine refuted seems to be an invention of primitive Christian polemic. Nowhere in the wide range of talmudic literature is the thesis expressly defended that material factors (like water or pork) can purify or defile a person's essential life. The standard rabbinical view accords with Ben Sira's pronouncement concerning the obligation to offer sacrifices—"all these things must be performed because of the ordinance" Ecclus. 35:5; see below, Chapter 6, re ritualism and ethics). The ritual is obeyed since (on talmudic presuppositions) God gave the relevant commandments. Also, it is significant that in Mark 7:5 the disciples, not their master, are the target of the criticism; cf. 2:18, 23.

The new doctrine is translated into action in 7:24ff., Jesus being allowed to practice what he preaches.

We might compare Acts 10:9ff., where Peter, after being divinely instructed in an *ekstasis* or trance that he must not regard as common what God has cleansed, goes to the house of Cornelius, the devout Roman centurion of Caesarea. He associates freely with him and those of his household, explicitly repudiating the old regulation prohibiting a Jew from visiting a Gentile (10:28). He proclaims the gospel of Jesus, Messiah and Lord (10:36), the Holy Spirit descends upon the auditors (10:44), and they are ordered to be baptised in the name of Jesus, Messiah (10:48). Thus the divine nullification of the laws of cleanness finds practical illustration in Peter's conduct at the house of Cornelius. So it is in Mark 7:1ff. The teaching enunciated in verses 1–23 is applied in verses 24–31: words become deeds, for Jesus actually imparts saving grace to a person who belongs to another nation.

2. Residual Superabundance. A further connection with St. Mark's general scheme is discernible in the conversation about bread in 7:27f., though here we need to be on our guard against possible misinterpretation. In the light of 7:27a it has not infrequently been argued that the feeding of the five thousand (6:30–44) is a feeding of Jews, and the feeding of the four thousand (8:1–10) a feeding of Gentiles: verse 27a reads, "Let the children first be fed"—the term "children" signifying members of God's chosen people. It is most unlikely, however, that the evangelist thinks of the matter in this way. There is no sure indication that the five thousand men (6:44) are Jewish, and indeed the pronouncement of 7:27a seems to mean that the process of feeding the Israelites is not an event of the past but is still proceeding. Also, according to the woman's reply in 7:28, the validity of which is accepted, the dogs under the table eat of the crumbs of the bread served to the children. On the other hand, the four thousand are not fed on the fragments collected after the feeding of the five thousand. Actually, the woman envisages a simultaneous feeding of the children and the dogs, and this is in accord with the evangelist's tendency to think of the miracles of the loaves as prefiguring the Christian eucharist;[15] for insofar as the two miracles are construed in such a sense the multitude would in each case be of a racially or nationally mixed constitution.

Thus, although the pronouncement of 7:27a provides no adequate ground for the view that the two miracles of the loaves are feedings of Jews and Gentiles respectively,[16] the conversation between Jesus and the Syrophoenician woman does have a significant bearing on St. Mark's accounts of the feeding of the multitudes. All three passages have eucharistic associations, the notion of the residual superabundance of the bread being especially prominent; and the same notion reappears in 8:14–21. According to 6:42f. the hunger of everyone in the thronging multitude is satisfied, and twelve baskets full of broken pieces are gathered; again, according to 8:8, the needs of the multitude are supplied, and seven baskets full of broken pieces are collected. In each instance, therefore, a crowd is adequately served with food, and there is enough

[15] See *M.R.*, pp. 106f.

[16] F. W. Danker in *J.B.L.*, LXXXII (1963), 215f., defends the reading "have come from afar" (Codex Sinaiticus, D, *etc.*) in Mark 8:3 and contends that the evangelist may have had Josh. 9:6 or Isa. 60:4 in mind in his endeavour to give the second miracle of the loaves a Gentile orientation. But in Isa. 60:4 "all" not "some" (as in Mark 8:3c) "have come from afar," and "all your sons" refers to members of the Israelite dispersion.

left over by those who partake of the meal to satisfy the needs of others; and this is the point made by the woman in the adroit reply of 7:28—the crumbs that fall from the children's table are sufficient to provide the dogs with a meal.[17]

3. The Bread of Life. That the miracles of the loaves are meant to have a mysterious significance is brought out in Mark 8:14–21, the pericope that follows the Pharisees' demand for a sign from heaven. Jesus and his disciples are crossing the Sea of Galilee to Bethsaida, and they have forgotten to take bread, although they have one loaf with them in the boat (v. 14). Seemingly out of the blue Jesus issues warnings against the leaven of the Pharisees and the leaven of Herod. Perhaps it is a case of the association of ideas: it was felt to be appropriate that a saying containing a reference to leaven (even in a metaphorical sense) should be introduced into a passage concerning bread (again in a predominantly metaphorical sense). Despite the fact that there is one loaf with them in the boat, the disciples begin to reason with one another because they have no bread. Jesus proceeds to rebuke them for their obtuseness by asking a number of questions—"Why do you reason because you have no bread? Do you not yet perceive, neither understand? Is your sensibility hardened? Though you have eyes, do you not see, and though you have ears, do you not hear?" (vv. 17f.). He then reminds

[17] If the extensive controlling importance of Mark 7:28 is pressed to the extreme limit, then the twelve and the seven baskets full of fragments gathered after the two miraculous feedings would be preserved for the benefit of Gentiles. But it is unlikely that the evangelist applied the principle entailed in the woman's reply with such mechanical consistency. He is content with the suggestion of residual superabundance: there is always more than enough for those who are fed.

them of the two miraculous feedings and of the residual abundance of fragments taken up in each instance, and ends the conversation by again asking, "Do you not yet understand?" Thus the material is so presented that the disciples are expected to discern the mysterious significance of the miracles of the loaves; that is to say, they ought to understand what the evangelist means his readers to understand, namely, that Jesus is none other than the Messiah and Son of Man, the Lord and Son of God, whose presence is mystically apprehended at the church's sacramental meals of fellowship and who imparts the eucharistic bread for the nourishment of the souls of those incorporated into the New Israel according to the spirit. To use terminology derived from John 6:22ff., he is the bread of life that comes down from heaven—and the one true loaf that is with the disciples in the boat.[18]

All this has an important bearing on the conversation in Mark 7:27f. Jesus declares: "Let the children first have their fill; for it is not good to take the children's bread and throw it to the dogs." To which the Syrophoenician woman makes the intelligent response: "Admittedly, Lord, but even the dogs under the table eat the children's crumbs." Of course in a literal sense this answer is quite unconvincing, for the crumbs normally dropped at a meal in a common household, while they might satisfy the hunger of a few small birds, would scarcely provide an adequate repast for a number of dogs—animals that (at least prior to the *eschaton*) are no-

[18] It seems clear therefore that the conversation of Mark 8:14–21 bears witness to a tension in the evangelist's own mind: according to St. Mark's basic philosophy the resurrection of the Son of Man inaugurates the period of enlightenment, and yet his faith in the Messiahship and Lordship of Jesus presses for overt recognition in his representation of the Messiah's earthly life of obscurity and dire humiliation; see *M.R.*, pp. 102ff., 172ff., 188ff.

toriously carnivorous rather than vegetarian. Such considerations, however, are wholly irrelevant, for it is the parabolic
significance of the language that is determinative. As in the
accounts of the miracles of the loaves, the evangelist is thinking in terms of the saving power of the sacramental bread, the
grace appropriated by believers at the church's eucharistic
celebrations. The capacity of such bread to satisfy the needs
of the world knows no intrinsic limitation. It is in superabun-
dant supply, and any curtailment in the impartation of its
healing potency is extrinsically conditioned by lack of faith
(cf. Mark 6:5f.). There is always more than enough for
others, be they Jews or Gentiles, besides those who have already received it.

Admittedly, a discrepancy is involved: in Mark 8:14b
Jesus is actually identified with the bread, whereas in Mark
7:27f. Jesus is represented as dispensing the bread to the children. Such a shift of standpoint, however, is in no way surprising since the same kind of ambivalence is present in the
earliest available literary sources concerning the eucharist,
and it may well exist in the common cultic tradition lying behind I Cor. 11:23–26 and Mark 14:22–25.[19] Both the Pauline
and the Markan reports imply that the eucharist was fundamentally a religious meal of communion. The members of the
holy fellowship were all one body as they partook of one loaf
(cf. I Cor. 10:15).

But paschal associations at an early date seem to have complicated thought on the subject, the consequence being that
the eucharistic bread quickly came to be construed as the
body of the sacrificed Lord. Thus the Messiah in certain influential circles assumed a dual role: besides presiding over the

[19] See *M.R.*, pp. 266ff.

eucharistic rite, he is also one with the sacred bread consumed by the Christian communicants. A second factor that may have been involved concerns the parallelism between the unifying function of the corporeal existence of Jesus during his earthly life and the unifying function performed by the eucharistic bread through which the oneness of believers is realized; just as the Messiah's bodily presence had been the rallying point of the fraternity of the disciples prior to the crucifixion, so in the interim period between the post-resurrection christophanies and the parousia in glory the bread of the holy table is the center and focus of Christian fellowship. A third factor which merits mention is the analogy between the Messiah's act of giving the bread and his act of giving himself sacrificially for the salvation of humanity; as the bread is broken and given to communicants, so the Lord surrendered his physical life in the fulfillment of his redemptive mission in the world.[20]

Accordingly, the discrepancy in question, so far from indicating that Mark 7:27f. and 8:14b are unrelated, actually bears witness to the affiliation of both passages with eucharistic doctrine, wherein the same ambivalence exists.

4. Reciprocal Visitation. A connection of a topographical character in St. Mark's general scheme may be contained in 7:24, 31, where the reference to Tyre and to Tyre and Sidon are perhaps intended to be understood in the light of Mark 3:7–12.[21] The latter is a generalizing passage, doubtless composed by the evangelist himself and designed to bring out

[20] Cf. Mark 10:45; 14:22; I Cor. 11:24; Gal. 2:20; also, G. Vermes, *Scripture and Tradition in Judaism* (Leiden, 1961), pp. 193ff.
[21] See S. E. Johnson, *A Commentary on the Gospel according to St. Mark* (London, 1960), p. 135.

something of the importance of the materials he is assembling in relation to his theologico-literary aims.[22] In 3:7f. Jesus and his disciples withdraw to the sea shore and a great multitude follows; also, there comes to him (his fame having spread) a great multitude from Judea, Jerusalem, Idumea,[23] Transjordania and from the district of Tyre and Sidon. Perhaps the doubling of the "great multitude" here arises from a concern on the writer's part to emphasize that those who resorted to Jesus were far more numerous and were drawn from a much more extensive area than those who resorted to John the Baptist.[24] But what is significant from our present standpoint is that in the course of St. Mark's narrative, with the exception of Idumea (which may exemplify a Markan tendency to hyperbole), Jesus operates in all the places mentioned in 3:7f. He is already in Galilee at 1:14; he visits Transjordania in 5:1, the regions of Tyre and Sidon in 7:24, 31, the territories of Judea and Transjordania in 10:1, and he enters Jerusalem in 11:11. Thus an active interest in the Lord's astonishing authority (cf. 1:22, 27) is awakened over a wide area, and he recognizes the validity of such interest by visiting the districts—even those in foreign countries— from which the great multitudes are drawn, thus anticipating and authenticating the church's mission to the world.

[22] See *M.R.*, pp. 62ff.

[23] "Idumea" is omitted in certain authorities, including the Sinaitic Syriac and some Old Latin MSS., and also in the parallels at Matt. 4:24f. and Luke 6:17f. The omission could have been made because Idumea remained *terra incognita* so far as the expansion of primitive Christianity was concerned. Cf. below, n. 33.

[24] See Mark 1:5. The evangelist indulges in literary extravagance when he writes that *all* the region of Judea and *all* the Jerusalemites were baptised by John.

5. Jesus as Lord. Commentators (among them the present writer) have been wont to argue that the title *kurios* in Mark 7:28 should be translated "sir"—that is, the Syrophoenician woman in her counter to Jesus' basic statement uses a polite rather than a religious form. In all three later gospels the disciples frequently employ *kurios* in the vocative when addressing Jesus, and no doubt the meaning "Lord" (a favorite Gentile equivalent of "Messiah") is intended; also, the third and fourth evangelists often refer to Jesus as "the Lord" in narrative. On the other hand, St. Mark never uses *kurios* in narrative and never employs the vocative except in the woman's reply;[25] moreover, this is the only miraculous healing recounted in his work in which the patient is definitely identified as a Gentile.

Hence, in view of the exceptional character of the account, it may well be that St. Mark means the vocative *kurie* to have its integral messianic import. The woman's knowledge then stands in dramatic contrast to the disciples' lack of insight, a motif greatly stressed in the general context of the story (cf. 6:52; 7:17; 8:14–21). And it is noteworthy that in the Matthean parallel the woman's form of address is understood messianically, the title "Son of David" being set in apposition with the *kurie:* she comes forth and cries, "Have mercy upon me, Lord, Son of David" (Matt. 15:22). So worded the woman's plea becomes reminiscent of Mark 10:47, where blind Bartimaeus cries, "Son of David, Jesus, have mercy upon me." Apparently, St. Matthew is associating Mark 7:24–31 with Mark 10:46–52, a presumption that finds some

[25] The evangelist may understand "the Lord" of the scriptural quotation in Mark 1:3 in its full Christian significance, applying it to Jesus rather than to God.

confirmation in the explicit commendation of faith at Mark
10:52 and at Matt. 15:28; and the likelihood is that the same
association is operative also in the thought of St. Mark himself.

As we have previously maintained,[26] Mark 10:46–52, being
immediately preceded by a report of the failure of the sons of
Zebedee to appreciate the moral implications of Jesus' Messiahship, may be meant to provide a significant contrast. In
two other passages in the second main section of the gospel
(8:34; 9:38ff.) favorable reference to outsiders has been made
after exemplifications of the disciples' incapacity to grasp the
import of the messianic secret. Further, besides having such a
retrospective connection, the story seems to have a prospective bearing on the account of the triumphal entry which follows. For, by appealing to Jesus as Son of David, Bartimaeus
supplies a foil to the acclamations of the public in 11:9–10.

Apparently the blind man calls out under the stress of
temporary emotional excitement and does not, as the evangelist interprets the matter, realize the full import of the title he
uses; at all events, when he comes near to Jesus he addresses
him simply as *"rabbounei"* (v. 51). Nevertheless, for a fleeting
moment, as though by a flash of insight, he provides the
multitude with an opportunity to apprehend and acknowledge the secret. But the opportunity is not taken. He calls out
loudly to the Son of David, yet the bystanders only remonstrate with him, and enjoin him to silence. Thus St. Mark
seems to be anticipating the paradoxical notion of John 9:39:
the Lord appears on the historical scene that those who do not
see may see and that those who see may become blind. The
blindness of those who see receives further illustration in the

---

[26] See *M.R.*, pp. 189ff.

cries of welcome in 11:9f. The mention of "our father David" in the third acclamation (v. 10a), at once so near to and so far from the ecstatic exclamations of blind Bartimaeus, gives striking proof that the people, though they have eyes, do not see.

It would seem, therefore, to be part of the evangelist's doctrinal intent to suggest that the Syrophoenician woman, in addressing Jesus as Lord, is a presage of things to come. Even during the earthly ministry, before the Messiah's final rejection by his own people, a representative of the religiously unprivileged world can, in a moment of deep insight,[27] recognize in Jesus the Lord of the Christian cultus who offers himself as the bread of life for the salvation of humanity.[28]

So we come to the end of the examination of Mark 7:24–31 in its bearing upon the evangelist's philosophical orientation, an examination conducted from the five different standpoints provided by the notions of defilement, residual superabundance, the bread of life, reciprocal visitation, and the Lordship of Jesus. The various investigations go to show that the story of the Syrophoenician woman is congruent with St. Mark's doctrinal scheme. Exemplifying characteristic themes evident elsewhere in the gospel, the report plays a significant role in the unfolding of the evangelist's ideas.

[27] We now hold that the Pauline pronouncement, "No one can say, 'Jesus is Lord,' except by the holy Spirit" (I Cor. 12:3), does not constitute a true parallel since it postulates a "revealed" (not a "natural") theology; see below, Chapter 6 (re reason and revelation).

[28] In Mark 5:19f. Jesus instructs the cured man to make known what "the Lord" has done for him, and it is noteworthy that he proceeds to announce what "Jesus" has done for him. It should also be observed that in Mark 15:39 the Roman centurion acknowledges the divine Sonship only *after* Jesus has breathed his last.

Hence there is warrant for the conclusion that the pericope appeared in the original edition of the work—especially so in view of the probability that the Matthean version of the story is based on the Markan.

Accordingly, a careful scrutiny of the gospel persuades us that Mark 7:24–31 follows directly from the design of the evangelist: he wishes to illustrate the Lord's freedom from the purity regulations and to demonstrate that the apostolic mission to the Gentiles was prefigured in the earthly ministry; and he infers from the tradition's reference to the woman's Syrophoenician connections that the journey beyond Palestine was an excursion into the region of Tyre and Sidon— totally disregarding the possibility that she may have been thought of by the tradents as an emigree resident in Galilee.

The assessment of the redactional situation to which we are led thus runs counter to that defended by W. Marxsen, who argues that the localization of the incident in the vicinity of Tyre is pre-Markan, and that the pressure of the tradition overcame a certain reluctance on the evangelist's part to include the story in his gospel.[29] Much of Marxsen's argument seems to presuppose the validity of Lohmeyer's thesis that, in St. Mark's interpretation, Galilee is the land of revelation and the scene of eschatological fulfillment. The people that sat in darkness saw a great light. So the predictions of Mark 14:28 and 16:7 are taken to envisage a Galilean parousia: the glorious manifestation of the exalted Son of Man is to occur in the region where he revealed himself amid the obscurity of his humble human life on earth (pp. 57ff.).

As we have shown elsewhere, however, a hermeneutics of

---

[29] See his work, *Der Evangelist Markus: Studien zur Redaktionsgeschichte des Evangeliums* (Göttingen, 1956), esp. pp. 36ff. The parenthetical page numbers in the text are references to this book.

this kind is open to weighty objections.[30] Marxsen even goes so far as to assert that Galilee alone is of interest to St. Mark (p. 61). But if this were really the case, there would be little possibility of giving an adequate explanation of the fact that the evangelist locates the most remarkable revelation of the Messiahship, the confession of 14:62, not in Galilee, but at a plenary session of the sanhedrin, at the residence of the high priest in the heart of Jerusalem.[31] That St. Mark is here to some extent prompted by anti-Semitic feeling can scarcely be doubted. But the form both of the high priest's question and of the confessional response betrays the operation also of a genuinely religious motive. The evangelist's faith in the reality of the Messiahship is pressing for overt recognition, the consequence being that the Lord's essential glory penetrates the encompassing gloom of the events to which the passion narrative bears witness, and the life of Jesus even at Jerusalem, despite its lowliness and shame, tends to become the actual sphere of his parousia in exaltation. Those who sat in the shadow of death, upon them did the light shine.[32]

But Mark 14:62 is not an utterly isolated phenomenon, for it exemplifies tendencies evident in other parts of the gospel; and, as we have seen, the same applies to Mark 7:24–31, a story which, despite its peculiarities, evinces characteristic recurrent motifs. On the other hand, Marxsen, who directs his attention for the most part on questions of doctrinal topography, judges the story to be of the nature of a discrepancy within the contextual framework of the gospel.

[30] See *M.R.*, 252ff.
[31] Regarding the climactic character of Mark 14:62, see P. Winter's paper, "The Marcan Account of Jesus' Trial by the Sanhedrin," in *J.T.S.*, n. s., XIV (1963), 94ff.
[32] Cf. *M.R.*, pp. 227f., 242f.

Regarding it as the only Markan pericope which reports events that are unambiguously located in Gentile territory, he contends that the evangelist, fully aware of the incongruence, hastens to restore the connection with the region of revelation by introducing among the stations of 7:31 a reference to the Sea of Galilee (p. 44). Such a contention is not made without difficulty, however, since it militates against Marxsen's general estimate of the redactional situation, according to which, the evangelist takes over the geographical data of the traditions and refrains from supplementing them with additions of his own (p. 61). This estimate itself seems to have no secure foundation,[33] but it has considerable importance in Marxsen's treatment of the redactional history of the gospel.

Moreover, even from a topographical standpoint, the Markan story of the Syrophoenician woman does not seem to be out of joint with the plan of the work. Already in 5:1ff. Jesus crosses the sea and wins fame as a thaumaturge in the country of the Gerasenes; subsequently, in 8:27ff. he enunciates the ethical principles of the gospel before the multitude (v. 34) in the vicinity of Caesarea Philippi. Marxsen would avoid such an objection by arguing that, for the evangelist, "Galilee" means much more than a political segment of the tetrarchy of Herod Antipas: Galilee is an extensive region around the Sea of Galilee (p. 42). So it is in this extensive sense that Galilee is, for the evangelist, the home of the gospel; and 1:28, where the fame of Jesus spreads all over the

---

[33] For instance, the reference to Idumea in Mark 3:8 evidently has little support in the synoptic traditions, and yet it would be rash to conclude from this, despite the omission in the Sinaitic Syriac and certain other authorities, that it was absent from the original text of the gospel.

surrounding region of Galilee is (after Lohmeyer) construed as paradigmatic, exemplifying a principle regulative of the form of representation in St. Mark's work as a whole (pp. 36, 40f.).

But, it may be asked, what of 3:7f., where the evangelist implies that Jesus' fame has become widely diffused, not only in Galilee, but also in Judea, Jerusalem, Idumea, Transjordania, Tyre, and Sidon? This passage seems to have just as much title as 1:28 to be understood in a regulative sense. Also, the story of the Gerasene demoniac, with its emphasis on pig-rearing in the district, seems to be no less unambiguous about its Gentile setting than the story of the Syrophoenician woman. And finally, when it is recognized that St. Mark's philosophy involves much else than topographical motifs, it becomes plain that the latter story, so far from being an incongruity in the contextual framework of the gospel, is integral to its doctrinal schematism.[34]

[34] Our thesis concerning the eucharistic dimension of such passages as Mark 7:24ff. and 8:13ff. finds noteworthy confirmation in Quentin Quesnell's treatise *The Mind of Mark: Interpretation and Method through the Exegesis of Mark 6:52* (Rome, 1969). This important work is viewed with disfavor in H. C. Kee's inadequate and misleading report "Mark as Redactor and Theologian: A Survey of Some Recent Markan Studies" in *J.B.L.*, XC (1971), 333–336; for a much more careful treatment, see J. H. Elliott's review in *The Catholic Biblical Quarterly*, XXXIII (1971), 135–138.

5

The Life History
of Mark 7:24–31

The story of the Syrophoenician woman dramatically recapitulates a primitive Christian controversy concerning the status of Gentile believers in the Messiahship of Jesus. Like the conflict story in Mark 2:18–20, it is apparently based on a tradition having an import contrary to the general significance of the pericope as it now stands. This is discernible in the opposition between the "children" and the "dogs" (v. 27) and in the remoteness of the exorcist's control of the demon (vv. 29f.). If we include the Matthean version (Matt. 15:21–28), four phases in the life-history of the story may be distinguished.

St. Mark's attitude to the Jewish nation is somewhat complicated, and it is noteworthy that, whereas in the fourth gospel the expression "the Jews" occurs some seventy times, in our earliest gospel, apart from the five instances of the title "the King of the Jews" (15:2, 9, 12, 18, 26), the expression is used only once, in the editorial comment of 7:3f.[1] St. Mark apparently believes that the Jews enjoy the divine prerogative of being the first among men to have the gospel addressed to them: the bread of life must be offered to Israel before it can

[1] Cf. *M.R.*, pp. 117ff.

be dispensed in the Gentile world (7:27). He also seems to take the view that the heathen can have the opportunity of knowing the way of salvation only after the Messiah has actually been rejected by his own people: so in 15:38 the veil of the temple is rent from top to bottom and in 15:39 a representative of the non-Jewish world testifies to the truth of the gospel when the Jews have done as they pleased with Jesus. On the other hand, the evangelist is anxious to make it clear that Jesus in some measure prefigures, already before the crucifixion, the work of the church's mission to the Gentiles. For in 5:1ff. the Messiah passes into pagan territory and, in consequence of the marvelous exorcism he performs there, his fame as a mediator of God's mercy is diffused among the inhabitants of the Decapolis; and in 7:24ff. he travels north to the region of Tyre, where he is addressed as "Lord" by a Syrophoenician woman and he effects a miraculous cure from a distance upon her ailing daughter. It may not be good to take the children's bread and throw it to the dogs, but there is no good reason why the latter should not eat of the bits of bread that fall under the children's table (7:28f.).

The doctrine of the divinely ordained precedence of the Jews comes to expression elsewhere in the New Testament and appears to have been widely held in the apostolic church. Thus, from Rom. 1:16 we learn that the gospel is God's power to salvation for everyone who has faith, for the Jew first, and also for the Greek.[2] Again, in Acts 13:46 it is reported that Paul and Barnabas address the Jews of Pisidian Antioch in the following terms: "It was necessary that the word of God should be spoken first to you. Because you have thrust it away and thereby shown yourselves unworthy of

[2] The omission of *prōton* ("first") in B and G may have been due to Marcionite influence. Cf. Rom. 2:9f.

eternal life, behold, we turn to the Gentiles." It seems, therefore, that certain influential exponents of the apostolic faith
saw an analogy between the rejection of Jesus, resulting in
the crucifixion, and the rejection of the church's messianic
proclamation, resulting in the Jewish perdition. And perhaps
the author of our earliest gospel is affected by such an ana-
logical mode of thinking: just as the church's gospel was rejected by the Jews before the apostolic missionaries could
turn their attention to the Gentiles, so the Messiah had to
come to the Jews and be rejected by them before a Gentile
could make the Christian confession of faith. Nevertheless, a
Syrophoenician woman was able to indicate the shape of
things to come. Her insight was foresight; she discerned in
advance the Lord of the Gentile churches, and duly received
a miraculous reward.

It must be noted, however, that St. Mark also thinks on a
different, more mundane, level and takes it for granted that
the conflict with the Jewish leaders arises from the evil
thoughts and malicious scheming of the Pharisees and others,
not because of any wrong on the part of Jesus (2:6–8; 3:6;
12:13; 14:1). Even the Roman procurator is aware of the
innocence of him who is called King of the Jews and knows
that the hierarchs have delivered him up because they are
envious of him (15:10ff.). Since Jesus fulfills a divine com-
mission he does not seek to subvert the God-given law of
Moses, but carefully complies with its requirements (1:44;
7:9–13; 12:28–34). Insofar as the moral and spiritual principles he enunciates are at variance with the enactments of the
law as these are commonly understood, his teaching is securely founded upon a deeper understanding of the true
meaning of the scriptures. He shows, for example, that it was
only on account of the hardness of men's hearts that the law

made provision for a husband's possible desire to divorce his wife; and a mere concession to human weakness should not be construed as a direct expression of God's will for men (10: 1ff.). In the evangelist's judgment, therefore, it is really the scribes and Pharisees who make void the word of God by maintaining and extending a tradition of purely human invention which perverts the real significance of scriptural statements (7:8-13); and, similarly it is the Sadducees who are seriously at fault in their hermeneutics when they fail to see that the God of the patriarchs is the God not of the dead but of the living (12:26f.). The standard of inward purity which Jesus propounds and explains (7:14ff.) is more fundamental in God's sight, so it is implied, than all the rules for ceremonial cleanness, for, as was revealed to the prophet Isaiah, a people may honor God with their lips, while their heart is far from him (7:1ff.). Although inaugurating the period of a new dispensation, the Messiah continuously has the sacred law on his side.

Thus, St. Mark's gospel illustrates the truth of Morton Smith's thesis that Christianity was differentiated as a distinct sect within ancient Judaism through a particular mode of legal interpretation.[3] The Deuteronomic codification of the prophetic moralism of Amos and his successors had led to the religion of the law, and this eventually formed the basis for the emergence of different schools of legal interpretation, resulting in the formation of different groups for worship and table-fellowship. It is true that the members of the early church had a fervid eschatological faith and asserted the Messiahship of Jesus, but this by no means excludes the legalistic character of Christianity's origin as a separate sect. As Morton

---

[3] See his article, "The Dead Sea Scrolls in relation to Ancient Judaism," *N.T.S.*, VII (1961), 347ff.

Smith puts it: "Even if one were to grant that in Christianity, by exception, a messianic belief was primary, one could still maintain that it was a legal dispute which precipitated the isolation of Christianity as a distinct sect."[4] The soundness of this view becomes clear when it is borne in mind that the alleged post-resurrection christophanies were not taken to constitute an intrinsically sufficient guarantee of the validity of the assertion of the Messiahship of Jesus. Scriptural corroboration was required, and, as Luke 16:29–31 shows, the apologetic inadequacy of the argument from the christophanies could itself be demonstrated by an appeal to Moses and the prophets.[5]

It is St. Mark's conviction, then, that the Messiah has the sacred law on his side, and the ways in which this conviction comes to expression bear witness to the truth that early Christian thought combined predestinarianism with a firm belief in the reality of moral responsibility. Jesus lived and died in accordance with the will of God disclosed in the scriptures, and yet the Jewish authorities are to be blamed for engineering the crucifixion. In the well-known parable of Mark 12:1ff. the wicked husbandmen betray their trust and are deprived of life and privilege; they eventually slay their lord's beloved or only son (cf. 1:11), and the vineyard is handed over to others. So, in the evangelist's usual mode of presentation, anti-Semitic feeling is tempered through an im-

[4] *Ibid.*, p. 360, n. 1.

[5] Cf. P. Winter, *On the Trial of Jesus* (Berlin, 1961), pp. 4f. In I Cor. 15:4ff. the statement "Christ was raised on the third day according to the scriptures" (v. 4) reinforces the appeal to personal experience in the words "Last of all . . . he appeared also to me" (v. 8).

plied distinction between the government and the people. Although the multitude cannot have the secret of the Kingdom of God (4:11f.), they recognize the remarkable authority of Jesus' words and deeds (1:22,27) and they seek him out wherever he goes. Neither the remoteness of rural districts (1:45) nor the walls of a house (2:1; 7:24) are a sure barrier against them, the result being that he does not have enough leisure in which even to eat (3:20; 6:31). Indeed, he is so popular with the general public that his enemies have to find a method of arresting him by stealth (3:6; 12:12; 14:1f.). And when at length the people do make vociferous demands for his crucifixion, it is only because members of the priestly aristocracy have maliciously stirred up the multitude against him (15:6ff.).

But a different kind of tendency was at work in the evangelist's mind. The ruin of Israel being thought of in terms of divine retribution, perhaps it was considered unjust that an entire nation should be condemned for an injustice allegedly committed by a handful of religious and political leaders in Palestine. Doubtless, however, other more influential factors were involved. Besides the progressive deterioration of the relations between church and synagogue prior to A.D. 66, there was a widespread desire among Christians—a desire intensified by the great insurrection (A.D. 66–70)—to make it clear to the Roman world that they were quite distinct from the hateful Jews—and particularly from the Pharisees, who assumed the leadership after the collapse of the state in A.D. 70.[6]

In any case, certain passages in the gospel betray a tendency on the part of St. Mark to equate the people generally with

[6] Cf. P. Winter, *op. cit.*, pp. 111ff.

the enemies of Jesus, especially the Pharisees and the scribes, that is, presumably, legal experts of the Pharisaic persuasion.[7] Thus in 3:20ff., by intercalating a story between the earlier and later parts of another, the evangelist suggests a significant parallel between the kinsfolk of Jesus, who assert that he is beside himself (v. 21) and apparently seek to prevent him from continuing his work (vv. 21, 31), and the scribes from Jerusalem, who attribute his extraordinary powers to the inspiration of Beelzebul, the prince of the demons (v. 22). It is further suggested that the blindness and the hostility of Jesus' physical relatives serve to bring out the real nature of the Messiah's family; those who are truly related to him belong to the spiritual community in which the will of God is performed (vv. 33–35). Whereas the mother and the brothers stand outside (v. 31), the multitude is an attentive audience seated within the house (vv. 20, 34), and this portrayal may well be meant to indicate in advance the spiritual fellowship of the churches resulting from the apostolic mission to the Gentiles.[8]

The Lord came to his own, and they that were his own did not receive him (cf. John 1:11), and such seems to be St. Mark's poignant reflection not only in 3:20–35 but also in 6:1–6, the story of the rejection of Jesus in his native place or

[7] Cf. Mark 12:28–34, where the scribe who agrees with Jesus concerning the two greatest commandments could have been a Pharisee of the school of Hillel. On the other hand, the scribes associated with the chief priests (11:27; 14:1, 43, 53; 15:1) are doubtless officials of the Jewish politico-religious administration. Cf. above, Chapter 3, n. 4.

[8] Cf. the favorable appeal to the multitude in Mark 8:34. According to the teaching of Gal. 3:23ff., faith in the Messiahship of Jesus obliterates the distinction between Jew and Greek; in the fellowship of the church all the members are one in Christ. Cf. Rom. 12:4; I Cor. 12:12f.

patris. This report has its immediate sequel in the account of the mission of the twelve (6:7–13, 30), and the intercalated story of the death of John the Baptist (6:14–29). Such a redactional arrangement of the three pieces of tradition suggests that the evangelist is concerned to indicate that the story of the rejection in the *patris* is a prefiguration of the final rejection of the Messiah by his own people, a collective action which resulted in the scandal of the crucifixion and the subsequent world-wide mission of the apostolic church.[9]

A third passage which must be mentioned in this connection is Mark 7:3f., an editorial parenthesis explaining—presumably for the benefit of Gentile readers—that the Pharisees and all the Jews practice the ritual of washing before meals and observe many other rules for ceremonial cleanness. Since, in the sections prior to Mark 14:1 the Pharisees are usually introduced as the paramount opponents of Jesus, the coupling of the Pharisees with all the Jews in this parenthetical comment may be a step on the way to the more sweeping kind of depiction we find in the fourth gospel. Apart from the five instances of the title "the King of the Jews" (Mark 15:2, 9, 12, 18, 26), St. Mark actually uses the expression "the Jews" only here at 7:3, whereas, as we have already observed, in the fourth gospel the expression occurs some seventy times, the Jews appearing in much the same role as that assigned to the Pharisees in Mark 1–13 and to the hierarchs in Mark 14–16. Thus the parenthesis of 7:3f. appears to provide further evidence of a tendency within the earliest gospel itself to

---

[9] Cf. *M.R.*, pp. 138f. The evangelist may have seen a parallel between the violent death of the Forerunner and that of the Messiah for whom he prepared the way; cf. Mark 9:11–13.

generalize beyond the particularity of Jewish responsibility for the ignominious death of Jesus.[10]

On historical and textual grounds, however, it has been argued that the parenthesis did not form part of the original edition of the gospel. Thus S. E. Johnson maintains that a Pharisaic notion of Israel as a holy people led to the application of the priestly laws of purity to laymen, and that such an extended procedure could not have been generally in force before A.D. 100—some twenty-five or thirty years after St. Mark produced his work.[11] Whether in fact the concept of

[10] Mark 14:55–65 should also be borne in mind, for the evangelist may have introduced this account of a nocturnal trial into the traditional form of the passion narrative, and the sanhedrin was a representative body, including Pharisees as well as Sadducees. Cf. *M.R.*, pp. 224ff., 280ff.

[11] See his *Commentary on the Gospel According to St. Mark* (New York, 1960), p. 131 (and p. 30 re Cod. 2427). Actually, the whole question of the laws of cleanness in the Judaism of the period is extremely complicated, as comes out clearly in J. Neusner's important paper "The Fellowship (*Haburah*) in the Second Jewish Commonwealth," *H.T.R.*, LIII (1960), 125ff., a study which makes use of G. Allon's equally important essay "The Application of the Laws on Ritual Purity" in *Researches in the History of Israel* (Tel Aviv, 1957), I, 148ff. Neusner points out that the *haburah* was a religious society founded in the villages and towns of Jewish Palestine during the Second Commonwealth to foster observance of the commonly neglected laws of ritual purity; that not all Pharisees belonged to such guilds or fellowships; and that members necessarily set up a barrier between themselves and outsiders, the latter being a source of ritual defilement (*op. cit.*, p. 125). Neusner further indicates that, according to Allon, "the following pattern is discernible in the disputes on ritual purity: the Sadducees demanded the strictest possible interpretation of the laws of ritual purity, but limited the application of these laws to the priests in the Temple itself; the Essenes likewise interpreted the laws very strictly, and applied them to every situation in daily life, but separated themselves into communes of observant men and women; among the Pharisees, the tendency to apply the laws of

Israel as a holy people, a nation of priests fenced off from the rest of humanity was the governing motive behind the transfer concerned, it remains that numerous Pharisees had come to apply *mutatis mutandis* the priestly laws of the Pentatuech to the Jewish laity. Obviously this program for Israel's reformation could not be effectively carried out so long as the Second Commonwealth existed, for it was only after the fall of Jerusalem that the Pharisees assumed a dominating position in the life of the widely scattered and now stateless (and tem-

---

purity to daily life conflicted with the impulse to limit severely the laws of purity." Neusner goes on to quote Allon thus: "There are two basic principles guiding the Pharisees, one, to make the law congruent to the needs of living, and the other, to extend the principle of sanctity to every man (not only the priests) and to every place (not only the Temple). The second principle obligated the sages to teach Israel to observe ritual purity, and to demand complete separation [from uncleanness]. However, life demanded the limitation of these laws, for it is not possible, or at least very inconvenient, to keep them. Therefore . . . the traditions, such as washing hands before a meal, which were not difficult to keep, or which were particularly crucial, such as the prohibitions concerning women in the menstrual period, were carried out" (Neusner, *op. cit.*, p. 137, n. 30; Allon, *op. cit.*, p. 176). As for Johnson's conjecture, we suspect that in the last resort it owes something to the thesis defended by A. Büchler in his *Der Galiläische 'Am-ha-'Ares des zweiten Jahrhunderts* (Vienna, 1906), namely, that the extension of the priestly laws on ritual purity to the common people took place as a result of the bitterness engendered by the Hadrianic persecutions in the thirties of the second century A.D., the rabbinical motive being radical *apartheid* between Jews and Gentiles. However, Johnson does recognize that the practice of washing before meals had been adopted by Pharisaic fraternities prior to the time when St. Mark wrote (A.D. 71–75—*op. cit.*, p. 20). But why "only recently" adopted? And regarding the general enforcement of the practice, why should he single out the year 100 A.D. for special mention (*ibid.*, p. 131)? Also, can we be sure that those responsible for the transfer of the Levitical laws acted on the principle that Israel is a holy people, a nation of priests?

pleless) Jewish communities. We know that, prior to A.D. 70, Pharisaic guilds or fellowships had been established in the towns and villages of Palestine to facilitate the strict observance of the Levitical purity laws. Among the observances involved was the ritual of washing the hands before meals, members of the guilds in question having made normative for their own ordinary eating habits the ruling of Lev. 22:1ff., according to which priests must perform an ablution before partaking of the sacrifices. But the extent to which such a situation obtained around A.D. 30 is difficult to determine. In all likelihood, during the last thirty years or so of the Second Commonwealth, Pharisees became less prone to eschatological enthusiasm. It was a time of great turbulence and social upheaval, and in the reign of Herod Agrippa I and again in the mid-sixties (in line with the policy of Herod Agrippa II) they exercised a moderating political influence, and sought to restrain the apocalyptic ardor of certain Palestinian groups, including the Christian. And perhaps alongside an increasing skepticism regarding the value of messianism went a growing concern for the application of the laws of ritual cleanness. Hence Christian communities during the fifth, sixth and seventh decades of the century would be exposed to Pharisaic attack because of their fervid eschatological expectation *per se* and, probably in most instances, because of a praxis that was taken to show a basic disrespect for the law of Moses.[12]

[12] Unless our argument is seriously at fault, Jesus himself must have stood much nearer to the Pharisaism of his time than is usually supposed. Even Morton Smith in his penetrating criticism ("A Comparison of Early Christian and Early Rabbinic Tradition," *J.B.L.*, LXXXII [1963], 169ff.) of Birger Gerhardsson's work, *Memory and Manuscript* (Uppsala, 1961) may give rise to misunderstanding when he argues that Jesus' teaching was not Pharisaic either in content or in method (p. 172). Such a contention is undoubtedly true if

Moreover, the view that the parenthesis of Mark 7:3f. is a later interpolation has textual grounds, for the passage is omitted, not only in the synoptic parallels at Matt. 15:1ff. and Luke 11:37ff., but also in Codex 2427. On the other hand, it is not impossible that the omission in this codex should be ascribed to the influence of St. Matthew, whose work provided the gospel text with which the early Christian scribes seem to have been most familiar. Also, it could be that the later synoptists omitted the Markan parenthesis because they wished to avoid an error, for they were fully aware that during the first century A.D. *all* the Jews by no means followed the Pharisaic rulings for ritual purity. Certain other Markan errors are avoided by the later synoptists. For example, the reference to the high priesthood of Abiathar in Mark 2:26 (a historical inaccuracy; see I Sam. 21:1ff.) is omitted in the parallels at Matt. 12:4 and Luke 6:4. Again, it seems unlikely that an interpolation made, say, in the middle of the second century (when rabbinical Pharisaism had become more or less normative among the scattered Jewish communities) would have won a place in all but one of the numerous textual authorities. Accordingly, there appears to be no good reason for supposing that the parenthesis was absent from the original text of

---

"Pharisaic" signifies the type of teaching which came to prevail in the rabbinical schools after 70 A.D. But—as indeed Morton Smith himself is well aware—the dominant doctrinal tendencies exemplified in the talmudic literature cannot be directly equated with the teachings of Pharisaic groups as they existed in the twenties of the first century A.D., and by the same token St. Mark's philosophical outlook is not to be identified with that of Jesus himself. Cf. above, Chapter 1, sec. 3, and P. Winter's review of Gerhardsson's same book in *The Anglican Theological Review*, XLV (1963), 416ff.; also, Winter's paper "Sadduzäer und Pharisäer" in *Die Zeit Jesu* (*Kontexte* III; Stuttgart, 1966), p. 47, and below, Chapter 7, n. 60.

the gospel; and hence it may be included in the evidence for
the Markan tendency to associate the people *in toto* with the
malice of their leaders in the assignment of responsibility for
the Messiah's shameful death.[13]

A careful study of the gospel as a whole suggests that St.
Mark distinguishes four principal periods in the historical
realization of God's saving purpose, namely: the preparatory
period of the old dispensation, which terminates with the removal of John the Baptist; the period of the Messiah's earthly
ministry, which is characterized by obscurity and suffering;
the post-resurrection period of enlightenment, in which the
gospel of the crucified Son of God is openly proclaimed to the
world with courage and confidence; and the final period of
eschatological fulfillment, which is to be triumphantly inaugurated by the Son of Man at his still-awaited parousia in
great power and glory.[14] During the first and second periods
Israel constitutes the sphere within which God's saving operations primarily take place, whereas during the third period,
because of the Messiah's rejection by his own people, Jewish
precedence no longer obtains. The vineyard has been given to
others. The spiritual community of the new Israel, the Lord's
true family, mediating God's salvation, spreads abroad in the
world of the Gentiles, and at the commencement of the fourth
and last period God's intervening power, involved in the vindication of the church's cause, will assume all-extensive cosmic
dimensions (13:24ff.).

Thus the Jews forfeit their long-standing priority, and our

[13] Another passage relevant to the present discussion is the story of
the withering of the fig tree in Mark 11:12ff., for the evangelist here
suggests that Israel stands under the Messiah's curse; see *M.R.*, pp.
120ff.

[14] See *M.R.*, pp. 168ff., 319ff.

earliest evangelist therefore echoes the Pauline doctrine that through Israel's trespass salvation has come to the Gentiles (Rom. 11:11). Before the occurrence of the trespass, however, the priority still holds, and so Jesus in the Markan portrayal can say to the Syrophoenician woman: "Let the children first be fed; it is not good to take the children's bread and throw it to the dogs" (7:27). Israelites are God's children in a special sense (cf. Exod. 4:22; Deut. 14:1; Isa. 1:2, *etc.*). As the Apostle Paul puts it, sonship belongs to Israel (Rom. 9:4), a statement implying that other peoples traditionally must have an inferior status. Although God reveals himself universally in his creation, the Gentiles gave themselves over to unworthy passions. They have become idolaters and thieves, sodomites and revilers of the truth (Rom. 1:18-32; I Cor. 6:9-11). So the opprobrious term "dogs" may be applied to them in their benightedness, a linguistic usage that has, of course, a scriptural basis.[15]

Hence commentators labor under a misapprehension when they seek—within the fundamental framework of the evangelist's revealed theology—to soften the harshness of the distinction between the children and the dogs in the pronounce-

[15] See S.-B., I (Munich, 1922), 724f., I. Abrahams, *Studies in Pharisaism and the Gospels*, II (Cambridge, 1924), 195f., C. G. Montefiore, *The Synoptic Gospels* (London, 1927), pp. 167f., and D. W. Thomas, "*Kelebh*, 'Dog': Its Origin and some Usages of it in the Old Testament," *V.T.*, X (1960), 410ff. Thomas shows that in the O.T. "dog" occurs in the language of self-abasement (*e.g.*, II Kings 8:13), and that its use in the sense of a devoted follower of a god helps our understanding of the term in Deut. 23:18, where it is the equivalent of "sacred male prostitute" (*loc. cit.*, pp. 417, 425); the Ishtar cult evidently had pederastic priests who played the woman sexually (*ibid.*, p. 426); cf. the usage of "dog" in Phil. 3:2 and Rev. 22:15. See also G. W. Ahlström, *Aspects of Syncretism in Israelite Religion* (Lund, 1963), pp. 32f.

ment of Mark 7:27. And, failing to treat the text *a posteriori* in the light of the cultural milieu from which it emanated, they not only force preconceived notions upon unwilling evidence, but also are liable to involve themselves in self-contradiction or fantastic explanations. Thus Bundy, following a suggestion made by Lohmeyer, stresses the overall coziness of the parable:[16] the pronouncement portrays a humble Galilean household, in which dogs are waiting under the table for falling crumbs. Bundy asserts that in such a homely verbal picture "no odious comparison" can be entailed, and yet, curiously enough, he goes on to argue that the third evangelist omitted the story because in it Jesus is reluctant to help a Gentile and because the word "dogs" on Jewish lips had unpleasant associations. Some commentators make much of the fact that *kunariois*, the diminutive for "dogs," is used on 7:27, and they distinguish between "little dogs" or "puppies" or "pet dogs" and "pariah dogs," the street scavengers *par excellence* in the ancient Near East.[17]

So Filson renders the saying in Matt. 15:26 (the parallel to Mark 7:27b): "It is not good to take the children's bread and toss it to the puppies."[18] That is, the Greek diminutive for "dogs" is taken seriously, although Filson's translations of Matt. 21:15 and 11:16 do not recognize a distinction between *paidas* ("children") and its diminutive *paidia*.[19] It is doubtless quite in order not to give "little children" in the rendering of

[16] See W. E. Bundy, *Jesus and the First Three Gospels* (Cambridge, Mass., 1955), pp. 280f., E. Lohmeyer, *Das Evangelium des Markus* (Göttingen, 1951), p. 148.

[17] Cf. C. E. B. Cranfield, *The Gospel according to Saint Mark* (Cambridge, 1959), p. 248.

[18] See F. V. Filson, *A Commentary on the Gospel according to St. Matthew* (New York, 1960), p. 178.

[19] *Op. cit.*, pp. 136, 218.

Matt. 11:16, for Hellenistic writers were liable to be inexact in their employment of diminutives, and attention might be called to Mark 4:1, where, accepting the D reading, the diminutive *ploiarion* of Mark 3:9 apparently becomes *ploion*, "boat." Why then should the *tois kunariois* in Matt. 15:26 be translated "puppies?" Presumably, it is due to a desire on the translator's part to mitigate the undemocratic inegalitarianism implied in the pronouncement. Filson evidently takes the story to be a report of an actual happening in the life of Jesus, and he argues that the effect of the saying would depend on the speaker's "tone and facial expression." The pagan woman "senses that his word is not final," and the "blunt answer" to the request for assistance is not to be understood as "a literal statement" signifying that Jesus called "her and her countrymen dogs."[20] Such argument so obviously savors of special pleading that it is likely to strengthen any suspicion lurking in the mind of the reader that in Mark 7:24–31/Matt. 15:21–28 we have to do with a dramatic representation of a primitive Christian controversy concerning *apartheid* or the segregation of Jewish from Gentile believers in the Messiahship of Jesus.

While recognizing the freedom with which St. Mark uses diminutives, Taylor nevertheless considers that the employment of the Greek diminutive for "dogs" in 7:27b softens "the apparent harshness of the saying of Jesus" to the Syrophoenician woman, and that "the word is not the only indication of a gentler tone. 27a ('Let the children first be fed') and the fact that the woman makes her witty reply, together with the reference to 'the children's bread' and the phrase *ta kunaria hupokatō tēs trapezēs* ('the dogs under the table')

[20] *Op. cit.*, p. 180. Why not "puppies" here, as in the translation of the text?

in 28, all show that He is speaking of household dogs."[21]
Taylor further contends that Jesus withdrew to the region of
Tyre "because the Galilean mission had failed" and that there
was "a tension in the mind of Jesus concerning the scope of
his ministry"—a tension coming to expression in Mark 7:27,
where Jesus "is speaking to himself as well as to the woman."
And—so Taylor concludes—"she is quick to perceive this."[22]

Such comments, however, belong to the realm of pure speculation. St. Mark nowhere gives any indication that Jesus goes
to the region of Tyre because the Galilean mission has failed,
or that he is prone to talking to himself, or that he is uncertain
about the nature and scope of his messianic task. It is true that
in the Gethsemane scene (14:32ff.), which greatly emphasizes the cost of the passion, the tremendous price that has to
be paid for human redemption, there is a moment of unsteadi-
ness or wavering when Jesus prays that the hour of suffering
might pass him by. But it is most unlikely that the evangelist
here means to convey the idea that there is some uncertainty
in Jesus' own mind about the character of the divine purpose.
Indeed the whole mode of presentation seems to imply that

[21] See V. Taylor, *The Gospel according to St. Mark* (London,
1952), p. 350.
[22] *Op. cit.*, pp. 636, 350. Taylor offers no explanation as to how the
woman comes to make her quick perception that Jesus is partly
talking to himself. On the other hand, Taylor resorts to telepathy in
his explanation of the cure of the woman's daughter as it is reported
in Mark 7:29f. While admitting that the evangelist himself probably
takes Jesus' assuring words ("the demon has come out of your daughter") to signify a cure wrought by Jesus, Taylor argues that the saying
may "mean a telepathic awareness of what is happening at a distance."
In support of this view he points to "the objective character" of the
Markan narrative, contrasting it with Matt. 15:28, where it is explicitly reported that the patient was healed from that hour—as in
Matt. 8:13 (*ibid.*, pp. 348, 351).

Jesus knows all along what the will of God consists in and, more specifically, that it entails the passion. Confronted by such an entailment, he shrinks from it in horror, and he overcomes his fear only by way of an agonizing inner struggle. Thus it is not any uncertainty in knowledge, but the weakness of the flesh, that conditions the one Markan instance of the Messiah's hesitancy concerning his vocation.

Furthermore, the various points made by Taylor in his attempt to soften the harshness of Mark 7:27 actually neither add to the biographical credibility of the conversation nor obliterate the radical character of the difference in ontological status between the children and the dogs.[23] We may safely

[23] It is interesting to notice how scholars, especially those unequipped with the form-critical method, betray their personal theological predilections in their treatment of Mark 7:24–31. Thus the Jewish writer, J. Klausner, in his *Jesus of Nazareth* (New York, 1925), pp. 294f., considers the saying of verse 27 to be "so brusque and chauvinistic that if any other Jewish teacher of the time had said such a thing Christians would never have forgiven Judaism for it." He also argues that since the evangelists wrote for Christians who were largely of Gentile origin, they could not have invented so rough a saying and ascribed it to Jesus. Klausner here does not appreciate the complexity involved in the motivation behind the gospels (see *M.R.*, p. 6., n. 4); he fails to realise: (*a*) that the story of the Syrophoenician woman had a history of its own prior to its incorporation into St. Mark's gospel; (*b*) that Mark 7:27 expresses a significant item of primitive Christian belief; and (*c*) that the story in question has its roots in a time when Christianity was a sect within Judaism. Similar insensitivity is betrayed by T. R. Glover (an English Baptist) in his work *The Conflict of Religions in the Early Roman Empire* (London, 1918), p. 127, n. 1., where he contends that the reference to dogs in Mark 7:27 must be a retrojection from the woman's reply in the following verse. That is, in this case, the saying is so chauvinistic that it could not *de facto* have been uttered by the Jesus of history, despite his Jewish birth and education—and yet it was taken up into a Gentile gospel. Strange indeed!

assume that any intelligent Hellenistic woman, addressed in such terms by a barbarian, would have immediately reacted by slapping the man's face. And, as in English, so in other languages, to call a woman "a little bitch" is no less abusive than to call her "a bitch" without qualification. In the parable the dogs may not be street scavengers, but the fact remains that they are not truly members of the household, as the children are; they are *under* the table, not *at* the table, and their consumption of the crumbs is an unintended consequence of the act of feeding the children. And the aptness of the observation derives from the circumstance that, according to an important apostolic belief, the Jewish rejection of the Messiah (Mark 8:31) or the Son of Man's self-sacrifice for many (Mark 10:45) has not yet taken place. Not until the inauguration of the post-resurrection period of spiritual illumination can the gospel be freely proclaimed among the Gentiles. Only then may those who were strangers to the covenants of promise become truly members of the household of God, the commonwealth of the new Israel (Eph. 2:11–22; cf. Rom. 8:15).

Nevertheless, as we have previously maintained,[24] in Mark 7:24–31 the evangelist wishes to illustrate the Lord's practical freedom from the laws of ritual purity and to demonstrate that the apostolic mission to the Gentiles finds some prefigurement in the earthly ministry; and he infers from the reference (in the story as he received it) to the woman's Syrophoenician connections that the travel abroad should be represented as an excursion into the region of Tyre and Sidon, disregarding the possibility that she was an emigree. Accordingly, the evangelist composed verses 24 and 31, introducing among the topographical details of verse 24 the characteristic motif that Jesus

[24] See *M.R.*, pp. 117f., 141, n. 51, and above, Chapter 4 (re defilement).

won widespread thaumaturgic fame despite his reticence and aversion to publicity.

In an important sense, therefore, Mark 7:24-31 is semantically bound up with the teaching of Mark 7:1-23, and the latter clearly presupposes a more or less protracted period of primitive Christian controversy regarding the status of Gentiles in relation to the gospel of the crucified Messiah.[25] Not Jesus himself but his followers are attacked by the critics, and this, as in the case of the conflicts concerning fasting and sabbath observance,[26] is an indication of the report's post-resurrection origin. Also, quite apart from the dogmatic tendencies to think of "the Pharisees" *en bloc* as the opponents of Jesus (7:1) and even to identify the Pharisees in this connection with all the Jews (7:3), there is the anomalous representation of Jesus as one who explicitly repudiates the Pentateuchal laws of ritual purity by asserting that it is only through the inner counsels of the mind that a human being can be defiled (7:15-23). As we gather from Gal. 2:1ff., the actualities of the situation must have been quite different, for the Apostle Paul had the utmost difficulty in persuading Peter and others

[25] S. E. Johnson, *op. cit.*, p. 130, also sees a long tradition of controversy behind Mark 7:1-23. But he thinks of the disputations as taking place between Gentile Christians and Jews, whereas it is much more likely that the controversy primarily eventuated within Jewish Christianity itself. One party in the church, representing the original Christian view, held that the Torah still remained in force and hence that membership of the new congregations was confined to those who complied with the Mosaic requirements. The other party, whose emergence may well have antedated the conversion of the Apostle Paul, contended that belief in the Messiahship of Jesus was *per se* sufficient qualification for acceptance to membership of the Christian communities.

[26] Mark 2:18-28. Cf. F. W. Beare's article in *J.B.L.*, LXXIX (1960), 130ff.

"reported to be pillars" of the original church at Jerusalem that the dietary laws of cleanness, which prevented them from having table fellowship with Gentiles, were no longer operative.

The third evangelist, who made an effort to produce a smooth and coherent narrative,[27] evidently sensed the grave historical problem raised by Mark 7:1–23. From Luke 11:37–41, the nearest Lukan parallel to Mark 7:1–23, we cannot infer that Jesus did in fact adjudge all foods clean (see Mark 7:19b). But what is especially remarkable is that St. Luke assigns the kind of soteriological nexus exemplified in Mark 7:1–31 to a situation in the post-resurrection period. For in Acts 10:9ff. Peter, through a special revelation and independently of the Apostle to the Gentiles, comes to see that what God has cleansed must not be called common or unclean, the consequence being that the gospel is proclaimed in the household of Cornelius, a Roman centurion stationed at Caesarea. As in Mark 7:1ff., words become deeds: a doctrinal nullification of the laws of ritual purity finds practical application, and saving grace is imparted in the non-Jewish world.[28] Thus a controversy that St. Mark has retrojected into the earthly ministry of the Messiah is thrown forward by the author of Luke-Acts into the life of the early church, where it properly belongs.[29]

[27] Cf. *M.R.*, p. 268, n. 18.

[28] Cf. above, Chapter 4 (re residual superabundance and the bread of life).

[29] St. Luke may have been aware not only of the limited nature of the approval given by the earliest Christian leaders at Jerusalem to the Pauline Gentile mission, but also of the persistence in Judea of a form of Christianity which continued to demand the observance of the Torah. Evidently Johnson errs when he urges that St. Luke fails to reproduce Mark 7:1–23 "partly because he regards its issues as already

Accordingly, we are now in a position to appreciate how the story of the Syrophoenician woman assumed its Markan form; and, if Matt. 15:21–28 is taken into account, four main phases in the story's evolution may be distinguished.

Phase 1. It seems to have been assumed by the first exponents of Christianity that Jesus' call to repentance was addressed to his compatriots, and, when Gentiles came to show an interest in their proclamation of the Messiahship, they argued that membership of their congregations was confined to those who submitted to the Mosaic law. They appealed to the authority of Jesus, who, as they alleged, recognized that he had been appointed to minister exclusively to God's chosen. The Messiah came to his own. They attributed the pronouncement of Mark 7:27b to him: "It is not good to take the chil-

---

settled and not relevant to the Gentile church for which he writes" (*op. cit.*, p. 130), for the question of the purity laws is dealt with in Acts 10:1ff. and 15:1ff. Also, there is scarcely sufficient warrant for Johnson's view that one of the most important issues between Jesus and the Pharisees was his rejection of their tradition (*ibid.*, p. 132). The existence of the diverse schools of Hillel and Shammai serves to show that there was no uniform tradition universally accepted among the Pharisees in the earlier decades of the first century A.D., and Jesus did not take the written law at its face value if, for example, the report of his condemnation of divorce may be trusted (Mark 10:1–12). Jesus was apparently in general agreement with Pharisaic teaching on the important matter of the resurrection of the dead (cf. Mark 12:18–27), while his summing up of the Torah in terms of the two great commandments would probably not have been inimical to the spirit of Hillel (cf. Mark 12:28–34). And, so far as Jesus' evident stress on the imminence of the final judgment is concerned, it should be noted that, in consequence of the dire experiences of 66–70 and 132–136 A.D., Pharisees, besides growing more embittered against Gentiles, became increasingly averse to eschatological enthusiasm; cf. above, notes 11 and 12.

dren's bread and throw it to the dogs." This saying could have been proverbial, somewhat corresponding to the English aphorism "Charity begins at home." They dramatized the situation, representing Jesus as making the pronouncement in response to an Aramean woman's request that he should heal her ailing daughter (vv. 25f.). The advent of the Messiah did not terminate Israel's election.

Phase 2. Certain elements in the Jewish-Christian groups came to feel that a belief in the Messiahship of Jesus was in itself a sufficient qualification for church membership, and they elaborated the anecdote of the Syrophoenician woman in the interest of their own theological interpretation, thereby giving the story a significance opposed to that of its nucleus in Mark 7:27b.[30] They ascribed the witty reply of verse 28 to the woman and depicted Jesus as acknowledging its validity: the pagan mother is commended for her intelligent response and her daughter is healed (vv. 29f.). Thus the advent of the Messiah meant the end of Israel's exclusive privilege, and the Torah was no longer an absolute soteriological imperative. On the other hand, concessions were made to the opposing party: it was conceded, in the first place, that Gentiles were not yet *at* the table, and, in the second place, that the Gentile girl was cured from a distance. That is to say, the Jewish upholders of the soteriological claims of non-Jews allowed that Jesus *de facto* confined his therapeutic and didactic activity to his own people, and yet they maintained that, as a side effect of his work, Gentiles on occasion did benefit from his saving grace: the Messiah in his earthly career prefigured the apostolic mission to the world, but the prefigurement was necessarily of a

[30] The same kind of phenomenon is discernible in the controversy story about fasting; see above, Chapter 2.

limited nature, for it was only after the crucifixion that non-Jews could truly become members of the household of faith presided over by the risen Lord. Although scandalous and foolish, the gospel of the crucified Messiah constituted the basis of the commonwealth of the New Israel, in which all, whether Jews or Gentiles, were united by a common faith.[31]

Phase 3. The story as St. Mark received it consisted substantially of Mark 7:25-30, but perhaps without the saying in verse 27a ("Let the children first be fed"). The evangelist added verses 24 and 31 to provide a topographical framework and connecting links, to show that Jesus' fame had spread beyond the bounds of Palestine (v. 24c), and to give a missionary coloring. He may also have added the saying in verse 27a, thereby making more explicit the implied doctrine that

[31] See I Cor. 1:22-24; 3:11; Gal. 4:26-29. The Jewish upholders of Gentile claims in this connection appear as "the elders of the Jews" who form a delegation on behalf of a legionary officer in the story of the healing (from a distance) of the centurion's son or servant (Luke 7:1-10/Matt. 8:5-13). which is the Q analogue of the Markan story of the Syrophoenician woman, and which adumbrates the same controversy. These elders, who recognize that Jesus' saving power can be proved effective even in a medical case of such seriousness that the patient is at the point of death (Luke 7:2-4), are clearly not to be confused with those elders who (in association with the hierarchs and scribes or civil servants) engineer Jesus' removal (Mark 14:43/Luke 22:52, *etc.*), or with the elders whose tradition maintains the laws of cleanness (Mark 7:3). The elders of Luke 7:3 are Jewish Christians and defend their integrationist position by drawing attention to the centurion's generosity: Gentiles, as well as Jews, can be virtuous, and this Roman officer has even made it financially possible to build a Jewish-Christian church; why then should he be refused membership of the congregation? In Luke 7:9/Matt. 8:10 Jesus is presented as personally recognizing the man's worthiness (specifically, his faith), just as in Mark 7:29 he is presented as personally acknowledging the virtue of the Syrophoenician woman (specifically, her intelligence).

the turn of the Gentiles to sit *at* the table would surely come—when the bread of life offered to the chosen people had been finally rejected by them.

Phase 4. This is presented in Matt. 15:21–28. St. Matthew based his account of the incident on the Markan, which he adapted and elaborated by making use of certain other traditions, including the Q story of the cure of the centurion's servant (Luke 7:1–10/Matt. 8:5–13), the Markan report of the healing of blind Bartimaeus (Mark 10:46–52), and a saying concerning the lost sheep of the house of Israel (Matt. 10:6), which may have been associated with the Q parable of the lost sheep (Luke 15:3–7/Matt. 18:12–14) and with the tradition about Jesus' eating with publicans and sinners, preserved in Mark 2:15–17.[32]

[32] See above, Chapter 4. For independent agreement with the basic thesis of the present study, cf. W. Schmithals, *Paulus und Jakobus* (Göttingen, 1963), p. 93, where it is maintained that the story of the Syrophoenician woman was designed to meet objections to missionary activity among non-Jews, and that it reflects a situation in which the church's Gentile mission was regarded as a new and exceptional development.

6

Theological Antinomies: Ben Sira and St. Mark

The selection of Ecclesiasticus and St. Mark's gospel in the present study is not to be taken to imply that any special relationship obtains between the two works. They are chosen simply as examples of important scriptural documents in an attempt to illustrate the thesis that biblical theology generally involves a number of fundamental doctrinal antinomies.

Ben Sira holds that the greatest good is wisdom, a divine quality to some extent displayed in all creation.[1] It can be detected in the world generally and in the law of Moses more particularly; by sustained endeavor men can progressively assimilate wisdom, and the sage would shed light on this highest of all human quests by offering his readers the results of his prolonged reflection on the basic conditions of human existence. By biblical standards Ecclesiasticus, which was probably written some time around 180 B.C., is not a short

[1] For a brief critical introduction (with bibliography) to Ben Sira's work, see our article "Ecclesiasticus" in *The Interpreter's Dictionary of the Bible*, ed. G. A. Buttrick (Nashville, Tenn., 1962), II, 13ff. It is remarkable that such an influential writer as Ben Sira has received little or no consideration in recent expositions of biblical theology; on the whole, much the same fate has been suffered by St. Mark—and this despite the likelihood that his gospel is the earliest connected literary witness to the life of Jesus.

work. The teachings set forth therein are quite comprehensive, and its many-sidedness may be brought out by a consideration of certain fundamental antinomies, contrary viewpoints which Ben Sira does not succeed in harmonizing with one another. That he is in some measure aware of the existence in his work of mutually opposing theses seems to be indicated in his emphasis on the limitations of the human understanding (3:23), an affirmation which dimly foreshadows the Kantian doctrine that the finite mind involves itself in unresolvable contradictions when it is allowed to operate in the uncharted regions beyond space and time. The antinomies exemplified in Ecclesiasticus include: (1) predestination and freedom, (2) optimism and pessimism, (3) retributive justice and factual truth, (4) universalism and particularism; (5) ritualism and ethics; and (6) reason and revelation. In varying degrees and manners they would seem to be encountered in most developed forms of biblical theologizing. Certainly their presence is discernible in basic documents of the New Testament, and in the discussions that follow we take the oppositions listed and seek to show in turn how they severally come to expression in Ecclesiasticus and in St. Mark's gospel.

1. Predestination and Freedom. Ben Sira takes over the ethical monotheism of Amos and his prophetic successors, a doctrine which is also assumed in many of the Psalms and in the book of Proverbs. Yahweh is the one and only God (36:5). He is "the All" (43:27), an expression which is not, however, to be understood in terms of strict pantheism, for God transcends his works, apparently as an artist transcends his materials (43:28). He is omnipotent and all-seeing (15:18), and knows what will be, as well as what has been (42:19). He created the cosmos, whose various parts are permanently adjusted to one another so as to operate in mutual harmony (42:23)—a conception that presumably precludes the possibility of a veritable eschatology. Good and evil alike proceed from God (11:14; cf. Isa. 45:7), and human destiny is in his hands (33:10ff.), not in man's (11:10ff.). The Creator rules with justice (35:12), requiting men according to their deserts (16:12) and controlling the course of events for the benefit of the righteous and the punishment of the wicked (39:22ff.). Yet in his compassion he forgives sins and saves in times of affliction (2:11). Wisdom itself is of divine origin (1:1); it suffuses all created things (1:9) and is supplied to all who love God (1:10).

On the other hand, man is a free being, and wisdom is acquired only by effort of will (6:18ff.). He can choose between good and evil, and therefore responsibility for sin is not attributable to God (15:11ff.). Ben Sira is quite confident that the human individual, on his creation, was left in the power of his own inclinations (15:14). Thus, although at times men may need divine help to overcome their evil propensities (23:4ff.), they alone are finally responsible for the way in which they severally work out their moral destiny. No one is without guilt, and all deserve punishment (8:5), and yet man enjoys the inherent volitional power to amend his ways and turn to goodness (17:26; 21:1).

St. Mark maintains that the whole career of Jesus, though outwardly one of tragic frustration, is in reality a continuous fulfillment of God's saving purpose as revealed in the scriptures.[2] Hence his frequent recourse to proof from biblical

[2] Since the Markan antinomy between predestination and freedom has been amply discussed elsewhere, we content ourselves here with a very brief statement; see *M.R.*, pp. 69ff., 103ff., 151ff., 171ff., 202f. and above, Chapter 1.

prophecy (1:2-3, *etc.*), and hence further—in view of the oneness between the messianic and the divine will[3]—the representation of Jesus as a clairvoyant (14:27ff.) and as a thaumaturge and teacher who deliberately conceals the truth from the public by enjoining the demons to silence (3:11f.) and by addressing the multitude in the cryptology of parables (4:11f.). When, at Caesarea Philippi, the messianic secret is eventually communicated to the disciples, they are at once, like the demons previously, enjoined to silence (8:30). Thereafter they constitute a vitally important elect group since, for the most part, they are destined, as the original exponents of the Easter faith, to be the nucleus of the apostolic church (14:28; 16:7). In the meantime they are privileged to receive esoteric instruction, and yet the deep significance of the secret persistently eludes their grasp (8:33; 9:34; 10:37). And this is evidently because, in the evangelist's interpretation, the Lord's resurrection mediates the transition from a predetermined period of obscurity to a predetermined period of enlightenment, in which the *mysterium Christi* is publicly proclaimed with understanding and confidence, pending the parousia of the Son of Man with great power and glory (9:9; 13:10, 26).

On the other hand, despite his predestinarianism, St. Mark, no less than Ben Sira, firmly believes in the reality of human freedom and responsibility. Although it is not the season for figs, the tree may nonetheless be cursed for its unfruitfulness (11:12ff.). Already in 1:15, at the outset of the Galilean ministry, Jesus calls upon the public to repent and believe in the gospel, an appeal reminiscent of those made in early Chris-

---

[3] In Phil. 2:8 this volitional harmony is explained in terms of the Christ's obedience; cf. Mark 14:36.

tian preaching as it is set forth in the Acts of the Apostles.[4] But from the standpoint of the predeterminism involved in the conception of the secret, the people are not yet in a position to make the required response to the gospel, a circumstance which immediately introduces a structural incongruity into the Markan presentation. Again, the evangelist sometimes gives the impression that he is expecting the disciples to come to a christological assessment of Jesus that is similar to his own (4:13, 40; 8:14–21). Evidently he is liable to forget that they are historically located in the period of obscurity and to treat them as if they were representative of the Christian readers of his work (cf. 13:14).

Moreover, there is a tendency to assimilate means to end, so that in certain instances St. Mark may be said to approach the kind of doctrine exemplified in the fourth gospel, where the hour of deepest humiliation is interpreted in terms of exaltation and glorification.[5] Presumably, the evangelist's confidence in the eschatological manifestation of the glorious Son of Man presses for characterization (with varying degrees of success) in his portrayal of the incarnate life. Hence on occasion the earthly ministry comes to be endowed with a glory of its own, and in a number of passages the true nature of Jesus, as St. Mark understands it, seems to be reaching out for some definite form of expression which it cannot yet receive. In 11:1ff. and 14:3ff., for example, St. Mark's belief is apparently calling for overt recognition, thereby putting great strain on the requirement of secrecy. And, notably, in the account of the nocturnal trial the pressure exerted by the evangelist's conviction subjects his doctrine of the secret to a strain it cannot withstand, the result being that in 14:62 there is ac-

---

[4] See Acts 5:31; 11:18; 20:21.   [5] See John 1:14; 12:23, 32.

tually a disclosure of the Son of Man outside the circle of the initiated.

Here, however, the urge to set forth the earthly ministry directly in the language of a high christological belief is probably reinforced by a desire to ascribe guilt to the Jews as represented by their leaders. For, although St. Mark holds that the passion is provided for in God's predetermining purpose, he nevertheless wishes to make it plain that the crucifixion takes place through the unwarranted hostility of the Messiah's compatriots. The same motive may be detected elsewhere than in 14:62, and it clearly makes for a certain inconsistency in the evangelist's treatment of his subject matter. Thus in 2:10 and 2:28 Jesus publicly refers to himself as the Son of Man; in 10:47f. blind Bartimaeus addresses Jesus as the Son of David; and in 12:12 the enemies of Jesus realize that the parable of the wicked husbandmen is spoken against them. In such passages as these the Son of Man is to a greater or less extent exposed to public view, and so it could be argued that the Jewish authorities were in an inexcusable position since they freely rejected Jesus not in ignorance but with an adequate knowledge of his claims.

2. *Optimism and Pessimism.* According to Ben Sira, man is created out of the dust of the earth (33:10), and to the dust he must eventually return (17:1). His span of life is short (17:2), inevitably terminating, though apparently with a few possible exceptions (48:9; 49:14), in the dismal existence of sheol, where there are no luxuries (14:10). Nevertheless, even death, the gateway to sheol, is welcome to those whose strength is failing.[6] Besides the fear of death, troubles are the

[6] See 41:2. The doctrine of sheol is made less gloomy in Greek I in certain passages (e.g. 7:17), and some of the glosses in Greek II go so

common lot of mankind—nightmares, famines, afflictions, plagues (40:1ff.). Times of happiness are liable to come to a sudden end (18:25f.). All men are sinful (8:5), women especially so (42:14), and it was through the sin of Eve that human beings became mortal (25:24).

On the other hand, good women do exist, and happy marriages are not unknown (26:1–4; 36:18–26). Humanity was made in the image of God and granted dominion over beasts and birds (17:3f.), being equipped with intelligence and skill (38:6). All the Creator's works are good, and he supplies every need (39:33): the world constitutes a magnificent unity in its rich variety (42:22ff.). Whatever misfortunes may exist, they are due punishments for the wicked (27:25–29; 39:25–31) or blessings in disguise (20:9ff.) or means of proving the genuineness of an individual's piety (2:5).

Unlike Ecclesiasticus, St. Mark's gospel is the product of a positive eschatological expectation, and so in this case indications of the writer's optimism are on the whole more obviously present. In general the evangelist is disinclined to dwell on the sufferings of the Messiah or on the afflictions of the church without drawing his readers' attention to the future in which, as he believes, they are to find their end and justification. Although he is for the most part dealing with events of the past and is setting forth the apostolic gospel in its historical aspect, his orientation has the prospectiveness characteristic of the religious optimist who believes that God's will must finally prevail over evil. He betrays something of the fervent hopefulness of the primitive church, being ever prone to look away from the humiliation and suffering of the past, the present,

---

far as to affirm that eternal bliss awaits the obedient beyond the grave *e.g.* 2:9; 19:19; cf. the glosses in the Latin version at 17:23; 21:10).

and the more immediate future, to the coming age, the aeon of fruition and open revelation. The best is yet to be.

Accordingly, St. Mark frequently gives the impression that he is interested in the Lord's earthly life, with its obscurity, lowliness and terminal shame, not for its own sake, but for the sake of the glory which it precedes and makes possible. The hidden Son of Man points out that what is secret must come to light (4:22); and it is in the post-resurrection period that the saving truth is propagated among the nations of the world (9:9; 13:10; 14:9). But even so, the end is not yet (13:7). The messianic *mysterium* may now be publicly proclaimed by the apostolic church, but the last triumphant confirmation of the gospel is still an object of optimistic expectation, and of such confirmation the tribulations of the elect are apparently a presage and a guarantee (13:24). Furthermore, even the parousia itself, despite the preceding tokens of cosmic dissolution (13:24f.) and the subsequent convocation of the elect (13:27), is not to be directly equated with the awaited consummation, but is to be included among the *tauta ginomena* ("these occurrences") that are preliminary thereto (13:29). Thus the evangelist is continually looking beyond the events he relates toward a future in which they are to have their triumphant outcome. Finality is a *fata morgana*, persistently elusive.[7]

---

[7] In P. Vielhauer's article "On the 'Paulinism' of Acts" in *The Perkins School of Theology Journal*, XVII (1963–64), 14ff. (a translation by W. C. Robinson and V. P. Furnish of the paper "Zum 'Paulinismus' der Apostelgeschichte" in *Ev.T.*, X, 1950–51, 1ff.—the translation is reprinted in *Studies in Luke-Acts*, ed. L. E. Keck and J. L. Martyn, Nashville, Tenn., 1966, and the original in Vielhauer's *Aufsätze zum Neuen Testament*, Munich, 1965), it is argued that, whereas, for St. Paul, the essential has already happened (Gal. 4:4), eschatology being a structural element of the christology of the risen

On the other hand, St. Mark is by no means an unqualified optimist. Despite his eschatological hope, there is a certain pessimism involved in his total attitude, just as there is in the case of Ben Sira. Thus he insists that the Messiah has to suffer (8:31) and that the faithful have to pass through dire tribulations (13:7ff.). The contemporaries of Jesus constitute an adulterous and sinful generation (8:38). Successful politicians are commonly motivated by unworthy ambitions (10:42ff.), and human nature is such that men are quite capable of committing the unforgivable sin of blasphemy against the Holy Spirit (3:29). As for the chosen race, its doom is sealed: the cursed fig tree must needs wither (11:21) or, as the matter is expressed elsewhere, the Lord's vineyard has to be given to others (12:9). The Son of God may rise from the tomb to which Jewish ill will has brought him (15:10, 39; 16:6), but it is nowhere suggested that there is any hope of restoration for the chief priests, the elders and the scribes; apparently their future is no brighter than that of Judas Iscariot (14:21). Henceforth the true kinsfolk of the Messiah are those who belong to the spiritual community wherein the will of God is performed (3:35), and yet even they need to be unceasingly

---

Lord (I Cor. 15:20ff.), for St. Luke the essential is still to come, at the restoration of all things (Acts 3:21), eschatology becoming the last phase of a continuous process of redemptive history. *Prima facie* perhaps, because of his forward-looking attitude, St. Mark's position may be thought to approach the Lukan point of view. However, when his work is considered in its entirety, account must be taken of his tendency to construe the earthly ministry directly in terms of the glory to be universally made manifest; and in this respect he approximates to the interpretation of the fourth evangelist, whose realized eschatology, unlike St. Paul's, antedates the passion so as to include the whole of the incarnate life. The essential is still to come, and yet to some extent it is already there in the career of Jesus. Cf. *M.R.*, pp. 172ff., 319ff.

vigilant (13:32ff.), man's capacity for holding out under stress being severely limited; the spirit may be willing but the flesh is weak (14:38), and so the prospective coming of the Son of Man must mean shame as well as joy (8:38).

3. *Retributive Justice and Factual Truth.* Convinced that God is just and impartial in the treatment of his creatures (35:12), Ben Sira argues that due benefits come to good people and hardships to the sinful or disobedient (39:25). Subscribing neither to the Platonic theory of the immortality of the soul nor to the Pharisaic doctrine of the resurrection of the body, he further affirms that just retribution operates wholly on this side of the grave. The requirements of justice are the requirements of God, the absolute Ground of all things; and, being all-powerful, the Creator could find no difficulty in recompensing a man on the point of death in precise accordance with the accumulated merit or demerit of his total moral performance (11:26). Admittedly, Ben Sira holds to the mercy as well as to the justice of God, and this necessarily imposes a significant limitation upon the effectiveness of the requirements of strict retribution as such. In his loving kindness the Lord forgives penitent sinners (2:11), accepting charitable deeds as an atonement for wickedness (3:3, 30). Nevertheless, it remains that so far as the unrepentant are concerned (34:26), the law of moral retribution is written into the constitution of the world. Providence smiles upon the righteous and frowns upon the wicked.

On the other hand, Ben Sira is by no means unaware of the sort of objections such as are raised against a theory of this kind, for example, in the book of Job. He evidently recognizes that the hard facts of common experience at least *prima facie* militate against it, and in this case he makes a deliberate attempt to overcome the antinomy by resorting to a distinction between appearance and reality. Things are not always what they seem to be, and are not therefore to be taken at their face value. The Lord may be slow to anger (5:4), yet his wrath rests upon sinners (5:6), and their day of calamity will inevitably come (5:8), whereas the fear of the Lord brings gladness and long life (1:12). The prosperity of the wicked lacks permanence (40:13), but the afflictions of the righteous are sent to test them (2:5) or to discipline them for their moral improvement (18:13–14; 32:14–15), and good fortune may be concealed in adversity (20:9). Moreover, the spiritual rewards of piety are not to be overlooked; the righteous man gains true friends (6:16), wins a good name that outlives him (39:9–11), and realizes that the fear of the Lord is better than intelligence or knowledge (19:24) and better than riches and strength (40:26). Perhaps here we may discern tentative approaches to Spinoza's doctrine that virtue is its own reward, a notion which figured prominently during the Enlightenment of the eighteenth century and came to notable expression in Lessing's theory of the education of humanity and in Kant's thesis that the good will alone has intrinsic value.

No less than Ben Sira, St. Mark believes that God is just in the treatment of his creatures, rewarding the righteous and punishing the wicked. God is the Creator of the world and it is he who ultimately presides over the whole course of history; with him all things are possible, and, for the sake of his elect, he can curtail the days of the eschatological tribulation (10:27; 13:19–20). Hence the divine will to justice must be finally effective; to use language derived from the Epistle to the Galatians (Gal. 6:7), God is not mocked, for whatever a man sows, that shall he also reap. So throughout St. Mark's gospel we find allusions to the retributive principle. Indeed,

like the idea of fate or necessity in the works of the great
Greek tragedians, it is woven into the texture of the evangelist's philosophy. Thus illness may be regarded as a punishment for sin, as in the case of the paralytic (2:1ff.); the man
is healed through the forgiveness of his sins—a therapy that
manifestly postulates a pathology with a moralistic foundation.

St. Mark is confident that the world is so constituted that
there must be measure for measure (4:24). A process of ethical atrophy is at work, so that the acquisition of little goodness
inevitably leads to still greater moral poverty, whereas an
abundance of virtue engenders a superabundance (4:25).
Such statements bring out the retributive presuppositions of
the call to repentance and faith at the commencement of the
ministry (1:14f.). It is assumed that men generally stand
under God's condemnation,[8] and that those who repent and
believe in the good news will not be punished for their sins.
The news is good because, with the announcement of the approach of the Kingdom, it couples an assurance that there is
still time for an effective change of heart. As with Ben Sira,
so with St. Mark, genuine repentance atones for sin. Hence,
in the evangelist's view, the eschatological announcement must
be an occasion for rejoicing: the Kingdom draws near, and
the repentant can look forward to the blessings of the coming
age in a future that is not far distant. *Metanoia* ("change of

[8] The saying in Mark 2:17, "Those who are healthy do not need
a physician, but those who are ill; I did not come to call righteous
people, but sinners," does not necessarily imply that there are in fact
certain individuals who are entirely without need of repentance. Cf.
Mark 10:18, where Jesus is represented as declaring that God alone is
good; but this may be understood by the evangelist as an illustration
of the Lord's modesty—he did not commit the sin of self-righteous-
ness.

mind") and *pistis* ("faith"), involving as they do confidence in the validity of the good news, guarantee participation in the glories of the age to come.

It must be observed, however, that usually in St. Mark's representation the object of saving faith assumes a more personal character and consists in the divine status of Jesus as Messiah and Son of God (1:1). This is the *mysterium* or secret of the Kingdom (4:11), vouchsafed to the disciples at Caesarea Philippi (8:27ff.) and to the Roman centurion when the earthly ministry has come to an end (15:39). The mysterious truth is communicated by the heavenly voice to Jesus himself at his baptism (1:11) and to Peter, James and John at the transfiguration (9:7), and it is known by the demons from the outset (1:24, 34; 3:11f.). Presumably, the demons are aware of the vital secret because their supernatural mode of being entails special capacities for insight into reality. Their knowledge indeed could scarcely spring from *pistis* as St. Mark understands it, for their behavior is wholly nefarious, whereas genuine faith must issue in action that conforms with the will of God (cf. 3:35). As one would expect, therefore, when demons recognize who Jesus really is they are disconcerted, convulsing with what should be construed as impotent rage or futile fear (1:23ff.). They realize that their doom is sealed, that the end of their reign is near, that Jesus will soon reappear as the victorious Son of Man to preside over the final judgment and to inaugurate the Kingdom of God with great power and glory (8:38; 14:62; 13:26). So far as the demons are concerned, the career of Jesus is a *Verdammungsgeschichte*, and the gospel is bad news.

The gospel is also bad news for unrepentant mortals, although, unlike the unclean spirits, they fail to recognize it as such. People who blaspheme against the Holy Spirit can never be forgiven, and so they must suffer the consequences of their guilt (3:29). To this category apparently belong the physical relatives of Jesus, who deem that he is beside himself and should be restrained, as well as the scribes from Jerusalem who declare that Jesus is possessed by Beelzebul, the prince of the demons (3:20–35). Such seems to be the intention behind the intercalation of the report of the Beelzebul controversy within the story of the opposition of the Lord's family, and it should be considered in relation to the account of the withering of the fig tree and the intercalated pericope regarding the cleansing of the temple (11:12–25): Israel stands under the Messiah's curse, a condemnation that involves Jesus' own accursed[9] death as well as the perdition of the Jewish nation.[10] Apparently the same kind of doctrine comes to light in the dramatic confession at the Jewish trial (14:62). The ominous truth is declared in their presence, but the judges do not realize that they are shortly to be judged by the prisoner who stands before them, when he reappears as the triumphant Son of Man with the clouds of heaven. Although the high priest rends his garments on hearing the momentous utterance, his is not the futile agitation of the silenced demon that knows the truth in the passage already noticed (1:23ff.). The presiding judge is given the opportunity to recognize or apprehend the *mysterium*, and yet he is only incensed at the preposterousness of the accused's syncretistic[11] asseveration and pronounces it to be blasphemy. In all probability St. Mark here means to imply that it is really the high priest himself in his official

---

[9] Cf. Deut. 21:23; Gal. 3:13.   [10] Cf. *M.R.*, pp. 120ff., 289.

[11] For the view that Mark 14:62 is a deliberate attempt to synthesize varying eschatological assessments of Jesus, current in the apostolic church, see P. Winter's paper "The Marcan Account of Jesus' Trial by the Sanhedrin" in *J.T.S.*, n. s., XIV (1963), 94ff.

capacity as representative of the entire[12] sanhedrin, the supreme
politico-theological organ of the Jewish people, who has
committed the unforgivable sin (3:29). The privileges conferred under the old dispensation are to be given to others
(12:9), and this means the end of Israel's exclusive rights; all
men are now to have open access to the divine presence
(11:17; 15:38f.).

As in Ecclesiasticus, therefore, justice must be done; apart
from genuine repentance or *metanoia* (which of course involves faith in God's readiness to remit sins) the righteous
are duly rewarded and the unrighteous are duly punished.
Whenever impenitence or *apistia* ("faithlessness") does not
obtain, appropriate sanctions are necessarily applied to human
conduct. Thus disease is a recompense for sin (2:5–12), and,
given *pistis*, sick people can be healed, whereas, in the absence
of faith, no cure is possible (6:5f.). Preventing the exercise
of God's pardoning grace, *apistia* allows retribution to take
its proper course. Again, Judas commits an atrocious offence
in betraying the Messiah, and so great is the punishment he
must suffer that it would have been good for him if he had
not been born (14:21). Evidently effective repentance is out
of the question in this instance, Judas aligning himself with
those whose hostility to Jesus is unpardonable.

On the other hand, St. Mark, like Ben Sira, is plainly aware
that the facts of general experience at least *prima facie*
militate against the doctrine that the world is in the control
of a divine Power that recompenses men according to their
deserts. Among the actualities of human existence are situations in which the wicked flourish while the righteous suffer
pain and loss. Tyrannical rulers among the nations lord it

[12] See 14:55, 64; 15:1.

over the oppressed masses (10:42), and corruption is rampant in high places, intrigue reigning in courts of justice (15:10). Wealthy people, who probably disqualify themselves for entrance into the Kingdom of God (10:23–25), enjoy material prosperity and hold on to their many possessions (10:21f.). Economic inequalities are an enduring feature of life in this world (14:7). John the Baptist, who preaches a baptism of repentance for the remission of sins and prepares the way for the Messiah (1:1–11; 9:11–13), suffers a violent death through the malice of an evil woman (6:14ff.). The priestly authorities at Jerusalem misuse their power, turning the house of God into a den of robbers (11:17). Thus, among Jews and Gentiles alike, evil flourishes, and, before the termination of the present order of existence, injustices will multiply to an unprecedented extent (13:5ff.).

St. Mark seeks to resolve the antinomy by maintaining that neither the prosperity of the wicked nor the suffering of the innocent is permanent. This age is soon to be superseded by the age to come, and at the moment of epochal transition, which is marked by the glorious reappearance of the Son of Man, all moral maladjustments will be rectified. The first shall be last, and the last first (10:31), and those who judge shall be judged (14:62). Thanks to God's omnipotence (10:27), the righteous must receive adequate compensation for their privations (10:28–31). And so it must be with those who prefer worldly gain to personal integrity (8:36), for whoever is ashamed of Jesus and his words amid contemporary sin and disloyalty, the Son of Man shall be ashamed of him, when he comes in the glory of his Father with the holy angels (8:38).

Thus there is to be a radical change of status at the consummation of the current cosmic aeon. The servant will enjoy exaltation, and the master will suffer humiliation (10:41ff.).

Such a conception of an eschatological double reversal has no place in Ecclesiasticus, for, as we have seen, its author contemplates neither a termination of the present cosmic order nor a resurrection of the dead. Nevertheless, St. Mark could subscribe to certain basic ideas that emerge from Ben Sira's reflection on the antinomy; while he could scarcely agree that the fear of the Lord brings gladness and long life, he certainly could agree that the prosperity of the wicked lacks permanence, that the afflictions of the righteous have a disciplinary value, and that good fortune may be concealed in adversity.

Indeed, the last-mentioned notion belongs to the essence of the evangelist's soteriology, for he holds that it is precisely through the Messiah's undeserved sufferings that a way of access to the divine Presence is opened up for the Gentiles (15:38f.). The crucifixion is the outcome of a miscarriage of justice, Pilate himself recognizing that the prisoner is an innocent victim of priestly ill will (15:10, 14). The wicked husbandmen deal treacherously with their Lord's emissaries, even to the extent of killing his beloved or only son. But recompense surely comes and good ensues, for the vineyard is given to others (12:1ff.). Moreover, the concept of affliction as an ordeal or disciplinary test is adumbrated in St. Mark's eschatology. As a prelude to the glorious appearance of the Son of Man and the convocation of the elect (13:26f.), there must be an intensification of suffering. Wars, earthquakes and famines will characterize the incipient phase of the travail by which the life of the new age comes to birth (13:8), and he who endures to the end will be saved (13:13). This clearly implies that all who come through the eschatological temptation with their loyalty intact thereby prove themselves worthy of the blessings of eternal life to be conferred by the victorious Son of Man at the parousia. The last tribulation is to be of

unprecedented severity (13:19), a *peirasmos* or test of such
enormity as to be an object of legitimate dread, since, despite
all good intentions, tenacity of purpose in the best of men has
its limits (14:38; cf. 13:20).

Dreadful though it is, the *peirasmos*, being an indispensable
means to a desirable end, possesses instrumental value, and in
this respect the eschatological ordeal has an axiological status
analogous to that of the crucifixion. For, in St. Mark's estimation, the sufferings of Jesus are the price that must be paid
for the imminent vindication of his cause at the parousia.[13]
Primarily, the evangelist's attitude is prospective rather than
retrospective; he looks beyond the humiliation of the past to
the coming age of fruition and open revelation, valuing the
earthly ministry, with its obscurity, lowliness and ignominious
termination in crucifixion, not for its own sake, but for the
sake of the glory which it precedes and makes possible. Thus
the passion, like the *peirasmos*, has instrumental value. It is, as
it were, a dark passage that has to be negotiated before the
light of a new day can be enjoyed.

But if ordinary events of a worldly future trail their shad-
ows, a supremely luminous event of a heavenly future should
gleam upon the antecedents that prepare the way for its
realization. And this is exactly the suggestion that is made in
certain Markan pericopes. Thus in the story of the transfiguration (9:2ff.) the three closest disciples are permitted to behold
their Master as he really is and in the form in which he is
destined to appear to the world when he comes again finally
to establish the Kingdom with great power and glory. And in
the account of the nocturnal trial (14:55ff.) there is actually
a disclosure of the *mysterium* outside the privileged circle of
the elect: Jesus gives open confession to the truth and declares

[13] See *M.R.*, pp. 173ff.

that his judges are fated to see the exalted Son of Man coming with the clouds of heaven. Amid the encircling gloom this dramatic announcement has a numinous character; it captures something of the resplendent glory of the parousia, and its reflected light penetrates the darkest depths of the humiliation to which the passion narrative bears witness. In other words, there is a discernible tendency in the mind of the evangelist to assimilate the means to the end, so that in the last resort the value or worth of the passion is not purely of an instrumental nature.[14]

A factor that is plainly involved in St. Mark's total assessment of the situation concerns the phenomenon of sacrifice. For while he regards the crucifixion as the result of a flagrant miscarriage of justice, he also regards it as the outcome of a voluntary act on Jesus' own part. The Son of Man freely gives his life for the ransom of many (10:45), a sacrificial act symbolized in the giving of the sacred elements at the last supper (14:22ff.). Whether the evangelist is here thinking in terms of Deutero-Isaiah's suffering servant may be disputed,[15] but in any event his interpretation exemplifies an appreciation of the atoning value of self-sacrifice voluntarily undertaken,

---

[14] It is sometimes argued that the propensity to confound means with ends is a sign of human waywardness, the case of the miser being cited as a clear illustration. Actually, however, the same disposition lies at the root of civilized activity in art, science and morality. For example, in fine art the capacity to make or construct is cultivated for its own sake, not merely as a means to the preservation of man's biological existence, so that we have the refinement of what Kant happily termed *Zweckmässigkeit ohne Zweck*—"purposiveness without purpose." Cf. our work *God and Reality in Modern Thought* (Englewood Cliffs, N.J., 1963), pp. 125ff.

[15] Cf. C. K. Barrett's contribution "The Background of Mark 10:45" to the T. W. Manson memorial volume, ed. A. J. B. Higgins, *New Testament Essays* (Manchester, 1959), pp. 1ff.

a mode of estimation which became increasingly prominent in Jewish thought in consequence of the numerous martyrdoms that occurred during the persecution under Antiochus Epiphanes in 168 B.C.[16] The notion that self-abnegation can compensate for sin is present in Ecclesiasticus, and almsgiving is a case in point (Ecclus. 3:30); but being more of an individualist than the author of the Servant Songs and having no eschatology in the apocalyptic sense, Ben Sira can scarcely set forth a radical doctrine of the saving efficacy of vicarious suffering.

The mention of almsgiving recalls Mark 10:17–22, a paradigm that vividly brings out the radicalness of the evangelist's ethical teaching: a wealthy man who would secure eternal life is instructed by Jesus that, in order to obtain treasure in heaven, he must sell all his many possessions and give the proceeds to the poor.[17] However, in the commentary appended to the paradigm (10:23–31) the basic doctrinal scheme concerning retribution undergoes a modification. Apparently the evangelist feels the inadequacy of the concept of a delayed (if imminent) double reversal, for in verses 29f. it is pointed out that those who renounce their families or properties receive ample compensation in the current epoch. This implies that the sacrifice of worldly goods is not merely a means to the attainment of celestial blessings in the age to come; the renunciation has its reward in the immediacy of the existing order of things.

The matter is put realistically in the verses under consideration, Jesus being represented as declaring: "There is no one

[16] See G. Vermes, *Scripture and Tradition in Judaism* (Leiden, 1961), pp. 193ff.

[17] Cf. Mark 12:41ff., where a poor widow is commended for depositing all her means of livelihood into the temple treasury. Like most moralists, Ben Sira would probably have regarded such an act as an instance of gross improvidence.

who has left home or brothers or sisters or mother or father or children or fields for my sake and for the gospel's, who shall not receive a hundredfold more now in this time, homes and brothers and sisters and mothers and children and fields with persecutions (*meta diōgmōn*), and in the coming age eternal life." Doubtless the relatives gained are members of the apostolic communities, societies animated by a strong spirit of mutual sharing and generous hospitality. Incorporation into the fellowship compensates for all the sacrifices made through the profession of the messianic faith, for it signifies adoption into the Lord's spiritual family. That is to say, the declaration should be understood in the light of the divided pericope in 3:20–21, 31–35, which reports that Jesus, estranged from his physical relatives, affirms in the presence of the multitude seated around him: "Whosoever does the will of God, he is my brother and sister and mother" (v. 35).

The mention of "homes" and "fields" in the list of immediate rewards is intended to emphasize that those who suffer privations because of their faith—through divisions in their household[18] or for some other reason—have their losses more than offset by the prevailing generosity that greets them within the fellowship of the apostolic communities.[19] But the stress on the superabundance of the recompense in the expression "a hundredfold more" is a hyperbole which lends no support to the view, mainly based on Acts 2:44; 4:34f. that, through its general practice of communism, the early church was rich in real estate. For, as Dibelius has shown,[20] these two passages are probably editorial, introduced by St. Luke to idealize the

---

[18] Cf. Matt. 10:34–36; Luke 12:51–53.

[19] Cf. Ben Sira's point that the righteous man gains true friends (Ecclus. 6:16).

[20] See his *Studies in the Acts of the Apostles* (London, 1956), pp. 123ff.

situation of Christianity in its pristine condition. Barnabas is singled out as one who puts the proceeds from the sale of his field at the disposal of the apostles, the implication being that this was a munificent gesture made on his own initiative (Acts 4:36f.). And Ananias is condemned not for failing to surrender all his money but for lying; apparently he played false by keeping back some of the proceeds from the sale of his property after giving the apostles to understand that all the proceeds were to be handed over (Acts 5:1ff.). Thus St. Luke is here generalizing from certain particular instances of generosity noticed in tradition, and he does this out of deference to a normative notion, adumbrated in Greek as well as in Jewish thought, that in any ideal or paradisal condition of human existence there could be no private property.

St. Mark's catalogue of the terrestrial rewards of self-sacrifice ends paradoxically with the words *meta diōgmōn*— "with persecutions."[21] The other synoptists omit this list, apparently taking it to be a needless duplication of the itemization in the catalogue of benefits renounced, and they content themselves with the "a hundredfold more" or a corresponding expression.[22] Also, perhaps they were both offended by the *prima facie* incongruity of the appendix. On the other hand, it might be argued that the *meta diōgmōn* was appended by a second-century scribe, affected by the developing craze for martyrdom and obsessed with the idea that persecution is a common privilege of those who profess faith in the Lordship

---

[21] D and the Syriac have the singular "persecution."

[22] In Matt. 19:29 some authorities (including Cod. Sinaiticus and D) have "a hundredfold more," while others (including B) have "manifold more." In Luke 18:30 most authorities have "manifold more"; but some (including D) have "seventyfold more" and others (including the Sinaitic Syriac) "a hundredfold more."

of Jesus. However, to cut the Gordian knot is not to solve the problem. There is no manuscript evidence for the view that the expression *meta diōgmōn* was absent from the original Markan text, and its paradoxical character, so far from being an isolated phenomenon, is but one indication among several of the evangelist's tendency to heal the breach between means and end. Indeed, the very fact that such a compensatory catalogue is supplied at all, points to a certain dissatisfaction with the doctrine that the earthly life of the Messiah and his followers, with all its trials and privations, has its only authentication in the celestial recompense which it precedes and makes possible.[23]

4. *Universalism and Particularism.* Following the teaching of prophets like Amos, with his stress on divine justice; Jeremiah, with his deep sense of personal responsibility; and Deutero-Isaiah, with his notion of a world-wide mission, Ben Sira holds that there is one universal God whose will is valid for all mankind. The Lord is the creator of the world who is everywhere present (16:26–30; 43:27), the ruler of the nations who requites all men according to their deserts (10:14–17; 16:11–14); and the conception of race can be construed entirely in terms of piety and morals (10:19).

On the other hand, Israel is the Lord's own portion (17:17; cf. Deut. 32:8), his first-born son (36:12; cf. Exod. 4:22) whose days are without number (37:25), and Jerusalem is his beloved city and dwelling-place (24:8–12; 36:13). So Ben Sira can pray that God will crush the foreign nations opposed to Israel (36:3–10) and vindicate the prophets by gathering together the scattered tribes of Jacob—his nearest

[23] Cf. *M.R.*, pp. 179ff., 208f., 241, 319ff.

approach to a characteristic messianic expectation.[24] And in an outburst of vexation he gives expression to a detestation of the Idumeans, the Philistines, and especially the Samaritans (50: 25f.).

Like Ben Sira, St. Mark takes it for granted that God is the creator of all things (13:19), whose will ultimately governs the entire range of cosmic evolution, determining its end as well as its beginning. The eschatological events *must* occur, and the controlling necessity derives from the divine volition, which compassionately shortens the days of the last tribulation (13:7, 20), the troubles preceding the signs of nature's dissolution, when the heavenly luminaries shall cease to shine and the celestial powers shall be shaken (13:24f.). Hence God is concerned about the whole of humanity, and he even intended that the temple at Jerusalem should be called a house of prayer for *all* the nations (11:17).

God's concern for all peoples is finally revealed in Jesus of Nazareth (1:9) and in the church's continuation of his mission. For this man, who is none other than God's unique or beloved Son (1:11; 9:7), appears on the scene of history to announce the approach of the Kingdom of God, an announcement that is at once a warning and a promise, and he calls upon his hearers to respond with repentance and faith (1:14f.). Also, he appoints twelve of his compatriots to be his immediate followers, that through them his saving activity might be extended and, after his death, perpetuated (1:16–20; 3:13–19; 6:7–13, 30; 14:28; 16:7). To these chosen few is committed the secret of the Kingdom (4:11), a truth that is evidently the mystery of their Master's divine status and soteriological function as the Messiah, the Son of God (1:1).

---

[24] 36:11–17; such passages as 47:22; 51:12:viii may well have been added later.

The secret, which is known by the demons all along (1:24, 34; 3:11; 5:7), is first disclosed to the disciples at Caesarea Philippi (8:29); and they are further informed that, as the Son of Man, Jesus must suffer rejection by his own countrymen before he can rise from the dead (8:31; 9:31; 10:33f.), that he has come to give his life for human redemption (10:45), and that he is due to return in glory at the end of the present age to conduct the final judgment (8:38; 13:26; 14:62).

Thus, in St. Mark's interpretation, Jesus is more than a proclaimer of the urgent need for repentance in view of the imminence of the Kingdom of God. He is actually the embodiment or personal agent of God's kingly rule in the twofold aspects of pardoning grace and retributive justice, and there are three distinguishable phases of his mediating activity. Firstly, in a career of lowly endeavor he serves his fellows even to the extent of offering his life as a ransom for many. Secondly, bestowing the Holy Spirit among his baptized followers,[25] he continues and extends the work of his earthly ministry through the apostolic church. Thirdly, representing the divine will to justice, he reappears in glory to rectify the moral maladjustments of the existing cosmic order.

[25] See 1:8, where Jesus is presented as one who baptizes with the Holy Spirit. On the other hand, in 1:10 Jesus appears in a different role: he is one who is himself baptized with the heavenly Spirit—as well as with water. This discrepancy is due to the fact that the evangelist sees Jesus from two contrary standpoints: (a) as the creator of the church, and therefore distinct from his creatures; (b) as the prototype of the Christian believer, and therefore corresponding to the church member. The same kind of discrepancy occurs in the account of the last supper (14:22–25): Jesus is one communicant among others and at the same time he represents the sacred bread; cf. M.R., pp. 266ff.

The Lord's mediating action in its first phase may be described as fundamentally particularist, whereas in the later phases a general interest in humanity is involved. But perhaps no real antinomy is present here, the evangelist regarding the world-wide mission of the church as the direct consequence of what takes place during the earthly ministry. Working on the principle that the children must first be fed (7:27), Jesus restricts his activity to his own people, and yet he is fully aware that after his resurrection the saving *mysterium* may be openly proclaimed (9:9), and that the gospel must be preached to the whole world before he can reappear in glory to judge the quick and the dead (13:10; 14:9). Moreover, even prior to the resurrection there are portents of things to come: for example, toward the end of the Galilean ministry Jesus travels into Gentile territory and heals the daughter of a Syrophoenician woman (7:24ff.); and on Golgotha immediately after the crucifixion the veil of the temple is rent from top to bottom, and a Roman officer openly acknowledges Jesus to be the Son of God.[26]

Nevertheless, valid though they are, such considerations by no means afford a demonstration that St. Mark finally avoids an unresolved dualism between universalism and exclusivistic particularism, for they leave out of account the basic concept of retributive justice. The evangelist thinks of this mainly in terms of an eschatological double reversal. The first shall be last, and the last first (10:31, 43f.). As this concept is applied in such a passage as 12:1–12, the privileged shall be deprived of their privileges, and the unprivileged shall be endowed with privileges. The wicked husbandmen kill the proprietor's beloved or unique son and in consequence they are condemned

[26] 15:38f. Cf. *M.R.*, pp. 247f.

to perdition, and the vineyard is given to others. The allegorical meaning is clear. The Jewish leaders, although they duly play their appointed role in the working out of the divine plan for human salvation, commit an odious offence in rejecting the promised Messiah, the result being that they are excluded from the joys of the consummated Kingdom. Their defection may redound to the benefit of the Gentiles to whom the privileges of the elect people are transferred, and yet it would seem to be tantamount to blasphemy against the Holy Spirit, for which there is no forgiveness either in this age or in the age to come (3:29).

Also, in certain passages, such as 3:20–35 and 11:12–21,[27] the evangelist inclines to think of the responsible leaders in their representative capacity, and this enables him to spread their guilt in a manner required by his evident conviction that the Jewish nation encompasses its own ruin in the crime of the rejection, as well as to suggest that Israel stands under the curse of the Messiah.[28] The chosen people are superseded by the new Israel, a spiritual community in which the will of God is performed and in which physical kinship counts for nothing (3:35). Prior to the crucifixion Jews still enjoy their privileges as members of God's elect people, and Gentiles are as dogs that can at best feed on the crumbs that fall from the children's table (7:28). But through their refusal of the bread of life[29] they forfeit their places at the table to those under-

[27] Cf. *M.R.*, pp. 120ff., 136f.
[28] The fig tree of 11:13f., 20f. seems to be intended as a symbol of Israel.
[29] If it be objected that this phrase, being derived from the fourth gospel (6:35), is inadmissible here, it may be replied that the expression is thoroughly consonant with St. Mark's ideology. He has the eucharist in mind in his accounts of the miracles of the loaves (6:34–43; 8:1–9) and of the conversation in the boat (8:14–21), as well as in

neath it, so that in this case the double reversal affected by divine judgement operates already in the present age—a facet of realized eschatology in early Christian thinking to which insufficient attention has been paid.

Of course the evangelist, like the Apostle Paul, believes in the existence of "a remnant according to the election of grace" (Rom. 11:15), and he makes it plain that the membership of the original Christian community was entirely Jewish (9:9; 14:28; 16:7). But, for a variety of reasons, the mutual relations between church and synagogue tended to deteriorate, and at the time of the composition of the gospel the apostolic doctrine of Jesus' Messiahship was meeting with wide acceptance in the Gentile world, whereas the Jews for the most part were showing themselves to be increasingly unwilling to respond to its appeal. Nevertheless, not all who belonged to Israel lost their seats at the table to the dogs at their feet, and St. Mark's recognition of this circumstance apparently comes to expression in 6:5f., where, despite the prevailing *apistia* or unbelief among his own folk, Jesus is able to perform a few miraculous healings.[30]

---

his rendering of the encounter with the Syrophoenician woman (7:24–31), in which the contrast between the children and the dogs appears. And in his report of the last supper the offered bread is equated with the Lord's body (14:22), the latter being the physical life that is freely offered for the ransom of many (10:45), as is indicated in 8:14, where Jesus is doubtless intended to represent the one true loaf with the disciples in the boat. So the offered body is the offered bread; and the *bread* guarantees eternal *life* when the Lord's archetypal sacrifice is supplemented by self-abnegation for his sake and the gospel's (10:29f.).

[30] Cf. *M.R.*, pp. 137ff. Conversely, St. Mark may show a recognition of the fact that not all Gentiles secure seats at the table when in 15:39 he singles out the centurion to make the confession.

5. *Ritualism and Ethics.* Ben Sira greatly respects the priest-hood and the ritualism of the temple. In one passage divine wisdom is personified and represented as ministering in the presence of the Creator in the holy tabernacle (24:10). The Lord bestowed special privileges upon Aaron the first high priest (45:6–22), and he established a covenant of peace with Phinehas that he and his descendants should always enjoy the dignity of the priesthood (45:24; cf. Num. 25:10–13). Simon the high priest made the court of the sanctuary glorious when, arrayed in his official vestments, he went up to the holy altar while presiding over ceremonies in the temple—perhaps on the Day of Atonement (50:11). Ben Sira therefore calls upon his readers to honor the priests and to pay the contributions due to them as ministers of the Lord (7:29–31), the festivals and sacrifices being divinely ordained (33:8; 35:4f.).

On the other hand, in line with the tradition established by Amos, Ben Sira so emphasizes the ineffectiveness of ritual performances *per se*, that in the last-cited passage the only justification he can give for the offering of sacrifices is that they are included among the requirements of the Law. A man who robs the poor in order to make an oblation is no better than one who kills a son before his father's eyes (34:20). In themselves sacrifices do not atone for sin (7:8f.); God will not accept the offerings of the unrighteous (34:18f.), and a man who fasts for his sins without genuine repentance gains nothing by his formal self-humiliation (34:26). It is the offerings of the righteous that are acceptable to God, par-ticularly when they are given generously (35:6–10), and it is the practice of justice and kindness—as in filial piety (3:3) and almsgiving (3:30)—that atones for sin. Also noteworthy is the fact that the Mosaic requirements regarding diet, lustra-tions, and the sabbath receive no mention at all.

In contradistinction to Ben Sira, St. Mark is opposed to the hierarchs and the ritualism of the Jerusalem cultus. The temple was divinely intended to be a house of prayer for all nations, but, thanks to the evil genius of the priestly authorities, it is *de facto* a den of robbers (11:17). Like the wicked husbandmen of the parable (12:1ff.), the hierarchs are selfish and murderous; they conspire to have Jesus removed without just cause (14:1; 15:10, 14), accepting the aid of Judas Iscariot, a man for whom it would have been good had he not been born (14:10-11, 21), and inciting the multitude to press for the release of Barabbas in preference to the Messiah, the Son of God (15:11). St. Mark also objects to the extended application of the laws of ceremonial purity, specifically the generalized practice of performing ritual lustrations before meals, regarding the Pharisaic hermeneutical tradition as a nullification of the commandment of God (7:1ff.). Indeed, in establishing a single standard of inward purity, he repudiates the distinction between clean and unclean meats, upon which much of the pentateuchal legislation is based, and holds that the Messiah makes all foods clean (7:14ff.). In the evangelist's view, he who is Lord of the Sabbath (2:28) has also made the one sufficient atonement needful for human redemption (10:45), an idea that is given dramatic confirmation in the rending of the temple veil immediately after the crucifixion.[31] The restrictions of the Levitical sacrificial cultus have had their day, and hence the Lord's prediction of the temple's ruination (13:2) can only be said to be eminently appropriate.

By no means, however, should all this be taken to signify that St. Mark is opposed to religious ritualism as such. Rather, his contention is that the ceremonial of the old dispensation

[31] 15:38; cf. *M.R.*, p. 247.

has been replaced by that of the new, and he takes it for granted that the church's observances of baptism, fasting, and the eucharist have their due authentication in the Messiah's earthly ministry. Regarding baptism, it is true that in 1:8 John's baptism with water is set in opposition to the Messiah's baptism with the Holy Spirit. But, as the following report serves to show, the evangelist can scarcely take the contrast to be mutually exclusive: Jesus receives the Spirit on his baptism with water at the hands of John (1:10)—a mode of representation which implies that baptism with water and baptism with the divine Spirit are closely interrelated. Jesus is here the model or prototype of the Christian initiate,[32] and the suggestion is that the church's rite of initiation, unlike John's baptism of repentance, has its proper concomitant in baptism with the Holy Spirit.[33]

So far as fasting is concerned, St. Mark finds the historical basis and justification of its ecclesiastical practice in the death of Jesus: so long as the messianic Bridegroom is physically

[32] Cf. above, n. 25. That the passive part assigned to Jesus in this passage could cause embarrassment is shown in Matt. 3:15f., where John is depicted as asserting that their roles should be interchanged. A further occasion for embarrassment in this connection would be the characterization of John's baptism as a baptism of repentance for the remission of sins (Mark 1:4). And it should be noted that St. Matthew reserves the phrase "unto the remission of sins" for his account of the last supper (Matt. 26:28); cf. Heb. 9:22 ("apart from the shedding of blood there is no remission").

[33] This doctrine comes out clearly in the Acts of the Apostles; see 8:14–17; 10:44–48; 19:1–7. Cf. John 3:5, where (according to the generally accepted reading) "birth of water and the Spirit" is a necessary condition for entrance into the Kingdom of God. Already according to Pauline teaching, baptism into the name of the crucified Christ (I Cor. 1:13–17,23) means incorporation into the body of Christ, the community informed and sustained by the divine Spirit he makes available (I Cor. 12:13). See also *M.R.*, pp. 12ff.

present with his attendant followers dietary restrictions are quite out of the question, but when he has been taken away from them they should mourn his loss by observing some ritual of fasting.[34] Also closely associated with the Messiah's death is the eucharistic rite, for the evangelist doubtless regards the supper reported in 14:22–25 not merely as the last earthly meal that Jesus takes in the company of his disciples, but more especially as the first celebration of the Christian eucharist, a ceremony intended to compensate in some measure for the Messiah's absence from his followers during the interim period between the passion and the awaited meal of reunion in the consummated kingdom. That the evangelist reproduces nothing corresponding to the command, "Do this in remembrance of me" (I Cor. 11:24), may well be due to the tacit assumption that his readers would at once realize that the report under consideration has to do with the institution of the eucharist. Taken as a whole the extant evidence points to the great importance of the communion meal in the early Christian cultus, and it is noteworthy that a number of passages in the body of St. Mark's gospel can scarcely receive satisfactory treatment in a hermeneutic that fails to take eucharistic imagery into account.[35]

On the other hand, not unlike Ben Sira, the evangelist can so emphasize the overruling authority of the ethical requirements of true religion as to suggest that ritualistic action of any sort is entirely devoid of value—and even that it is per-

[34] 2:18–20; cf. above, Chapter 2.

[35] The passages in question are 6:34–43 (the feeding of the five thousand; 7:24–31 (the Syrophoenician woman); 8:1–9 (the feeding of the four thousand); and 8:14–21 (the conversation in the boat concerning bread). For the exegesis of these passages, see above, Chapters 3–5; and for a general discussion of the Markan account of the last supper, see *M.R.*, pp. 258ff.

nicious in its influence. Admittedly, in passages explicitly dealing with the opposition between cultic and moral obligations, he usually has Mosaic taboos specifically in mind. Thus in 2:15–17, 23–28; 3:1–6 it is the dietary and the sabbath restrictions of the old order that are subordinated to the pressing claims of the sick and the hungry. In certain passages, however, subordinationism of this kind is presented in such a manner as to admit of a generalised application beyond the ritualistic taboos of the Mosaic dispensation.

Thus in 7:1–23 the repudiation of Jewish lustrations before meals is made the occasion for the radical contention that, true religion being an affair of the heart, ceremonial observances can only serve to promote the vice of hypocrisy.[36] The standard of inward purity which Jesus propounds and explains (vv. 14ff.) constitutes the one thing it is needful to recognize, for, as was revealed to the prophet Isaiah, ritualistic regulations encourage people to honor God with their lips, that is, to all outward seeming, while their heart remains far from him (vv. 1ff.). And, for example, an institution like that of corban, the authorized dedication of wealth for cultic purposes, is calculated to prevent men from fulfilling their divinely ordained filial obligations (vv. 10ff.). Moreover, if evil thoughts or vicious designs, proceeding from the inner recesses of the mind, alone can defile a man (vv. 21ff.), then only wholesome thoughts can make him worthy of the Kingdom of God. External observances have no valuable contribution to make in the cultivation of the religious life.

[36] Cf. Matt. 6:16–18, where religious hypocrites are alleged to show a sad countenance in public that they may make demonstration of their fasting, and thereby acquire a reputation for piety. But in this case no radical conclusion is drawn. Fasting as such is not condemned; it is merely proposed that fasting should be practiced without ostentation.

Positively they do not count, but negatively they do, being conducive to the establishment of an *Ersatzreligion*, a counterfeit substitute for the real thing.

Again, in 12:28–34 it is maintained that the correct attitude to the divine Law is determined by the regulative principles of love to God and love to one's neighbor, practical adherence to which is of far greater religious importance than the offering of all the holocausts and sacrifices ever prescribed. Involved here is doubtless the notion that the proliferation of cultic formalities has the effect of obscuring God's essential requirements so that—to use phraseology derived from St. Matthew's gospel—people are induced to strain out the gnat while swallowing the camel (Matt. 23:24). Such a line of exegesis receives confirmation in a number of passages occurring in the section which St. Mark introduces with a report of Peter's confession at Caesarea Philippi (8:27ff.). Stress is laid on the unique importance of self-abnegation in the life of genuine discipleship (8:34ff.). For the achievement of true greatness there must be humility, a readiness to become the servant of all (9:33ff.); and such virtues as tolerance, sympathy with the weaker and self-control are to be cultivated (9:38ff.). Eternal life is conditioned by sacrifice for the welfare of others (10:17ff.), and the crucial question concerns not baptism with water, but one's capacity to be baptised with the Messiah's sufferings.[37]

---

[37] 10:35ff. It should be noticed that the story of the anointing (14:3–9) at an early stage of its life-history may have been used by some Christian group that maintained the superiority of the claims of the cultus to those of almsgiving. But as the story now stands this motif has been overshadowed because of a desire (probably on St. Mark's own part) to bring out the dual appropriateness of the woman's act: first, it is fitting that the Messiah's head should be anointed; second, it is fitting that there should be some compensation

6. Reason and Revelation. Ben Sira's ethics are largely derived from a study of the writings of the sages, particularly the book of Proverbs, and from his own rational reflection upon his varied experience of the world. Much of his practical wisdom is sound enough, as when for example he argues that gluttony should be avoided because of its deleterious effects on physical health (31:20), but his moralistic generalizations are not always convincing and his pronouncements are not always consistent. Thus he sometimes postulates that women are inherently evil (25:24; 42:14) and at other times that this is not the case (25:1; 26:3). While it has to be borne in mind the counsels were given on various occasions and reflect different moods and circumstances, such inconsistencies betray certain serious inadequacies in Ben Sira's rationalistic prudentialism. For one thing he persistently refuses to try to see things from any other standpoint than that of a man who is the somewhat despotic head of a family. Thus when he condemns the sparing of the rod (30:1), he does not carefully scrutinize the pertinent evidence for his judgment, but simply jumps to the conclusion that a son who is brought up strictly will turn out to be a person of whom his father can boast in the presence of his acquaintances (30:2f.). In the metaphysical realm Ben Sira's intellectualistic aspirations are perhaps most easily discernible in his repeated attempts to demonstrate that the doctrine of God's retributive justice does not conflict with the facts of common experience.

On the other hand, he freely owns to the limitations of the human understanding (3:17ff.) and assumes as axiomatic that God came to man's assistance by declaring his will in the

---

for the failure of the women in 16:1ff. to fulfil their purpose of anointing Jesus' corpse. See *M.R.*, pp. 229ff.

Mosaic law (45:5), a set of revealed truths that can fill the
finite mind with wisdom. So it is in terms of respect for the
Law rather than in terms of rationalistic prudentialism that
the sage defines wisdom (19:20; 21:11). And he holds that,
just as wisdom is older than creation (24:9; cf. Prov. 8:22ff.),
so the Law antedates Moses, it being already known to Abraham (44:20) and even to primordial humanity (17:11ff.).
Here of course a natural theology is entailed. Man was originally so constituted that he enjoyed an immediate knowledge
of his Maker, presumably in virtue of a native mode of rational intuition. But thanks to sin—more specifically, the
initial sin of woman (25:24)—corruption set in. The species
became subject to death and, as it seems, man's pristine capacity for comprehending God's will was seriously, if not
wholly, impaired. To meet the situation of general degeneracy God eventually offered guidance in the special revelation
made on Mount Sinai, and thereafter it could be said that the
law of Moses and supreme wisdom are one and the same thing
(24:23).

Accordingly, with such an identification of wisdom with
the Mosaic law, the sum of spiritual truth comes to be found
not in any sort of rationalistically argued ethics, but simply
in obedience to the will of God as disclosed in the scriptures.
Nevertheless, Ben Sira is far from regarding the pentateuchal
legislation as being all on the same level: the ritualistic rulings
are taken to be secondary to the ethical, and the requirements
concerning diet, lustrations, and the sabbath are passed over
in complete silence. Thus his moral rationalism and his religious faith in the special revelation of God to Israel are not
integrated in a consistent scheme of thought. He does not seek
to justify his view concerning the primacy of the ethical in
the Law, any more than he tries to show that the counsels of

his general prudentialism can be deduced from the Pentateuch by legitimate exegesis. It is true that he goes beyond the position represented in the book of Proverbs by identifying Wisdom with the Law vouchsafed to Moses, and in certain passages he anticipates talmudic developments as when, for example, he seems to approach a juristic distinction between intentional and unintentional wrong oath-taking (23:11). However, because of his relatively generous allowance of scope to natural theology and an associated ethic, Ben Sira's teaching has a balance that is quite foreign to typical rabbinics; and it is perhaps significant that in his enumeration of the great men of the past (44:1ff.), there is not so much as a fleeting reference to Ezra, the legal expert who tended to be regarded as the ideal scholar in the pharisaic and talmudic tradition, especially among the Amoraim.

More obviously than Ben Sira, St. Mark is preoccupied with revealed truth rather than with a natural theology involving a general concept of divine immanence or availability and a rationalistically argued ethics. He firmly believes in a special mode of divine self-disclosure operated in accordance with a transcendent design for human salvation. The Creator himself has chosen to intervene on man's behalf in a remarkable sequence of outstanding events, and broadly the evangelist appears to distinguish four principal stages in the historical realization of God's saving purpose; firstly, the period of preparation which terminates with the removal of John the Baptist; secondly, the period of Jesus' earthly ministry, which is characterized by obscurity and suffering; thirdly, the post-resurrection period in which the redemptive secret of the Messiahship is openly proclaimed to the world; and fourthly, the period of eschatological fulfillment in a new age or order of existence which is to be triumphantly inaugurated by the

Son of Man at his still-awaited parousia for the final judgment.[38]

This whole scheme of revealed theology clearly presupposes that all is far from well with the human situation. Not
only are there grave moral maladjustments in the present age,
the wicked prospering and the righteous suffering (6:14ff.),
but men are in a state of degeneracy that has evidently rendered them incapable of saving themselves (10:45). The
evangelist's pessimistic assessment of the human condition already comes to expression in the preface to his work, where
John the Baptist, who prepares the way of the Lord, is presented as proclaiming a baptism of repentance for the remission of sins (1:4). The same kind of assessment is evinced in
1:15, where the Messiah himself at the commencement of his
ministry makes a public appeal for repentance in view of the
imminence of the Kingdom of God. None is good except the
Being through whom all things are possible (10:18, 27); or,
to put the matter otherwise, men suffer from a deep-seated
illness that calls for the healing touch of the divine Physician
(2:17). St. Mark nowhere offers a diagnosis of the widespread sickness and its debilitating consequences on the moral
constitution; and, unlike Ben Sira, he makes no explanatory
reference to the original sin of one or other of man's primordial parents. But, particularly when St. Paul's stress on
original sin is borne in mind (Rom. 5:12–21; I Cor. 15:21–
22), the evangelist may be understood as taking it for granted
that Adam is to be charged with ultimate responsibility for
the sorry plight of his total progeny.[39]

[38] See *M.R.*, pp. 173ff.
[39] It could be that St. Mark, like Josephus, includes the demons in
this progeny; see *M.R.*, p. 48. Of course such a doctrine of Adam's
ultimate responsibility (on the human level) does not preclude the

Presumably, it was out of compassion[40] for man in his ca-
lamitous predicament that God decided upon revealing himself in a special way through the mediation of an elect people,
Israel, the seed of Abraham.[41] As we have already implied, the
revelatory action is understood to be effected under two
principal dispensations—that of preparation via the law and
the prophets, and that of fulfillment via the humiliation and

---

evangelist from assigning proximate blame for particular evils to
individuals and groups; cf. the antinomy between freedom and
predestination.

[40] In the story of the wicked husbandmen (12:1ff.), which would
seem to be an allegorical *resumé* of significant elements in the doctrinal scheme of St. Mark's revealed theology, the motif of the divine
mercy suffers radical subordination to that of God's retributive
justice. This is doubtless due to the fact that the evangelist is here
primarily concerned with the troublesome problem occasioned by
what Loisy called *l'échec de l'évangile auprès des juifs*, and he wishes
to show that the chosen people, as represented by their appointed
leaders, are liable to punishment at the hands of God for rejecting the
Messiah and the prophets who were sent before him; see *M.R.*, pp.
116, 201f. Like the account of the trial before the sanhedrin (14:55–
65), the allegory (12:1ff.) is strongly anti-Semitic in tone, and it is
not impossible that St. Mark himself actually composed it. For the beloved or only son (v. 6), cf. 1:11; 9:7; 14:61; 15:39. For the notion
that the Jewish authorities rejected the Messiah because they selfishly
wished to be the sole inheritors of God's covenanted promises (v. 7),
cf. 11:17; 13:2; 14:58.

[41] Cf. Gen. 12:3, where the divine promise is made to the first of the
patriarchs that through him all the tribes of the earth shall be blessed.
In Gal. 3:16 St. Paul argues that the reference to Abraham's seed in
such passages as Gen. 18:18 is specifically to Jesus, through whom—
as is asserted in Gal. 3:14—the blessing of Abraham comes to the
Gentiles. So, according to Pauline teaching, those who are united to
the Christ by faith must be Abraham's seed since they are heirs in the
sense of the divine promise (Gal. 3:29). St. Mark apparently adopts
the same general view, although in certain important respects his
doctrine differs from that of his influential predecessor.

exaltation of the Messiah, the Son of God. In his work St. Mark is primarily concerned with the first main phase of the revelatory action under the second dispensation. He seeks to delineate the earthly career of the Messiah, the Son of God, showing that it was in complete accord with scriptural prophecy and that it constituted a necessary prelude to the church's open proclamation of the gospel, pending the parousia of the Son of Man with great power and glory. Having assembled a number of traditions current in certain apostolic communities, the evangelist arranges them in such a manner as to subserve his theological design. To a greater or less extent he adapts them to the ideological framework of his philosophy of history, and in a few instances perhaps he actually composes the constituent pericopes.

Thus attention is focused on the earthly ministry as the overture of the final phase in the drama of God's remedial action for human salvation, and St. Mark introduces Jesus to his readers in the capacity of a divine plenipotentiary. He is the Mightier One for whom the prophets of the first dispensation have prepared the way (1:1ff.), and, after the incarceration of John the Baptist (1:14), Jesus can publicly appear in Galilee preaching the gospel of God. For all has duly been made ready. Elijah *redivivus* has performed his appointed task; the voice from heaven has confirmed that the Mightier One is God's unique Son; and Jesus has proved his fitness for the messianic work before him by overcoming the temptation of Satan in the wilderness. The glad announcement that can now be made is clearly an anticipation of the gospel proclaimed by the apostolic church, and as such it is, by strictly historical standards, out of its proper season, for the Son of Man is not yet risen from the dead (9:9). But, for the evangelist, historical representation is subservient to theology, and he here wishes to make it plain that Jesus makes his first public appearance as the Messiah, the Son of God, in whom the divine intention for Israel finds its veritable realization, and in whom the deepest needs of all peoples find satisfaction. The long-awaited moment has at last arrived—the moment of transition from the age of promise to the age of fulfillment. To use Pauline language, the fullness of time has come since God has sent forth his Son for the salvation of the world (Gal. 4:4).

In St. Mark's interpretation, Jesus meets the soteriological needs of degenerate humanity in various ways. He demonstrates his effective power by waging victorious war against the demons, healing the sick and forgiving their sins, and by expounding a new teaching with an authority which clearly differentiates it from scribal hermeneutics (1:22, 27; 2:5ff.). More specifically, he entrusts his disciples with the secret of the Kingdom of God (4:11; 8:29), and, after his resurrection, it is their vocation publicly to proclaim its saving content (9:9). Their reunion with the risen Lord, who goes before them into Galilee (14:28; 16:7), means the foundation of the apostolic church and its world-wide diffusion of the gospel (13:10; 14:9).

But instruction as such, no matter how authoritative, is not in itself soteriologically efficacious. The truth has to be appropriated by repentance and faith (1:15; 11:22), and there are some whose *apistia* ("faithlessness") is so deep-seated as to render them incapable of making the required response (6:5f.). The demons belong to this class, the category of the damned. They know the mystery of Jesus' veritable identity,[42] but their discernment holds no consolation for them. On the contrary, it involves a recognition of their im-

---

[42] See 1:24. 34; 3:11–12; 5:7. On the other hand, St. Paul holds that demonic powers cannot have known the true nature of Jesus. See I Cor. 2:6ff., and *M.R.*, p. 174. n. 9.

pending perdition; they recognize that the coming of Jesus means the imminent destruction of their power (1:24). Thus, like those who commit blasphemy against the Holy Spirit (3:29), the demons are past redemption. But whereas the former are blind to the truth and confound good with evil (3:22, 30), the demons, although grasping the truth, are, as it would seem, volitionally so corrupt that they cannot bring themselves to repentance and faith; they are not without spiritual insight, but they suffer from a defect of will which precludes them from making the required creative decision.

Furthermore, in St. Mark's view, Jesus also meets the soteriological needs of the world by freely offering his life as a ransom for many (10:45; 14:24), a doctrine which implies that the crucifixion cannot be understood merely in terms of the provisions of a heavenly purpose that overrules all earthly affairs. It was a punishment eminently undeserved and voluntarily undergone, so that, considered under the rubric of justice, the death of Jesus possesses compensatory or atoning value, facilitating the remission of penalties which men rightly deserve.[43] But the evangelist is just as anxious to emphasize that the Lord's sacrifice constitutes a model for human conduct. Besides having fateful implications for Jesus himself (8:31; 9:31; 10:33–34), the fact of his Messiahship has moral implications for all who would be his followers. Thus in 8:35 it is laid down that whoever loses his life for the gospel's sake will save it, and in 9:35 that if anyone wishes to be first he must be last and servant of all (10:43f.). In 10:13ff. the presence of children is used as an occasion for illustrating that the blessings of the Kingdom must be received in a childlike spirit (cf. 9:33ff.), while in 10:17ff. the incident about the

[43] Cf. *M.R.*, p. 212, n. 4.

rich man, who alleges that he seeks eternal life, serves as an opportunity for pointing out that entrance into the Kingdom calls for renunciation and great efforts of will. Thus St. Mark in this connection makes the same point as that made in Phil. 2:5ff., where the readers of the epistle are exhorted to cultivate the same kind of mentality as that exemplified in the Messiah who took the form of a servant and humbled himself even to the extent of enduring the shame of death on a cross.

According to the evangelist, however, Jesus also provides a norm for conduct in his hermeneutics, for he is a teacher, the rabbi *par excellence*, who shows how the Mosaic law has a continuing ethical validity under the new dispensation. Thus the Pauline doctrine that the coming of the Messiah spells the termination of the law (Rom. 10:4), is not subscribed to by St. Mark, who presents Jesus as clarifying the Law and drawing attention to what is of permanent moral importance therein. On the negative side, by setting forth a standard of inward purity, he renders obsolete the ceremonial regulations which enjoin ritual lustrations and compliance with the distinction between clean and unclean meats (7:1ff.); and, by his atoning death he renders cultic sacrifices unnecessary as means of access to the divine presence and favor.[44] On the positive side, the Master clearly indicates that the correct attitude to the law is determined by the regulative principles of love to God and love to one's neighbor, practical adherence to which is of far more worth than the offering of all the cultic sacrifices ever prescribed (12:28ff.). Thus, in the evangelist's judgment, Jesus by no means subverts the God-given Law of the first dispensation, and in so far as his ethical pronouncements are at variance with Mosaic enact-

[44] 15:38; cf. Heb. 6:19–20; 10:19–20; also, *M.R.*, pp. 247f.

ments, his teaching is securely founded upon a deeper appreciation of the true meaning of the scriptures. He shows, for
example, that it was only on account of man's hardness of
heart that the law made provision for a husband's possible desire to divorce his wife; and a mere concession to human insensibility should not be construed as a direct expression of
the Creator's will for men (10:1ff.). It is really the Pharisees
who make void the word of God by upholding a tradition of
purely human invention, which obscures the genuine significance of scripture (7:8ff.), and, similarly, it is the Sadducees
who are seriously at fault in their exegesis when they fail to
realize that the God of the patriarchs is not the God of the
dead, but of the living (12:26f.).

Like Ben Sira, then, St. Mark holds that Israel was chosen
to be the instrument of God's special revelation, and thereby
to mediate remedial action from above to a degenerate humanity. But, unlike Ben Sira, the evangelist maintains that
under the second dispensation Israel, in its capacity as the
chosen instrument of God's saving purpose, is superseded by
an eschatological community whose membership transcends
all racial barriers. The supersession is attributed to responsible
Jewish defection, and is interpreted in terms of divine retribution. The fig tree stands under the Lord's curse because it
has failed to bring forth the fruit expected of it (11:12ff.),
and it is because the wicked husbandmen selfishly wish to
keep the precious inheritance to themselves that they are
liquidated and the vineyard is given to others (12:1ff.). The
custodians of the law, the heirs of Moses and the prophets,
have betrayed their trust, and hence they must suffer replace-
ment. The temple at Jerusalem, which was really meant to be
called a house of prayer for all nations, has been turned into a
den of robbers (11:17), while prevailing Pharisaic practice

betrays that the authorities are much more concerned to uphold a tradition of their own contrivance than to observe the commandment of God (7:8). And when at length the promised Messiah appears, the chosen people do not recognize him. His kinsfolk deem that he is beside himself (3:21), scribes from Jerusalem assert that he is possessed by the prince of the demons (3:22), and in due course the assembled members of the supreme Jewish court unanimously condemn him to death (14:64).

In the evangelist's thinking, therefore, the distinction between Jews and Gentiles, evidently a racial one,[45] is bound up with the principles of a revealed theology. God chooses Israel to be the instrument of his remedial action for the restoration of a degenerate humanity, and such divine intervention introduces a crucial differentiation of status among the peoples of the earth. Descendants of Abraham are creatively constituted as a privileged nation. They become God's children in a distinctive sense (cf. Exod. 4:22; Deut. 14:1; Rom. 9:4), and their ontological superiority continues from the time of the first patriarch's call to that of the Messiah's final rejection at Jerusalem. Throughout this period Israel is the sphere in which God's saving operations primarily take place, and the Messiah himself clearly recognizes that, since the children must first be fed, it is not good to take the children's bread and throw it to the dogs (7:27). But Israel persistently fails to fulfill the obligations associated with its privileged position, and there are limits even to the long-suffering

[45] Of course the racialism entailed here (as in the case of the Pauline opposition between Abraham's "children of the flesh" and his "children of the promise") is misleading since it disregards the fact that a Gentile could become a Jew by undergoing certain rites of initiation. Cf. below, Chapter 7, n. 78.

of God. The place of Abraham's seed must be taken by others
(12:9), and God's elect reconstituted on a new foundation.

Thus St. Mark would seem to imply that the general calamity of Adam's primordial sin, resulting in the choice of
Israel, is succeeded by the more specific calamity of Jewish
defection, resulting in the establishment of the apostolic
church, through whose agency the gospel is openly proclaimed among all nations (13:10; 14:9). This means that,
under the new dispensation, after the crucifixion, Jewish priority no longer obtains, and that the racial discrimination,
valid under the first dispensation and during the Lord's
earthly ministry, gives way to a class distinction founded
upon a spiritual principle. For the reconstituted Israel is an
integrated community composed of those who perform the
will of God, and in its fellowship racial distinctions count for
nothing (3:33; cf. Rom. 10:12). Nevertheless, continuity
with the old Israel is secured, not only through the Messiah's
Jewish birth,[46] but also through the disciples, who, after wit-
nessing the post-resurrection christophanies in Galilee
(14:28; 16:7; cf. I Cor. 15:4ff.), become the foundation pillars of the original apostolic community (cf. Gal. 1:18; 2:9).
To use Pauline terminology, there persists a remnant, chosen
by grace (Rom. 11:5), a Jewish minority that actually com-
prises the foundation membership of the Christian church.

Moreover, as certain representatives of the old order are
incorporated into the newly formed society of the elect, so
the Mosaic law, as clarified and interpreted by the Messiah,
retains its validity under the second dispensation, and in this
respect Markan doctrine differs quite definitely from St.

[46] Cf. above, n. 41.

Paul's. As P. Vielhauer has pointed out,[47] the Apostle, taking Moses to be a messianic antitype, a personification of the covenant of death (II Cor. 3:4ff.), contends that the Messiah's coming means the end of the Law (Rom. 10:4). The evangelist, however, is opposed to such dogmatic extremism and the historical discontinuity it entails, for, while believing in the obsolescence of the time-honored dietary and cultic regulations, he postulates the enduring worth of the ethical directives contained in the Law—at any rate when exegesis is guided by the Master's teaching.[48] St. Luke in this connection seems to put still greater stress on the uninterrupted continuity of the various stages in the historical realization of God's saving purpose, holding that the Mosaic laws of ceremonial purity remain in some sense operative for Jewish Christians, and in a more limited way even for Gentile members of the apostolic churches.[49] Thus, so far as the status of the Law is concerned, the Markan point of view mediates be-

---

[47] See his paper "On the 'Paulinism' of Acts" in *The Perkins School of Theology Journal*, XVII (1963–64), 10ff. (previously referred to above, n. 7).

[48] See 10:28ff. Thus E. Schweizer ("Mark's Contribution to the Quest of the Historical Jesus," *N.T.S.*, X [1963–64], 429) errs when he argues that, for St. Mark, the crucifixion means the termination of the Mosaic law. It should also be noticed that *de facto* St. Paul finds his theory of the complete abrogation of the Law quite unworkable in practice, and, when certain converts take his antinomianism to warrant what he deems to be licentiousness, he is driven to appeal to the law as supplying a criterion of conduct that possesses a continuing validity (Gal. 5:14). Indeed, it appears that legal regulations of some sort, as integral to social organization, are a necessary prerequisite for the establishment of moral values; cf. our work *God and Reality in Modern Thought* (Englewood Cliffs, N.J., 1963), pp. 112ff., 125ff.

[49] See Acts 15:1ff., and Vielhauer, *loc. cit.*, pp. 11f.

tween the positions occupied by St. Paul and by the author of Luke-Acts.

On the other hand, St. Mark, not altogether unlike Ben Sira, shows intellectualistic tendencies which compete with his concern to expound a theology of revelation, and so his total philosophy of history cannot be adequately elucidated merely in terms of his doctrine of God's saving action through the mediation of a chosen race. Thus in 7:14ff., where a direct appeal is made to human intellection, it is assumed that in principle the ethical criterion of inward purity admits of a form of rational demonstration. The evangelist intends his readers to apprehend what he himself apprehends, namely, that the ancient distinction between clean and unclean meats has no real bearing upon the question of an individual's moral worth; and he does not simply rely on the authority of Jesus as God's earthly emissary, but feels that a physiologically based consideration will clinch the issue for any normally constituted adult. The foods a man eats pass into his stomach; and it is the dynamic ideas engendered within the mind, not the digestive processes of the physical organism, that determine a person's character, making him either vicious or virtuous.

It is true that in this case the mode of presentation is affected by a conception integral to the Markan scheme of revealed theology, according to which the apostolic gospel cannot be understood and publicly proclaimed prior to the Lord's resurrection. But such dogmatic influence on the form of the report should not blind us to the underlying rationalism of its content, especially when the same respect for man's natural insight and intelligence is exemplified in a number of other passages. Thus in 7:24ff. a non-Jewish woman is commended for her readiness of wit in quickly perceiving that even the dogs under the table may eat of the children's crumbs; in 10:28ff. a scribe is congratulated for his perspicacity in immediately agreeing that the commandments of love to God and love to one's neighbor are of far more importance than all the demands of the sacrificial cultus; and in 10:35ff. the great multitude listens with pleasure when, by a felicitous inference from Psalm 110:1, Jesus shows that the scribes must be wrong in postulating the adequacy of "the Son of David" as a messianic title or designation.[50]

Accordingly, although St. Mark, unlike St. Luke in Acts 17:28,[51] does not explicitly lay claim to pagan culture for Christian pre-history, he assumes that man's ability to grasp divine truth is not wholly lost. Humanity in general is still *capax Dei*, and this implies that Adam's primordial sin has not brought total spiritual ruin upon his descendants, who, though alienated from paradise, can in principle detect the authentic lineaments of their Maker. Men aspire after God, and, if their endowments have suffered impairment from the fall, the damage done by no means amounts to total depravity among the masses of the world's population. Admittedly, there are some persons who think that the Messiah's work borders on madness (3:21), and others who fail to see that a house divided against itself cannot stand (3:25) and who call good evil (3:30), but such specimens of humanity are exceptions that prove the rule.

[50] This piece of tradition was probably circulated by a section of the primitive church that preferred the christology of the Son of Man; cf. P. Winter's observations in his article "The Trial of Jesus" in *Commentary*, New York, September 1964, p. 41.

[51] See Vielhauer, pp. 7f.

It is the evangelist's assumption, therefore, that men are one, not merely in a negative fashion through their common need for repentance, but positively in virtue of their restless searchings for fellowship with the Divine. In 7:24ff., a passage to which allusion has already been made, it would seem to be presupposed that there is an uneffaced presentiment of the one true God.[52] A Syrophoenician woman intuits that Jesus can heal her daughter, and her insight into his status falsifies the racial dichotomy which is bound up with the Markan scheme of revealed theology. This is no "dog" who speaks. The *mysterium* that is hidden from the multitude and has to be given to the disciples (4:11) is here discovered by a non-Jewish person on her own initiative.[53] Even during the earthly ministry, before the Messiah is finally rejected by his own people, a representative of the allegedly unprivileged world proleptically discerns in Jesus the Lord of the Hellenistic cultus, who offers himself as the bread of life in the interest of human salvation. Thus what is tentatively suggested in 5:19f. comes out plainly in 7:28. For in the earlier passage Jesus instructs the cured demoniac to make known how the *Lord* (that is, God, presumably) has shown mercy to him, whereupon he proceeds to announce in the Decapolis what *Jesus* has done for him. This suggests that the healed man apprehends the Lordship of Jesus, and it is noteworthy that the evangelist may take him to be a Gentile. For in his demented condition the man dwells amid a pig-rearing population (5:11), and, after the exorcism, when he returns to his

---

[52] Vielhauer (pp. 6f.) rightly sees in such a presentiment a fundamental characteristic of "natural" in contradistinction to "revealed" religion; and he notices that in Acts 17:26ff. man's search for divine truth is directly attributed to humanity's kinship with God.

[53] Cf. above, Chapter 4 (re Jesus as Lord).

own folk, he goes into the Decapolis, a region largely inhabited by non-Jews.[54]

Hence, on one side of his teaching, St. Mark approaches the kind of doctrine exemplified in certain important passages of Lukan composition.[55] For example, according to Acts 17:22ff., it is the fact of man's existential derivation from an all-encompassing creative power that conditions his restless searchings for the Divine; distractions have led man astray, but, in view of his finitude, ignorance is in this case excusable, and the superstitions of idolatry may be transcended by repentance—that is, by his awakening to a self-awareness of his basic kinship with the one true God. Again, in Acts 10:35 it is declared that God shows no partiality, so that in every nation any person who venerates him and does what is right is acceptable to him. Clearly, the doctrinal implications of Mark 7:24ff. possess something of the same naturalistic tenor. In virtue of her native intelligence and perspicacity the Syrophoenician woman senses that God's plenipotentiary is in her neighborhood, and, although he would remain in seclusion, she seeks him out. On being confronted by him she at once recognizes his essential Lordship, and her earnest request is duly granted, her afflicted daughter being promptly cured by an exorcism effected from a distance.[56]

All this, however, runs counter not only to St. Mark's own

[54] St. Mark may intend the *Kuriou* ("of [the] Lord") in 1:3 to allude to Jesus, despite the fact that in the scripture cited (Isa. 40:3) the reference is to God.

[55] See Vielhauer, pp. 6ff.

[56] Of course St. Luke's naturalism is more explicit than his predecessor's, as may be directly illustrated by comparing Mark 12:28ff. with Luke 10:25ff. In the former passage the scribe agrees with Jesus' proposal, whereas in the latter it is the lawyer who proposes, Jesus merely concurring with him.

primary scheme of revealed theology, according to which, open access to God's presence has to be secured through the crucifixion (Mark 15:38), but also to the teaching of St. Paul, for whom no one can say "Jesus is Lord" except when he is renewed by the Holy Spirit (I Cor. 12:3). In the Apostle's view, natural man is utterly alienated from the creative Source of existence, and his saving connection with God is established only through the Messiah's death (Rom. 3:25–26; II Cor. 5:20–21), an extremity of humiliation that precedes and makes possible the new life engendered by mystic communion with the risen Lord (Rom. 4:25; I Cor. 15:20–23; Phil. 2:5–11). By nature men are but negatively united in sin (Rom. 3:23), and the oneness of humanity cannot be realized on a positive basis otherwise than by the incorporation of corrupt human beings into the body of the living Christ (Rom. 10:12; I Cor. 10:16; Gal. 3:28), through whose informing Spirit human nature is regenerated (I Cor. 12:12–13; II Cor. 5:17–19). Admittedly, in Rom. 1:18–23 St. Paul does refer to a natural knowledge of God; but if the passage is carefully studied, it will be seen that such knowledge, far from inducing men to venerate the one true God, has led to a suppression of the truth, so that they have brought themselves into an inexcusable situation. Thus natural theology is here used merely to support a thesis which asserts mankind's radical culpability. On the other hand, in Mark 7:24ff., already before the Messiah's final rejection, the Syrophoenician woman witnesses to the fundamental oneness of humanity in a positive sense, subverting the racial opposition between the children and the dogs which is entailed in the concept of divine election—a crucial motif in the evangelist's scheme of revealed theology. Accordingly, as in the case of the Law, so in the case of natural religion, St. Mark's philosophy, when considered as a whole, may be said to mediate between the contrasted doctrinal positions held by St. Paul and the author of Luke-Acts.

It would seem, then, that hovering in the background of the evangelist's thought, and competing with the scheme of revealed theology which is usually to the fore, is a mode of theological naturalism that links him with St. Luke and with the religious cosmopolitanism of Stoic rationalism.[57] And, associated with this hovering ideology, there is a class distinction which cuts across the racial barrier between Jews and Gentiles and applies to peoples everywhere. It is as though the rich and the powerful were pre-eminently affected by the deleterious consequences of Adam's sin. For, just as the Jewish masses are misled by their leaders (15:11), so it is with the masses of all nations, oppressed as they are by tyrannical politicians who have ruthlessly forced their way to power out of an inordinate lust for personal aggrandizement (10:42f.).

Doubtless, a number of factors helped to determine St. Mark's attitude in this connection. For one thing, in line with the prophetic tradition established by Amos, numerous sayings of Jesus, preserved in the gospel tradition, seem to have been directed specifically against the rich and the powerful (*e.g.* 10:25). And it should also be borne in mind that the membership of the apostolic communities, both Aramaic and Hellenistic, was mainly drawn from the lower social orders (1:16–20; cf. I Cor. 1:26–30). In any case, whatever the

---

[57] For some valuable observations on Stoic teaching, see the article "Paulus und die Stoa" by M. Pohlenz in *Z.N.T.W.*, XLII (1949), 83ff. Strictly, a complete rejection of natural religion would evidently exclude the possibility of a free human response to saving truth; hence St. Paul is induced to maintain that God predestines those whom he really calls to salvation (Rom. 8:30).

causal factors involved, the evangelist holds that it is primarily the Jewish leaders who are to be blamed for bringing about the crucifixion.[58] They are the wicked husbandmen, destined to perdition for the betrayal of their trust (12:1ff.). Hence, in the evangelist's usual mode of presentation, anti-Semitic feeling is tempered through the influence of an implied distinction between government and people. Although the multitudes cannot yet receive the secret of the Kingdom of God (4:11f.), they recognize the remarkable authority of Jesus (1:22, 27), and they pursue him wherever he goes (1:45; 3:7; 6:31). Indeed, he is so popular with ordinary folk that his enemies—who belong to the higher ranks of society—have to wait for an opportunity to arrest him by stealth (3:6; 12:12; 14:1–2). And when at length the common people do clamor for his crucifixion, this is only because their emotions have been maliciously aroused by the chief priests (15:6ff.). Clearly, St. Mark's sympathies are on the side of the masses as opposed to those of high estate.[59]

The lower orders among whom Jesus wins popularity are both Jewish and Gentile, a point made clear in 3:7f., the introductory part of a significant editorial note, in all likelihood of the evangelist's own composition. The Lord is fol-

---

[58] Cf. above, Chapter 5.

[59] Nevertheless, certain passages in the gospel do show a tendency to equate the Jewish people with the enemies of Jesus. 3:20–35 is a case in point; see above, Chapter 5. E. Trocmé (*La formation de l'évangile selon Marc*, Paris, 1963, pp. 108f.) argues that 3:20–35 is a polemic directed specifically against James, the Lord's brother, who soon became prominent in the original church at Jerusalem (Gal. 1:19; 2:9). But that the polemic is of wider application seems to find some confirmation in the Markan account of the rejection in the *patris* (6:1ff.), which may be meant to represent in advance the Messiah's final rejection at the hands of his own compatriots; see below, Chapter 7 (re Markan antipathies).

lowed by a great multitude from Galilee, and also by a great multitude from Judea, Jerusalem, Idumea, Transjordania, Tyre and Sidon. Thus, whereas, according to 3:8,[60] the common Idumean is favorably disposed towards Jesus, the Idumean nobility, as represented by the Herodian family, is hostile to him (3:6; 8:15; 12:13). The early defenders of the apostolic faith appear to have shared with most other Jewish factions a pronounced antipathy for Herod the Great and his offspring. According to Josephus, he was hated as a friend of the Romans, as an Idumean, and as a half-Jew (*Ant.* 14:15:2), and leading Pharisees saw in his dominion a divine judgment that had to be borne with patience (*Ant.* 15:1:1); his death at Jericho in 4 B.C. was by no means an occasion for public or private lamentation (*Ant.* 17:8:1). The Christian aversion seems to have remained fairly constant throughout the first century, and it comes to forcible expression in Matt. 2:1ff., where the tormented king appears as a monstrous butcher of innocent little children.[61]

The first of the two warnings in Mark 8:15 ("Beware of the leaven of Herod") may be meant to be understood in the light of 6:14ff.—the report of the Baptist's decapitation at the order of Herod Antipas, the tetrarch of Galilee and Perea.[62] It is true that in the report Herodias plays the role of the evil genius behind the dreadful affair, her husband taking

[60] The omission of "Idumea" in certain MSS may be due to the combined influence of Matt. 4:24f. and Luke 6:17f., which renderings could have been affected by the circumstance that Idumea was not among the territories covered by the early Christian mission.

[61] Cf. P. Winter, "Jewish Folklore in the Matthaean Birth Story," *H.J.*, LIII (1954–55), 34ff.

[62] Herod (Antipas) is called "king" in Mark 6:14, but the correct title is used in Matt. 14:1 and Luke 3:19; cf. the words "my kingdom" in Mark 6:23 and "the king" in Matt. 14:9.

action with great reluctance. In fact the function of the lady in this case is similar to that assigned by St. Mark to the chief priests in his account of the condemnation of Jesus: Pilate does not wish to have the Messiah put to death, but his hand is forced by the multitude, whose emotions have been manipulated by the priestly aristocracy (15:6ff.). Thus we are here confronted with a mixing of motives, a concern to exonerate the masses being combined with a concern to exonerate the supreme political authority embodied in the person of the procurator. The evangelist is *for* the masses (both Jewish and Gentile) and *against* their leaders (both Jewish and Gentile). But when he has to choose between Jewish and Gentile (Roman) leadership, he prefers the latter. For he wishes to show that, despite the manner of Jesus' death and the superscription on the cross, there are no valid reasons for supposing that Christianity is in any way a seditious movement.[63]

A passage that requires more detailed consideration in this connection is Mark 10:42ff., where a contrast is drawn between the way to greatness in the world of politics and the way to greatness as it is exemplified in the career of the Son

[63] The motif of Herod's reluctance in Mark 6:26 may reflect a similar concern—to show that the Baptist movement is politically innocuous. Also, it could be that the evil role assigned to Herodias in the story was to some extent affected by the figure of Jezebel in the scriptural tales about Elijah (I Kgs. 16:29ff.). On the other hand, in view of the evidence supplied by Josephus, it seems that Herodias was in fact an ambitious and strong-willed person. Thus, in 39 A.D. when her brother (Agrippa I) received the title "king" from the emperor Caligula, she became extremely envious and urged her husband (Antipas) to seek the royal title for himself. He apparently yielded to his wife's persistent pestering, the upshot being that the emperor ordered his banishment to Spain (*Ant.* 18:7:1f.) or to Lugdunum in Gaul (*Bel.* 2:9:6).

of Man, who came not to be served but to serve and to give his life for the redemption of many. T. W. Manson[64] argues that the phrase *hoi dokountes archein* in verse 42 should be construed in a sense analogous to that of "whoever wishes to become great among you" (v. 43), and he proposes the following translation: "You know that those who aspire to rule over the Gentiles (*tōn ethnōn*) subjugate them and the greatest of them (*hoi megaloi autōn*) rule them despotically. Not so is it among you; but whoever wishes to become great among you shall be your servant. And whoever wishes to attain primacy among you shall be the slave of all."

Such a rendering, however, is open to objection. In the first place, there are various types of causal explanation in St. Mark's total philosophy, and he shows much facility for suddenly shifting his frame of reference from one type to another. Thus, with regard to the origination of evils of one sort or another, on a primary level of causation, they can be produced by human volition (as in 2:1ff.); on a secondary level, by demonic agency (as in 5:1ff.); and, on a tertiary level, by the ultimate predetermination of God (as in 8:31). Hence in 10:42 the evangelist could be thinking on the secondary or even the tertiary causal level of explanation, in which case to translate the words *hoi dokountes archein* with "those who seem to rule" or "those who are supposed to rule" would be quite correct. It is a common hermeneutical error to assume that Markan thought is excogitated from a single standpoint, and in this instance he may well be interpreting the affairs of secular politics much in the way St. Paul appears to do in I Cor. 2:8, where "the rulers of this age" could denote the demonic forces of Satan as constituting the real power behind the thrones of the world.[65]

Moreover, it seems wrong to assume that in verse 42 *tōn ethnōn*, the object of *archein* ("to rule over"), should be rendered "the Gentiles." For, in the evangelist's opinion, irresponsible leaders and ruthless tyrants are by no means confined to the non-Jewish political scene. The bane of the common people everywhere lies in corrupt religious and political leadership. The Herods and their supporters, like the hierarchs, the scribes and the prominent Pharisees, are types of the *megaloi* ("great ones") of the nations, who ruthlessly cut their way to power with the edge of the sword and subjugate the masses in the furtherance of their selfish ambitions. The ordinary Jew is just as much a victim of political misrule as the ordinary Gentile. He is subjected to the cruelty of such a man as Herod, who promptly has a Godsent messenger decapitated to satisfy the desire of a worthless woman (6:14ff.); he is misled by the Pharisees, who pervert the word of God in the maintenance of their own all too human exegetical inventions (7:8, 13); and he is deceived by the chief priests who play on his worst instincts (15:11). Nevertheless, even though thus exposed to corrupt leadership, the common man is not wholly depraved, and the light of natural reason still flickers in his heart. Hence a Syrophoenician woman can discern in the person of Jesus the proleptic Lord of the Hellenistic Christian cultus.[66] And a blind beggar can

---

[65] In this case the passage must contain anti-Roman feeling—a rare phenomenon in the gospels. The use of the word *legion* in Mark 5:9 may also betray such sentiment; see P. Winter, *On the Trial of Jesus* (Berlin, 1961), p. 129.

[66] 7:24ff. The reading "widow" instead of "Greek" in the Sinaitic Syriac (v. 26) may indicate that the translator thought of the woman as belonging to the class of the poor and oppressed. It should also be noticed that in 12:41ff. a poor widow is commended for contributing

perceive that Jesus is the Son of David, the promised messianic
bringer of health and salvation; although physically blind he
has the spiritual sight to see the truth, and in consequence is
cured of his somatic disability.[67]

On the other hand, just as there are a few members of the
chosen race who make a positive response to the Messiah's
teaching (6:5), so there are exceptions that prove the rule
with regard to the opposition between the *megaloi* and the
oppressed masses. Thus, in 12:28ff. one of the scribes, unlike
the great majority of his influential colleagues (1:22; 2:6, 16;
3:22; 7:1; 8:31; 9:11; 10:33; 11:27; 12:35; 14:1, 43; 15:1)
agrees with Jesus; he recognizes the supremacy of the commandments of love to God and love to one's neighbor, and he
is authoritatively informed of his proximity to the Kingdom
of God. Again, in 14:3ff. an unnamed woman, evidently of
great wealth, lavishly pours a whole phial of costly perfume
upon the head of Jesus; she thereby performs a generous action that is eminently appropriate—and this, despite the fact
that rich people the world over usually cling to their possessions, excluding themselves from entrance into the Kingdom
of God.[68]

---

more to the temple treasury than all the wealthy people, the reason
being that her act involved great self-sacrifice—which, according to
10:23ff., is a necessary condition for the attainment of eternal life.

[67] 10:46ff. In 12:35ff. the title "Lord" is preferred to the designation
"Son of David," but this does not mean that, in St. Mark's judgment,
the blind beggar's use of the Davidic title is without legitimacy.

[68] It may also be observed that in 15:42ff. Joseph of Arimathea, "a
respected member of the council," is represented as being favorably
disposed toward Jesus—a passage which may contradict 14:64, according to which the sanhedrin unanimously condemned the prisoner
to death. Re Markan inconsistency generally, most scholars still
seem strangely reluctant to do more than skim the surface; see, for
example, H. Riesenfeld, *The Gospel Tradition* (Philadelphia, 1970),
p. 74.

7

The Formation of
St. Mark's Gospel

In the present study a brief exposition of Etienne
Trocmé's contentions in *La formation de l'évangile
selon Marc* is followed by a tripartite critique, where
an attempt is made to show: (1) that the Markan
gospel betrays no dualism between rustic miracle
materials of Galilean provenance and more academic
traditions derived from the original church at Jerusalem; (2) that, while the evangelist is averse to the
Jewish leadership generally, he tends to regard the
Pharisees as the principal opponents of Jesus; (3) that
St. Mark's work did not pass through two editions,
but was authored *c.* 70 A.D. by a person who composed the first thirteen chapters to provide a relatively
prolonged introduction to an adapted version of the
traditional passion narrative.

La formation de l'évangile selon Marc,[1] by E. Trocmé of
the University of Strasbourg, is an erudite and highly original
investigation that has hitherto received insufficient attention
in the English-speaking world. The main body of the work is
divided into four chapters, which deal respectively with the
earliest evangelist's sources, his antipathies, his positive con-

[1] Paris: Presses Universitaires de France, 1963; page references to
this work are usually given parenthically in the text of what follows.

cerns, and the redactional history of the gospel. An extensive bibliography is appended. The discussions throughout are both lively and informative, besides being in continual touch with research in France, Germany, Scandinavia, England and North America.

In his defense of the two-document hypothesis (Matthew and Luke used Mark and Q), Trocmé critically considers (pp. 7ff.) Vaganay's rendering of the proto-Matthew theory,[2] the notion of a primitive Petrine gospel,[3] and Dodd's contention that the apostolic preaching *ab initio* entailed a schematic outline of the Christ's earthly career.[4] The various types of traditional material utilized by St. Mark are scrutinized in the light of form-critical research, and the point is made that the evangelist, so far from being a colorless compiler, was a man of initiative with definite convictions of his own, an individual who was prepared to move outside official Christian circles in order to secure additional information regarding the historical Jesus.

Trocmé greatly stresses the difference in significance and tone between the miracle stories, which figure so prominently in Mark, and the *logia* (sayings, parables and pronouncement-stories), and he proceeds to infer that each of these species of material must have emanated from a radically different milieu: whereas the latter are essentially moralistic and derive from the Jerusalem ecclesiastical tradition guaranteed by those closely associated with Jesus prior to the crucifixion,

[2] L. Vaganay, *Le problème synoptique: une hypothèse de travail* (Tournai, 1954).

[3] As, for example, in A. T. Cadoux's work *The Sources of the Second Gospel* (London, 1935).

[4] C. H. Dodd, "The Framework of the Gospel Narrative" in *The Expository Times*, XLIII (1932), reprinted in his *New Testament Essays* (Manchester, 1953), pp. 1ff.

the former are of a popular character, being in a general way more sensational than edifying; presenting Jesus in the role of an agent of thaumaturgic power, such stories as those of Mark 4:35–5:43 reflect the quasi-animistic culture that prevailed in the rural districts near the frontier between Galilee and Syria.[5] However, the Galilean provenance of St. Mark's *Wundergeschichten* is taken to afford no justification for the supposition that there existed a Galilean form of Christianity independent of, and as ancient as, that of the church at Jerusalem;[6] it merely shows that the activities of Jesus had made a deep impression upon the villagers of north-eastern Palestine (people only on the way to being Hellenized), as well as upon his immediate followers (pp. 37–44). Moreover, the lack of refinement in the evangelist's thinking is matched by the rusticity of his linguistic style, his failure to set forth an

[5] In this connection Trocmé (pp. 39f.) seeks to render more plausible R. Bultmann's hypothesis (See *Die Geschichte der synoptischen Tradition,* ed. 4, Göttingen, 1958, p. 256; English translation, Oxford, 1963, p. 240) that the Markan miracle stories for the most part had a Hellenistic origin, betraying a mythical notion of Jesus, while the *logia,* with their presupposed concept of the Lord as a sage and eschatological prophet, derived from a Palestinian Jewish environment. Trocmé agrees that there exist striking differences between characteristic talmudic accounts of miracles attributed to rabbis and the typical Markan miracle story, wherein the dominating personality of the thaumaturge stands out with singular vividness.

[6] At this point Trocmé (p. 43, n. 159; p. 195, n. 72) has in mind the much-discussed theory of E. Lohmeyer (see his *Galiläa und Jerusalem,* Göttingen, 1936), which is based upon the double localization of the christophanies and upon the respective roles of Peter and James, the Lord's brother; cf. R. H. Lightfoot, *Locality and Doctrine in the Gospels* (London, 1938); W. Marxsen, *Der Evangelist Markus: Studien zur Redaktionsgeschichte des Evangeliums* (Göttingen, 1956, 2nd ed., 1959); L. E. Elliott-Binns, *Galilean Christianity* (London, 1956).

explicit statement of his theological design being due to the poverty of his literary capacities (pp. 54–57). He nevertheless was a person of independent judgment who opposed the normative Christianity of his day and argued forcibly against the apostolic establishment at Jerusalem by utilizing exoteric traditions in making an earnest appeal to the veritable ecclesiological intentions of the Galilean Christ (p. 68).

As for St. Mark's antipathies, Trocmé contends that he did not regard the Pharisees as the principal enemies of Jesus (p. 71); they simply figure in the role of a Galilean syndicate concerned to uphold the purity of personal morality (p. 73), the writer still cherishing a limited hope of their acceptance of Christianity (p. 74). The evangelist was especially ill-disposed to the scribes, the hierarchs,[7] and the physical relatives of Jesus; and in those passages directed against the scribes a certain anti-intellectualist tendency may be detected (p. 80). The likelihood is that the evangelist was here making an oblique attack on prominent spokesmen of the church, whose legalistic scruples and naively apocalyptic Messianism deterred them from turning to the masses that were attracted by the church's gospel; more specifically, he was censuring the venerable leadership in Jerusalem, an apostolate whose sectarian narrowness is still discernible in Acts 1–5—and this despite St. Luke's desire to bring out the essential continuity entailed in the triumphant spread of Christianity (p. 89). Thus St. Mark is to be regarded as an individual who upheld

---

[7] According to Trocmé, St. Mark in this connection tends to identify the hierarchs with the temple under their control (pp. 83f.): *de facto* it is not the house of God (Mark 11:17), but the seat of the priestly aristocracy (14:49), the place where the latter brook no authority other than their own (11:18–28; 12:1–12); its splendor is as suspect as its economic organization (13:1–2; 11:15–16).

a popular missionary form of the new religion and displayed
an adventurousness that ran counter to an officialdom he
deemed unduly intellectual and apologetic. For example, in
Mark 9:11–13 Peter, James and John find in scribal hermeneutics (relating to the eschatological role of Elijah *redivivus*) an argument with which to contradict the Master
himself; the three disciples fail to understand what Jesus
teaches (Mark 9:10), and readers of the gospel were meant to
realize that in paying too much attention to academic eschatological speculations certain influential spokesmen of the
apostolic church distanced themselves from the authentic
thought of the historical Christ. Again, in Mark 12:35–37 the
scholastic refinements of rabbinical exegesis only end in frustration;[8] what is here being opposed is not a simple faith in
Davidic christology (see Mark 10:48–49; 11:10), but the
argumentational subtleties of prominent exponents of Christianity who were adjudged to be excessively concerned to
defend the gospel before the intellectual elite at the headquarters of Judaism (pp. 93–95). But if the evangelist wished
to point out the limitations of Peter and his colleagues, he was
no less anxious to set James, the Lord's brother, in a still more
unfavorable light, the consequence being that in Mark 3:20–
35 Jesus' physical relatives figure as nefariously as the scribal
leaders from Jerusalem who declare that the Lord is possessed

[8] Trocmé holds (p. 94, n. 81) that the small collection of controversy stories in Mark 12:13–40 were, with the exception of vv.
35–37, derived from the Jerusalem ecclesiastical tradition. The evangelist found the *ensemble* a little too conciliatory with respect to the
scribes (or experts in the Mosaic law), and therefore added the
pericope in question to express his disaccord with those who had
organized the tradition, and implicitly to accuse them of collusion
with the representatives of scribal learning.

by Beelzebul, the prince of the demons.[9] And in the story of Jesus' rejection in his native place it is authoritatively stated (Mark 6:4) that a prophet is not without honor, except among his own kin and in his own home (pp. 104–9).

Thus, in Trocmé's estimation, besides drawing on authorized ecclesiastical tradition in which Jesus appeared as a messianic rabbi and founder of a new Jewish sect, St. Mark availed himself of popular Galilean reminiscences. These latter, suffused with legend and pagan religiosity, represented Jesus in the form of an astonishing healer, at once beneficent and fleeting, who, having broken with the narrow prejudices of strict Jews, had aroused their nagging opposition. So it may be said that the earliest gospel resulted from a literary effort to weld two different images of the Christ's person and work in a portraiture with a distinctive style of its own.[10] Moreover,

---

[9] Trocmé (p. 108) takes the severe condemnation of Mark 3:28f. to apply both to those (members of Jesus' family—cf. v. 31) who declare that the Lord is beside himself (v. 21) and to those (scribes from Jerusalem) who claim that he is possessed by Beelzebul (v. 22). But Trocmé (p. 147, n. 123) objects to the use of the term "anti-Semitism" in characterizations of St. Mark's attitude; see above, Chapter 4, n. 11, and below, n. 84.

[10] P. 119. Of course Trocmé denies that the evangelist was a systematic writer with a talent for speculative thought (p. 168); and he charges (p. 112, n. 10) that J. M. Robinson (*Das Geschichtsverständnis des Markusevangeliums*, Zürich, 1956; English translation, *The Problem of History in Mark*, London, 1957) and W. Marxsen (*op. cit.,*) each make the mistake of seeking to thrust the Markan message into the sophisticated framework of twentieth-century theological categories, the former's interpretation being governed by O. Cullmann's theory of *Heilsgeschichte*, the latter by R. Bultmann's version of Existentialism. On the other hand, Trocmé (p. 112) considers that both Robinson and Marxsen rightly stress the evangelist's identification of the historical Jesus with the risen Lord, the past being

in working out his synthesizing project the evangelist brought in the notion of the Christ's redemptive purpose, adding Mark 10:45b ("and to give his life as a ransom for many") as an appendix to a passage (10:42–45a) of quite a different kind.[11] The motif of sacrificial atonement is absent from the traditional material reproduced in verses 42–45a, and its introduction at verse 45b may well have been prompted by association through the proximity of verses 38–39, which concern the cup of suffering and the baptism of death. A connection was thereby established between the Lord's prophetic and thaumaturgic service or ministry, the main theme in Mark 1–8, and his function as sacrificial victim, the basic schematism of which is presented in 8:31–10:45, largely by means of the three predictions of the passion and resurrection (8:31; 9:31; 10:32–34). Such a *rapprochement* (at 10:45) was intended to set forth the preaching and healing aspects of the ministry in their true light, the crucifixion being understood as a voluntary self-sacrifice willed by God in the fulfillment of his redemptive purpose, not as the defeat of an incomprehensible personality endowed with supernatural powers (pp. 124f.).

However, Trocmé holds that the evangelist thought of

---

construed in terms of the present: what *was* said and done (by the crucified One), *is* said and done (by the living Christ among believers). And it is noticed (p. 112, n. 10a) that the author of the Markan gospel uses the historic present more frequently (151 times) than the other canonical evangelists.

[11] Trocmé considers (p. 124, n. 66) that Mark 10:45b alludes to Isa. 53:10–12, and appeals to the arguments put forward by H. W. Wolff in his *Jesaja 53 im Urchristentum* (3rd ed., Berlin, 1952), pp. 60ff. He further considers (p. 125, n. 67) that the *logion* must have had its origin in a Palestinian *milieu*, and appeals to the discussion by E. Lohse in his *Märtyrer und Gottesknecht: Untersuchungen zur urchristlichen Verkündigung vom Sühnetod Jesu Christi* (Göttingen, 1955), pp. 116ff.

Jesus, not in the loneliness of his towering personality, but in the solidarity of his relationship with the faithful, a relationship which, thanks to his resurrection, was perpetuated in corporate Christianity. In the earliest connected account of the ministry the hero appears in the capacity of One who enjoys the status of unique leadership. Jesus was the chief of a group (pp. 125f.) and, in the Markan view, the church came into existence when, after a brief interval of three days (Mark 8:31; 9:31; 10:34), fellowship with the leader was resumed on a spiritual level; and such a conception of Jesus' single and continuing hegemony was evidently directed against James, the Lord's brother, and the Jerusalemite tendency to endow the new religion with a dynastic organizational structure analogous to that which Islam was to adopt some six centuries later. Less obvious perhaps, but involved nonetheless, there obtained a certain animadversion for Peter, a vociferous disciple (8:29; 9:5) who was deliberately associated with his colleagues as frequently as possible and made to appear no better than they (8:33; 9:2; 10:35–45; 13:3)—the point being that the church must remain under the unique and ever-active guidance of the Risen Christ (pp. 137f.). So it may be legitimately inferred that the evangelist was the spokesman of an enterprising movement, which, having broken with the mother church at Jerusalem, had launched a mission among the ordinary folk of Palestine and in so doing was armed with the enduring conviction that it thereby conformed with the ecclesiological orders of the living Lord, as well as with the example of the earthly Jesus (p. 168).

In the final chapter of his work Trocmé contends that the Markan gospel went through two editions which, for convenience, we will designate PM ("proto-Mark") and CM ("canonical Mark"). PM consisted substantially of Mark 1–

13, and CM was created in the main by the simple device of appending to PM a passion narrative which probably originated in Jerusalem and consisted essentially of Mark 14–16; this we will designate JPN ("Jerusalem passion narrative"). St. Luke used PM, whereas St. Matthew used CM. In support of this hypothesis it is argued that while Mark 14–16 relates a history, Mark 1–13 exhorts the reader to make history, and that, in view of the three predictions of the passion and the account of the transfiguration, anything corresponding to JPN as a conclusion would be quite unnecessary from the standpoint of the author of PM; it was the bare eventuation of the passion-resurrection, not the historical details thereof, that constituted the hidden center of gravity in PM (pp. 176f.). On the other hand, the redactor responsible for CM had a different purpose: he aimed at fixing the night of Thursday-Friday and the day Friday for a festival that had hitherto been made to coincide with the Jewish passover. It was felt to be a case of intolerable subordinationism that the church each spring should have to depend on the astronomical calculations of the rabbinical authorities; hence the redactor's desire for a liturgical emancipation (p. 184). Trocmé thinks it likely that CM was produced in Rome towards A.D. 85—around the same time as the composition of Luke–Acts (which probably took place in the Aegean region). When uniting PM with JPN, the final redactor touched up the two texts with chronological notes and with a few explanatory observations, such as those of Mark 3:17; 7:11, 34; 12:42; 15:16, 42 (pp. 190ff.). Both PM and JPN had been in use at Rome for some time. The latter served liturgically for the annual commemoration of the passion, and was attributed to St. Mark, whose name was eventually transferred to CM; this procured for CM a quasi-apostolic authority and, indirectly, a reflection of the authority of

Peter, with whom tradition associated John Mark, the Jerusalemite. But the person who combined PM with JPN must remain unidentified (p. 194).

In support of his view that JPN primarily fulfilled a liturgical purpose Trocmé cites the works of Bertram, Carrington and Schille.[12] However, Bertram's thesis is alleged to be far too vague: while he rightly insists on the creative influence of early Christian worship in the constitution of a document wherein the stature of the hero infinitely surpasses that of a martyr pure and simple, Bertram nowhere offers a concrete definition of the cultic framework he has in mind (pp. 48f.). As for Carrington, his hypothesis regarding JPN is viewed with more favor, despite its alliance with a general explanation of the Markan structure that is adjudged to be rather adventurous;[13] and Trocmé, who thinks that the book of Esther (a work doubtless drawn up with a view to the feast of Purim) provides an interesting parallel, maintains that JPN was originally designed as the *megillah* ("roll") to be publicly read on certain special occasions in the *Urgemeinde* at Jerusalem; more specifically, as it is contended (p. 49), one may legiti-

---

[12] G. Bertram, *Die Leidensgeschichte Jesu und der Christuskult: eine formgeschichtliche Untersuchung* (Göttingen, 1922); P. Carrington, *The Primitive Christian Calendar: A Study in the Making of the Marcan Gospel*, I: *Introduction and Text* (Cambridge, 1952); G. Schille, "Das Leiden des Herrn: die evangelische Passionstradition und ihr Sitz im Leben" in *Z.T.K.*, LII (1955), 161ff.

[13] Carrington surmises that St. Mark's gospel is a collection of pericopes set in the order of a liturgical year that was derived from Judaism by the Galilean church. But, as Trocmé notices (p. 49, n. 184), Carrington has to admit that the passion narrative in its extant form accords ill with his proposed scheme and is compelled to treat it as an independent document, whose limits are indicated somewhat waveringly: 13:1 to 16:8, of which the primitive nucleus could have been 14:3 to 15:41 or 15:47.

mately suppose that the text of JPN was translated into Greek and amplified here and there in order to promote a regular celebration of the Christian passover (such as obtained in the mother church) in those Hellenistic communities where there existed some resistance to the fixed observance of sacred seasons.[14] Accordingly, if not without qualification, Trocmé refers approvingly to Schille, who argues that the crystallization of the passion reminiscences was due to a yearly celebration at Jerusalem that commemorated the first Good Friday and Easter Sunday, a crystallization effected around three poles: (a) a recollection of Jesus' last earthly night, bound up with an annual *agapē* or love-feast (Mark 14:18–72); (b) a liturgy affiliated with the three hours of Jewish prayer, for a solemn commemoration of the crucifixion (15:2–41); and (c) a matutinal celebration of Easter, perhaps involving a visit to the empty tomb (15:42–16:8); these three elements were assembled to form a continuous narrative (before St. Mark's reception of the work) by means of redactional notices like those of 14:1–2, 10–11, 17; 15:1. Such a thesis, so it is maintained (p. 50), while excessively conjectural in many details, succeeds in showing that the Markan passion narrative had its roots in the cultic life of the Jerusalemite church;[15]

---

[14] Trocmé is of the opinion that churches under Pauline influence were particularly in mind (cf. Rom. 14:5–6; Gal. 4:10–11; Col. 2:16–17 and P. Carrington, *op. cit.*, pp. 38ff.), and that, when JPN was put into Greek certain Petrine passages were added to reinforce the authority of the text in the Hellenistic churches concerned; thus Mark 14:12–16, 27–31, 37–39, 54, 66–72, which doubtless stemmed from eye-witness testimony on the part of Peter, would lend the latter's apostolic prestige to the ecclesiastical practice implicitly defended in JPN (p. 49, nn. 186f.). Cf. below, n. 96.

[15] In Trocmé's view (p. 50, n. 189), it was not only as the place of residence of the "pillars" (Gal. 1:18–2:10) or of the "twelve" (Acts 1–5), as the center of ecclesiastical authority (Gal. 2:12–13; Acts 15),

inter alia it accounts for the narrative's relative abundance of topographical and chronological notices, as well as for its dramatic features. Hence it may be inferred that Mark 14:1–16:8 (JPN) is fundamentally a liturgical text, originally designed for use in cultic commemorations of the Messiah's sufferings, death and resurrection;[16] that the document was already in Greek when it was incorporated into the gospel; and that the process of translation from Aramaic had included the addition of certain details calculated to enhance the reputation of the document in extra-Palestinian churches and thereby

---

or as the religious capital of Judaism and the goal for great pilgrimages (Acts 21:23–27; 22:17), that Jerusalem fascinated St. Paul; it was also because the church there, on the occasion of certain important Jewish festivals, held services in commemoration of the passion, an event that was absolutely decisive in the eyes of the Apostle to the Gentiles (I Cor. 2:1ff.). The latter's keen desire to make his visits to Jerusalem coincide with some Jewish feast or other thus becomes more easily explicable (cf. Acts 18:20–22; 20:16).

[16] It is argued (pp. 51ff.) that Mark 16:1–8 formed the natural conclusion of JPN: the Master's glorification has been recalled in the audacious self-affirmation of 14:62 (p. 51, n. 196), and, in view of the multiplicity of available persons to whom post-resurrection christophanies had been vouchsafed (p. 51, n. 195; I Cor. 15:5f.), an allusion to his victory over death—such as we find in the story of the empty tomb—would have been liturgically sufficient; the women may have held their peace (Mark 16:8), but the triumph nonetheless became known to countless witnesses! As for the abrupt ending *ephobounto gar* ("for they were afraid") at 16:8d, this must have been due to a post-Markan redactor who was more closely bound to the ecclesiastical tradition than the evangelist himself; the appendix was added to explain the women's silence, an addendum that was made without much attention being paid to the question of its harmonious integration with the work as a whole; no other Markan pericope ends with a *gar* ("for"), and while St. Mark's literary talents were modest enough, he would scarcely have been satisfied with such an awkward conclusion (p. 54).

help forward a more widespread regular observance of the Christian passover.[17]

As already pointed out, according to Trocmé, JPN was attributed to St. Mark; in fact, without necessarily being its author, the latter could have been the translator, amplifier and propagator of the document (p. 194). It is deemed likely that the mention of Alexander and Rufus, sons of Simon of Cyrene (Mark 15:21), and the picturesque report about the young man who fled naked (14:51f.) are Markan additions to JPN. Neither detail would seem to have liturgical value, and neither appears in the other synoptics; they were deliberately omitted by St. Matthew, and they were absent from the passion narrative received by St. Luke. The second of the two details may well be autobiographical, in which case it would constitute the signature, so to speak, of the witness who presented JPN to the Greek-speaking churches. A nephew of the Cypriot Barnabas (Acts 4:36; Col. 4:10), with whom he collaborated at Syrian Antioch and in Cyprus (Acts 12:25; 13:5, 13; 15:29), and attached from time to time with the missionary group led by the Apostle Paul (Acts 13:5, 13; Col. 4:10; II Tim. 4:11; Philem. 24), John Mark was probably more conversant with Greek than with Aramaic. A native of Jerusalem (Acts 12:12, 25), a clandestine witness of the arrest of Jesus (Mark 14:51f.), and certainly closely associated with Peter (Acts 12:12; I Pet. 5:13), he was admirably suited for the

---

[17] Trocmé maintains that the only element in Mark 1–13 that shows affinity with Mark 14:1–16:8 is the account of the triumphal entry at 11:1–10. The implicit influence of the Old Testament, the combination of dramatic and liturgical features (especially at vv. 7–10), the curious parallelism of 11:1–6 and 14:12–16 are obvious points of comparison. Perhaps the combined influence of Mark 14:12–16 and Zech. 9:9 was responsible for the production of a liturgical document of which use was made in Mark 11:1–10 (pp. 50f.).

task of translating and editing JPN for the benefit of the Hellenistic churches, a document of which Peter, if not the author, was at least the principal guarantor. While the prominence of the latter in Mark 14–16 may result from additions made to a more primitive form of JPN, the supplementations are supposed to have preceded the Markan intervention, which may well have taken place at Rome soon after Peter's death[18] —that is to say, between the years 65 and 70 when the Christian groups in the imperial capital were dressing the wounds they had sustained during the Neronian persecution (p. 194, n. 70).

So far as PM is concerned, Trocmé contends that its author was a Palestinian, Greek-speaking, Christian Jew, hostile to the hierarchical and scribal elite at Jerusalem, as well as to James, the Lord's brother; while allowing a certain authority to Peter and the Twelve, the positivity of his attitude was definitely not without qualification, but he had no particular connection with the Apostle Paul, for his orientation scarcely extended beyond the bounds of Palestine (pp. 197f.). It could well be that he belonged to the company of the Hellenists who, after lodging a complaint with the Twelve, were allowed to appoint a diaconate of Seven.[19] It is observed that the

[18] This accords with the tradition preserved by Irenaeus and by the anti-Marcionite prologue, although it is applied by these witnesses to CM, not just to the Greek form of JPN. As for the view that the translator of JPN was more conversant with Greek than with Aramaic, Trocmé observes (p. 194, n. 70) that there are mistakes in the rendering at Mark 14:3 and 41, and he refers to M. Black, *An Aramaic Approach to the Gospels and Acts* (ed. 2, Oxford, 1954), pp. 159ff.

[19] See Acts 6:1ff. Regarding the Seven and the *milieu* they represented, Trocmé refers (p. 199, n. 85) to M. Simon, *St. Stephen and the Hellenists in the Primitive Church* (London, 1958); O. Cullmann, "Secte de Qumran, Hellénistes des Actes et Quatrième Évangile" in

appearance of this group in Acts coincides with serious quarrels in the church of Jerusalem (Acts 6:1) and led to a limitation of the powers of the Twelve (6:2–6), who subsequently, even in the face of persecution, were apparently not disposed to identify themselves with the Seven (8:1). In the years that followed the relations between this group and the leaders of the original Jerusalemite church were far from being cordial: Peter and John reaped what Philip (one of the Seven) had sown in Samaria (8:5ff.); Peter went to Caesarea without troubling to arrange a rendezvous with Philip, who had established himself there (10:1–48; cf. 8:40; 21:8–9); and the Hellenists still resident at Jerusalem toward A.D. 60 continued to lead an existence somewhat aloof from the great church directed by James, the Lord's brother.[20]

With one exception, a proselyte of Antioch, the Seven of Acts 6:5 were Jews by birth. They all bore Greek names and operated among Greek-speaking Jews (6:8–10; 11:19). They were not universalists: if Philip turns to Samaritans and to an

the symposium *Les manuscrits de la Mer Morte, Colloque de Strasbourg—1955* (Paris, 1957), pp. 61ff., and the same scholar's "L'opposition contre le temple de Jérusalem, motif commun de la théologie johannique et du monde ambiant" in *N.T.S.*, V (1959), 157ff.; C. Spicq, "L'epître aux Hébreux, Apollos, Jean-Baptiste, les Hellenistes et Qumran" in *R.Q.*, III (1959), 365ff.; and P. Geoltrain, "Esséniens et Hellenistes" in *T.Z.*, XV (1959), 241ff.

[20] Trocmé notes (p. 199, n. 86) that the disciple of long standing (Acts 21:16) to whom the Christians of Caesarea—a community under the leadership of Philip, one of the Seven—bring the Apostle Paul, after having escorted him as far as Jerusalem, is a Cypriot named Mnason; and it is thought significant that the Apostle spends the night at the Cypriot's house before presenting himself to James and all the elders of the Jerusalem church (21:18). Of course Trocmé takes the Western reading at 21:16 (a variant that locates Mnason's residence in a village on the route traversed) to be a later emendation.

Ethiopian (8:5–39), his concern is still only with Jewish heretics and with a proselyte, at least in intention. Apparently, it was only circumstances that led some of them to deal with pagans, in the relatively distant region of Syrian Antioch (11:20f.). Their field of action was limited to Palestine, Phoenicia, Cyprus and Syrian Antioch (8:4–40; 11:19–20). As for their missionary method, it allowed a large place to wonder-working (6:8; 8:6–8, 13), to public appeals (6:8; 8:6), as well as to verbal violence (6:10–11, 13–14; 7:2–53). In all these respects, they practiced the sort of thing that PM teaches (pp. 199f.).

Their theological ideas were also reminiscent of doctrines exemplified in PM. The temple at Jerusalem was condemned as contrary to the will of God and doomed to destruction (Acts 6:14; 7:44–50); and the leaders of Israel were attacked for resisting the Holy Spirit (7:51–59), after the manner of Aaron (7:40f.) and of Solomon (7:47–50): so far from conserving the law of God (7:53), they even showed their will to disobedience before they had actually received it (7:39). Hence the most venerable of customs are modifiable (6:11, 13–14)—a notion that recalls the teaching of Mark 7:1–23 and 10:2–9 (p. 200).

The christology of the Hellenists as indicated in Acts seems to have been somewhat rudimentary. Such titles as "Prophet" (Acts 7:37), "Righteous One" (7:52) and "Lord" have nothing distinctive about them; and as for the vision of "the Son of Man standing at the right hand of God" (7:56), it is reminiscent of the synoptic sayings regarding the eschatological appearance of the Son of Man, the title here being employed only to menace Stephen's enemies with the prospect of imminent punishment. Apparently, the group was not greatly interested in christological speculation; its members stressed

the unmerited sufferings which Jesus had accepted with humility (7:52; 8:32–35), and they were mainly preoccupied
with the ultimate triumph of the Righteous One over the
wicked husbandmen,[21] a triumph that would open the eyes of
the nation that had been abused and misled. On these points
there are possible resemblances to the ideas of PM—at all
events no opposition exists (pp. 200f.).

The doctrine of the Holy Spirit professed by the Seven was
also somewhat analogous to that exemplified in PM; and this
is all the more striking in view of the fact that St. Luke's own
ideas on the subject were quite different. For the Hellenists,
the Holy Spirit signified the force that inspires the disciple
who bears witness to his faith with irresistible words (Acts
6:10, 15; 7:55; 8:29–39). It was also the spirit of prophecy
vouchsafed to certain believers (cf. 7:55; 8:39; 21:9–14),
but it was certainly not a gift granted to *every* believer, and in
this respect there existed an important theological divergence
between the apostles of Jerusalem and the Hellenist Philip
(Acts 8:14–17), whose position in this connection was similar
to that of the author of PM (p. 201).

Accordingly, Trocmé is persuaded that PM originated
among the Hellenists. The situation in which these latter
found themselves over against official Judaism and basic Palestinian Christianity sheds light on certain characteristic features of the gospel: the forthrightness of some of its polemical
passages, its confident zeal, its curiously limited orientation,
its mixture of liberalism and conservative respect for the Jerusalemite tradition. Such a situation also explains the redaction,
the plan and the presiding intention of the work. Brutally
persecuted by the Jewish authorities, the Seven and many of

---

[21] Trocmé compares the *lutrōtēs* ("redeemer" or "deliverer") of
Acts 7:35 with the *lutron* ("ransom") of Mark 10:45.

the group they represented fled beyond the reach of their mortal enemies, but in their various places of refuge, not far from Judea, they maintained the restless mentality of emigres, preparing for reconquest and seeking the most advantageous points of attack for their religious revolution. Expelled from Samaria by their rivals of Jerusalem, they took counter action in Galilee and its neighboring regions, where they went forward in the company of the Risen Lord and treading in the footsteps of the earthly Jesus. Hence the hostility shown by PM to the Jerusalemite church becomes quite understandable, especially when the evidence of Acts 1–5 is taken into account, for the traditions behind these chapters seem to imply that the mother-church at an early date had developed into something of a closed community, rather narrowly sectarian and doubtless tinged with the stringency characteristic of Essenism. So it appears to have come about within the first few years of Christian history that the official leaders at Jerusalem had hardened themselves against free and open missionary endeavor: James and his associates were largely preoccupied with theological debates and with the maintenance of order and the conservation of the purity of sound doctrine (pp. 201f.).

Trocmé is finally led to infer that the author of PM must have been Philip the evangelist (Acts 8:4ff., 26ff.; 21:8f.), who drew up the document as a literary defence of his audacious missionary expeditions across Samaria and the northerly parts of Palestine. One of the Seven, Philip possessed originality and an enterprising spirit. Established at Caesarea after fleeing Jerusalem (Acts 8:40), he was still residing there with his family toward the year 60 (Acts 21:8f.). From this base —a convenient one because of the mixed character of the town's population and the usual presence of the procurator there—one may suppose that he undertook his independent missionary journeys. And in all likelihood it was to justify and enlist support for his efforts that he decided to compose PM, expounding therein what he took to be the veritable ecclesiological intentions of Jesus. With regard to the date of the composition, it could not have taken place earlier than the collusion between Agrippa I (A.D. 41–44) and the Pharisees (an alliance that threatened the church—Mark 3:6; 12:13), or than the project of Caligula (A.D. 39–41) to set up a statue of himself in the temple at Jerusalem (a plan reflected in the last chapter of PM—Mark 13:14). Moreover, the composition could scarcely have occurred later than A.D. 57, for St. Luke probably came across PM at Caesarea during the protracted period of St. Paul's imprisonment there (Acts 24–26). Hence it may be supposed that the document first saw the light of day at Palestinian Caesarea toward the year 50 (pp. 202f.).

The foregoing exposition should make it clear that Trocmé's work merits assiduous consideration; in addition to being highly original, the main argument is closely reasoned in a manner that exemplifies insight and scholarship. Nevertheless, despite the forcefulness of the author's lucid presentation, his central theses are open to serious question. For one thing, of dubious validity is the contention that our earliest gospel exemplifies a dualism between unrefined miracle stories of Galilean provenance and traditions of a more sober character derived from the Jerusalemite church, for a strong sense of the supernatural, coupled with a lively belief in the reality of thaumaturgic power, would seem to have been well-nigh universal in primitive Christianity; and did not James, the Lord's brother, as well as Peter and the other apostolic "pillars" at Jerusalem, have their origins in Galilee? Also, Trocmé's discussions of the evangelist's antipathies are not altogether satisfactory: it is arguable, for instance, that in Mark 1–13 there is a tendency to make the Pharisees the principal opponents of Jesus, that the Herodians of Mark 3:6 and 12:13 represent the policy and administration, not of Agrippa I (A.D. 41–44), but of Agrippa II (A.D. 50–100), and that the Lord's physical relatives in Mark 3:21, 31 symbolize in some measure the chosen race as a whole. Moreover, while there are significant differences between Mark 1–13 and Mark 14–16, is it likely that the former ever circulated as a separate entity? And, in a general way, can the philosophy behind the earliest gospel be adequately dealt with when its complicated leitmotif of secrecy is treated as a side-issue? In the pages that follow Trocmé's fundamental theses are in turn subjected to critical examination under three main heads: (1) thaumaturgical traditions; (2) Markan antipathies; and (3) redactional history.

1. Thaumaturgical Traditions. It would seem that Trocmé scarcely succeeds in making more plausible Bultmann's hypothesis that the divergence between the *logia* of Q and the typical miracle material of St. Mark is to be attributed to the opposition between Jewish or Palestinian Christianity and the form of the new religion that developed in Hellenistic circles.[22] Admittedly, such *Wundergeschichten* as those of Mark 4:35–5:43 differ significantly from those that usually figure in talmudic literature, but this difference may be largely due to the dissimilarity in temper and outlook between primitive Christianity (Jewish as well as Gentile) and the type of Judaism that consolidated itself in the rabbinical schools after the

---

[22] See above, n.5. In general, cf. Morton Smith's important article "Prolegomena to a Discussion of Aretalogies, Divine Men, the Gospels and Jesus" in *J.B.L.*, XC (1971), 174ff.

collapse of the second commonwealth. For one thing, after the dire experiences of 66–70 and A.D. 132–136—experiences that were understood to result from excessive messianic ardor— there developed a dominant tendency to frown upon all expressions of fervid eschatological enthusiasm as at once foolish and dangerous;[23] and with this went a certain inclination to discountenance anything calculated to encourage a cult of prophetico-thaumaturgic personality, a mode of devotion that had so frequently been involved in the numerous abortive insurrections of the troubled period extending from the death of Herod the Great (4 B.C.) to the fall of Jerusalem (A.D. 70), and finally in the Bar Kokhba revolt that was terminated under Hadrian with unmitigated savagery in A.D. 136.[24] It is in no way surprising, therefore, that characteristic talmudic accounts of wonders performed by rabbis should have a different tenor from that possessed by the typical Markan miracle story, wherein the dominating personality of the thaumaturge is made to stand out with singular vividness.

Moreover, the Markan material generally displays a popu-

[23] It is noteworthy that in this respect *mutatis mutandis* the normative Judaism that emerged after 70 A.D. is analogous to the hierarchical Sadduceanism that obtained before the fall of Jerusalem, not to primitive Christianity—or even to certain movements within Pharisaism as it existed during the lifetime of Jesus.

[24] Cf. *M.R.*, pp. 288f. It should be borne in mind that no less a dignitary than R. Akiba acknowledged the validity of the ill-fated Bar Kokhba's messianic pretension, an acknowledgement which in the long run would hardly have contributed to the rabbi's reputation for wisdom or soundness of judgment. Regarding the involvement of thaumaturgy in the uprisings of the decades preceding the fall of Jerusalem in 70 A.D., an illustration is provided in the case of Theudas who, as it appears, gave proof of his divine vocation by assuring some of his followers that he would part the waters of the Jordan and lead them across on dry ground (see Josephus, *Ant.* 20:5:1; Eusebius, *Hist. Eccles.* 2:11; cf. the anachronistic reference in Acts 5:36).

lar and a prophetic character which on the whole distinguishes it quite definitely from the contents of the talmudic tradition. Apparently, Jesus himself proclaimed the nearness of the end of the present world, an *eschaton* in which signs of cosmic dissolution would bring in their train the final judgment and the inauguration of the Kingdom of God in the glory of a new and transcendent order of existence: all earthly institutions were destined shortly to pass away. And, after the crucifixion, the apostolic exponents of the resurrection faith, both in Aramaic and Hellenistic quarters, continued to live in an atmosphere of lively eschatological expectation, although evidently they made the Master's original proclamation more concrete, announcing that the Risen One would return in triumph either as the conquering Messiah to restore Israel's political independence or as the glorious Son of Man displaying an efficacious Christhood that would effect a renewal of the conditions of existence in general and of sin-scarred humanity in particular.[25] In any case, existing institutions as such were still being disparaged. On the other hand, the material preserved and commented upon in the rabbinical tradition as it perpetuated itself after the fall of Jerusalem, issued from a unique institutional form that was prized for its antiquity and for its continuing resilience through centuries of change. Although it is a supposition for which there is little or no direct evidence, literary or archeological, synagogues could have been established not long after the Deuteronomic reform of 621 B.C., and the associated rabbinical schools may well have developed during the Persian period which began in 539 B.C. These latter had essentially an educational and a hermeneuti-

---

[25] See above, Chapter 1, Sec. 3; and cf. P. Winter's article "The Trial of Jesus" in *Commentary* (New York), XXXVIII, 3 (September, 1964), p. 41.

cal function to perform, the main concern being to interpret and apply what was taken to be the declared will of God as presented in the pentateuch. This meant that oral teaching was conserved and elaborated to supplement the written and sacrosanct word, a word that was fixed for all time, and, by the middle of the second century A.D., various mnemonic techniques had been devised for the maintenance of an ancient tradition that served as a bulwark against the constant threat of disintegration among the scattered congregations of a proud people now completely bereft of statehood. The situation was a precarious one; and an ever-present care appertained to the struggle for existence in an alien and enduring world.

We are thus confronted with a significant contrast. Primitive Christianity possessed no documentary basis for its distinctive soteriological proclamation, the consequence being that its oral tradition regarding the historical Jesus had a flexibility and an openness that did not belong to the talmudic Judaism which survived the catastrophes of A.D. 70 and 136. Also, the apostolic gospel had a popular and prophetico-eschatological character which distinguished it sharply from the legalistic spirit that subsequently came to predominate in the rabbinical schools. There is no evidence that Jesus founded an academy and engaged in formal scholastic teaching; he operated in public places, and his closest followers were not post-graduate students who had successfully pursued certain specified courses of required instruction, but who, for whatever reason, had spontaneously responded to his call for repentance in view of the imminence of divine judgment. And the early upholders of the Easter faith could not possibly have had any deep concern for long-standing survival in a cosmos that was doomed to an impending death, or for the perpetuation of an institutionalized form in a social order that was passing away.[26]

Hence, in view of the difference in situation and outlook between the tradents in the two cases, it is not surprising that such narratives as those of Mark 4:35–5:43 should display a dramatic pointedness and a novelistic interest in personality that are absent from the miracle material normally to be found in talmudic writings. And this dissimilarity would seem to have little or no bearing on the question of whether, say, the story of the Gerasene demoniac (Mark 5:1–20) was first transmitted and developed among Palestinian-Aramaic or among Hellenistic representatives of the apostolic gospel. Nothing strictly analogous might appear in the extant literary productions of the rabbinical schools, and yet, on internal grounds,[27] it is arguable that the story *de facto* took its rise in a Jewish-Palestinian environment; indeed, perhaps it had a pre-Christian Judaic ancestry, having been originally told among certain Jewish admirers of a compatriot who won thaumaturgic fame in a foreign country. So the story could have been taken over and applied to Jesus in some Aramaic-speaking Christian community, wherein it was supplemented by the addition of verses 18–20, an appendix meant to bring out the importance of the family in the work of propagating the gos-

[26] Cf. above, Chapter 5, n. 12; see also E. P. Sanders, *The Tendencies of the Synoptic Tradition* (Cambridge, 1969), pp. 26ff., 294ff.

[27] Features of the story which seem to suggest a Palestinian-Jewish-Aramaic origin include: (a) the association of an unclean spirit with graves (v. 2); (b) the use of the Latin word "legion" of a host of unclean spirits (v. 9), a usage which seems to betray deep-seated antipathy for the imperial occupying forces; (c) the sense of appropriateness apparent in the demonstration of the reality of the exorcism: the unclean spirits enter the pigs, animals which, by Jewish standards, were technically unclean (v. 13). Cf. *M.R.*, pp. 49, 86ff.

pel: it had been discovered in the course of missionary activity that, when a person received benefit from the new faith, other members of his household were also liable to respond to its appeal—a motif that finds further exemplification in such passages as Acts 16:14–15, 31–34.

Trocmé (p. 41, n. 150) agrees that Mark 5:18–20 did not belong to the original form of the tale, but maintains that the verses were added by the evangelist himself to domesticate, so to speak, the savagery of the story's rather vulgar sensationalism by bringing it into line with the moralism of the regular ecclesiastical tradition. Of course this view is bound up with Trocmé's general contention that the material of Mark 4:35–5:43 exhibits a certain rustic artlessness which precludes the possibility of its having been derived from the relatively sophisticated *milieu* of an urbanized society, whether Jewish or Hellenistic: that is to say, the stories in question must be taken to reflect the quasi-animistic culture that prevailed in the rural districts near the frontier between Galilee and Syria, and they serve to indicate that the thaumaturgic activities of Jesus had made a deep impression upon the uneducated and somewhat simpleminded folk who inhabited that region. But is a thesis of this kind really satisfactory? The available evidence suggests that a lively belief in supernatural intervention pervaded the various strands of primitive Christianity, a movement founded upon implicit confidence in the miracle of the Lord's resurrection. The apostolic communities generally flourished in a tense atmosphere of eschatological enthusiasm, and in such a cultural environment wonder-working was taken for granted, the tendency being for the miracles of the present to be construed as prefigurements of God's awaited intervention at the end of the world.[28]

[28]See, for example, Matt. 12:28 and its parallel in Luke 11:20, where the exorcisms of Jesus are interpreted as signs of the inbreak-

Furthermore, a strong sense of the miraculous would appear to have been widespread in the Judaism within which Christianity emerged to become in the first place a sectarian development, as well as in the wider sphere of Hellenistic culture.[29] What we understand by the scientific attitude may to some extent have been foreshadowed in the philosophical schools among Stoics, Epicureans and Sceptics—and perhaps a minority element within Sadduceanism was affected by their teaching.[30] Generally, however, the thought of the time did not exemplify that interest in the abstract and the impersonal which is required for the systematic scrutiny of the operations of natural phenomena. Primitive man's division of events into the categories of the usual and the unusual was still largely determinative of the human understanding of the world, and, judged by scientific standards, this is an extremely inexact method of differentiating the multifarious items of experience. Any kind of object could be included in the category of the unusual and attributed to a transcendent cause, providing that the manner of its presentation was not consciously expected by the experiencing subject. The mind tended to pass lightly over the frontier between the organic and the inorganic spheres, and nonliving things, besides animals and human beings, were frequently thought to be acting under the direct influence of a supernatural agency. Also, an occurrence might be unusual to one person, but not to another; and it was partly

---

ing Kingdom of God; but the intervention of such authority in power and glory is still prospective, being awaited with eager expectation (Mark 9:1; 13:26; Rom. 8:19; cf. Mark 13:30; Matt. 10:23; Luke 22:18).

[29] Cf. *M.R.*, pp. 41ff.

[30] It may be recalled here that Greek philosophy of the type here in view is perhaps already discernible, for example, in Eccles. 1:14–18; 3:1–8, 22; 7:16–17; 8:15; 9:3, 7; 10:19. These passages could have been composed around 250 B.C.

because of the vagueness of the notion of the unusual, and partly because of the imperfection of contemporary knowledge concerning proximate causes, that there was ample room for the free exercise of the imagination in the interpretation of phenomena and the assignment of their causal conditions. What is deemed to be invalid or fantastic or merely sensational is dependent upon the criteria of truth which the judging mind adopts, and those criteria are largely determined by the intellectual climate of the prevailing culture.

Hence if there still obtains a more or less unrestrained tendency to understand causation anthropomorphically as effectual action informed by a purpose, the mind is prone to seek an explanation of any striking disturbance of familiar routine not in the impersonal conception of a particular concurrence of proximate causes as such, but by resorting to the teleological idea of a transcendent being who has decided for some purpose to interfere with the ordinary course of events. The transcendent being may be considered good or evil according to the character of the occurrence which calls for explanation; but on certain occasions an injurious occurrence could be ascribed to the intervention of a beneficent being as, for example, when it is construed to be a punishment inflicted for some offense committed against divine law. And it was evidently through an inclination to systematize such primitive notions that in Jewish thought during the closing centuries of the pre-Christian era there arose the dualistic doctrine of an evil spiritual Kingdom opposed to the Kingdom of God. The numerous supernatural beings of early Semitic belief were swept into the service of one or other of the two conflicting forces which were continuously striving against each other for the domination of mankind. Each of the transcendent Kingdoms was taken to be organized after the manner of an oriental state, having a supreme commander who stood at the head of a vast hierarchy of subordinates and directing the strategic operations of his hosts. The arch-demon (or evil or unclean spirit), who had various names assigned to him (Satan, Beelzebul, *etc.*), corresponded to God, the commander in charge of the Kingdom of righteousness, who would eventually vanquish the forces of Satan at the termination of the present cosmic order.

Of course it is not to be supposed that the Jews of the period subscribed in this general connection to a carefully defined body of doctrine. But there were certain commonly accepted beliefs of wide application which helped to shape the prevailing outlook on the world. Furthermore, despite the exclusivism of the Jews and the uniqueness of their ethical monotheism, their ways of thinking were not unaffected by the cultural traditions of other nations. Doubtless, indeed, the development of the cosmic dualism and eschatology just delineated already bears witness to an infiltration of ideas from Persian sources. But in the first century of the Christian era the interaction of cultures had become much more extensive and complicated. Greek was now the general language of commerce and of civilization in the eastern empire, and the Roman government had established an order that facilitated travel on an unprecedented scale. The consequence was that ideas could be diffused over wide areas with remarkable rapidity, and this stimulated the evolution of what has been termed "the Hellenistic theology"—that complex amalgam of ideas and practices derived from primitive magic, Greek philosophy, Orphic religion, Babylonian astrology, doctrines from Egypt and Persia.[31] Jewish religion, too, made its contribution to this

[31] See E. Bevan, *Hellenism and Christianity* (London, 1921), pp. 91ff.

comprehensive syncretism especially through the synagogues of the dispersion and the translation of its sacred literature into Greek. Thus there came to exist a certain community of beliefs among the people inhabiting the eastern mediterranean region. It is true that Judaism, thanks largely to the spirit of Pharisaism, was not basically modified by the welter of Hellenistic notions, but on the level of popular thought beliefs were current among the Jews which also found currency in the surrounding world of Hellenistic civilization.

Thus the belief that demons cause human ills was prevalent both in Jewish and in Gentile society, and with it went a number of associated ideas regarding the practical means of resisting and overcoming demonic power. It seems to have been commonly held that such power could not be successfully dealt with independently of divine assistance, and an assumption of this nature underlies Eph. 6:10–20, where the author[32] exhorts his readers to be strong in the strength of the Lord since their struggles are not against flesh and blood, but against the world rulers of this darkness, the spiritual hosts of wickedness in the heavenly places. The writer here offers an ethical interpretation, implying that the required divine power was made available through the practice of a virtuous life or through a personal recognition of God's moral demands. But in general perhaps it was more commonly supposed that supernatural assistance against demonic forces was to be gained by specialized knowledge of occult truths and by mysterious magical techniques, such as those briefly indicated in Mark 8:23 (the use of saliva and manual contact). However, in this

---

[32] If the Epistle to the Ephesians was not written by St. Paul, its author seems to have been familiar with Pauline thought. Cf. I Cor. 2:6–8, where "the rulers of this age" are doubtless demonic forces that were understood to be responsible for current evils.

particular case there is no reference to the demon pathology, and the fact is that in such redactional passages as Mark 1:34; 3:10–11; 6:13 the suggestion is made that illnesses fell into two categories, namely, those that were occasioned by demon possession and those that had other causes.[33] The unsystematic character of prevalent thought in this connection finds further illustration in many instances when one tries to determine whether or not the supernatural action was taken to be subject to human mediation. The resurrection, for example, was taken to have come about through the direct action of God (see Gal. 1:1; Acts 3:24), whereas in the Markan miracle stories divine power seems to have been basically regarded as something mediated through the person of Jesus. At all events, as in the wider world of Hellenistic religion, so in primitive Christianity, there was a tendency to merge the idea of mediation into that of identity, so that miraculous deeds could be related of an individual not merely to show that he was an instrument of transcendent power but to prove that he was really a divine being.[34]

[33] Cf. *M.R.*, pp. 52ff., where an attempt is made to classify the typical miracle stories of the synoptic traditions.

[34] Cf. M. Dibelius, *From Tradition to Gospel* (London, 1934), pp. 96f. Of course a distinction needs to be drawn between the Markan interpretation of any particular story and the way in which it was probably understood among those responsible for its transmission before its incorporation into the gospel. Thus, assuming that Mark 5:18–20 already belonged to the Gerasene story as the evangelist received it (see *M.R.*, pp. 86ff.), the word "Lord" in verse 19 could have meant "God" to the tradents and "Jesus" to the evangelist, for the demon's declaration in 5:7 does not *necessarily* imply the high christological doctrine of the Son of Man. Again, it seems that in 1:34 the evangelist interprets what was originally understood to be an apotropaic utterance (specifically, the demon's address in 1:24) as a mode of supernatural witness to the Lordship of Jesus in his christological capacity as the Son of Man; see *M.R.*, pp. 74ff.

Accordingly, there seems to be no justification for Trocmé's thesis that reports like those of Mark 4:35–5:43 must have emanated from the allegedly quasi-animistic culture of rural districts in northern Palestine. The characteristic presuppositions and motifs of these narrations were widely current in the Jewish thought of the time; and so far as the early church is concerned, Jesus was regarded not only as a sage and eschatological prophet, but also as a worker of wonders. Hence stories of his marvelous accomplishments would circulate in the apostolic communities because of their instrumental value in the service of apologetics, for it was felt that they afforded demonstration of his divine status and office.[35] Moreover, such tales would have a certain intrinsic value derived from the deepseated human interest in things strange or unfamiliar, an interest that would seem to be involved in the psychological root of all religion, so that in an important sense the concept of divine power is always liable to be resorted to in attempts to account for life's discrepancies.[36] As common experience teaches, what is extraordinary in its magnificence can easily evoke strained attention mingled with fear, and even in the form of the bizarre or grotesque, what is unfamiliar tends to command a certain fascination which no amount of educational discipline can completely eliminate. Thus general considerations of a psychological nature militate

[35] The apologetic function of miracle stories is brought out plainly, for example, in Mark 2:10–12, where the healing of a paralytic is deliberately effected to prove Jesus' authority to forgive sins. Admittedly the present form of the narrative shows signs of having been subjected to editorial treatment (see *M.R.*, pp. 126ff.), but this by no means excludes the likelihood that an implicit apologetic purpose has been rendered more explicit.

[36] Cf. our work *God and Reality in Modern Thought* (Englewood Cliffs, N.J., 1963), pp. 158ff., 244ff.

against the contention that St. Mark's gospel—a stylistically unrefined literary production—exemplifies a dualism between popular miracle stories of rustic Galilean provenance and esoteric *logia* of a more sober character, derived from the normative tradition of the church at Jerusalem.[37]

The fact is that the new faith was founded upon the sensational proclamation of the Christ's resurrection (I Cor. 15:1ff.); and a vital expectancy of the miraculous seems to have suffused all sections of primitive Christianity. The apostolic communities known to St. Paul were charismatic societies inspired and sustained by the divine Spirit, and thaumaturgic activities, no less than teaching and preaching, were counted among their accepted functions (I Cor. 12:10, 28). And in the hypothetical source Q, which is composed mostly of *logia*, Jesus puts his own victories over the demons alongside those of other Jewish exorcists, and he is permitted to discern in his own thaumaturgy a sign of the inbreaking Kingdom of God (Matt. 12:27f./Luke 11:19f.). Also, Q contains the account of the healing of the centurion's son or servant (Matt. 8:5ff./Luke 7:1ff.), and this, apart from the story of the Syrophoenician Woman (Mark 7:24ff./Matt. 15:21ff.), is the only synoptic account of a cure that takes place telepathically. Again, the passion narrative (Mark 14:1ff.), a document which, according to Trocmé, derived from the

---

[37] Trocmé may have overlooked the circumstance that the so-called "pillars" of the Jerusalem church (Gal. 2:9) were themselves Galileans (cf. Mark 14:70; Matt. 26:73). It should also be noticed that, in St. Mark's view, the Twelve were appointed not only to preach, but also to cast out demons (3:15), a function which, despite one noteworthy failure (9:18, 28), they could successfully discharge (6:7, 13). Moreover, the evangelist locates the efficacious cursing of the fig tree in the urban district of Jerusalem (11:12–14:20).

church at Jerusalem, is by no means bereft of miracle material. The pericopes concerning the finding of the upper room (14:12ff.), the designation of the betrayer (14:17ff.), and the prediction of the disciples' cowardly flight (14:27ff.) are impressive enough in themselves; but then we have the notices regarding the impressive daytime darkness (15:33) and the rending of the temple veil (15:38). It is true that in the first three of these passages Jesus appears as a clairvoyant, but depicted instances of foreknowledge can be no less dramatic than accounts of exorcisms, especially when, as is the case here, there is a tendency to assimilate prescience to predetermination, so that the Master comports himself as if he were actually the ultimate arbiter of the future course of events.[38]

Evidence that the prevailing thought of the time did not divorce the ethico-philosophical wisdom of the sage from the techniques of the thaumaturgical art, is provided by Josephus, and he was neither a rustic nor an eschatological enthusiast. In *Ant.* 8:2:5 it is stated that Solomon—traditionally respected as the father of Jewish wisdom literature—could expel demons and was the author of incantations by which distempers might be alleviated. And in the same passage Josephus reports that he had himself witnessed a certain Jewish exorcist named Eleazar giving a demonstration in the presence of a group that included no less a person than Vespasian. Eleazar inserted a ring with a root of those sorts mentioned by Solomon (as was supposed) into the nose of the demoniac,[39] and, while reciting formulae of allegedly Solomonic authorship, he dispossessed the demon, drawing it out through the

[38] Cf. *M.R.*, pp. 232ff.
[39] Re the magical root of Baara, see *Bel.* 7:6:3, where Josephus also explains that the demons are the souls of the wicked who have departed this life.

patient's nostrils. By way of offering further proof of the reality of the strange extraction, he commanded the demon to knock over a bowl of water, placed a little way off, as it fled from the scene of the operation.[40]

In the reporter's own judgment Eleazar's astonishing achievements afforded confirmation of Solomon's pre-eminence in wisdom and virtue. And, we submit, if an urbane intellectual like Josephus could assess thaumaturgy so highly, how much more must this have been the case with the "pillars" of the primitive church at Jerusalem—Galileans not renowned for their learning (cf. Acts 4:13; I Cor. 1:27), who lived in an atmosphere of intense emotional excitement, continually proclaiming the resurrection of the crucified Christ and the imminent termination of the present world-order? Of course the linguistic form of the report concerning Eleazar's exploits differs from that of the Markan miracle stories. But this is scarcely surprising seeing that Josephus deliberately sought to fashion his style on Greek literary models, whereas St. Mark's tales are mainly transcripts of oral traditions that were preserved and elaborated in the apostolic communities for apologetic purposes, and doubtless to some extent for the sake of their intrinsic hedonic interest.[41]

[40] In all likelihood, therefore, the upsetting of the bowl in this instance corresponds to the wild stampede of the swine in Mark 5:1ff., where the exorcized demons are extremely numerous: appropriately enough the unclean spirits take up lodgings in about two thousand unclean animals—hence they must all have vacated the Gerasene!

[41] Trocmé (pp. 42f.) rightly stresses the entertainment value of Mark 4:35–5:43; 7:32–37; 8:22–27; 9:14–29. But he errs in suggesting that it was only among the uncultivated inhabitants of north-eastern Palestine that such value was ascribed to the stories. Entertainment value in the present context more or less corresponds to what M. Dibelius (*From Tradition to Gospel*, London, 1934, pp. 70ff.)

2. *Markan Antipathies.* St. Mark's gospel is fundamentally a popular work. Its style is rough, simple and direct, and its author sympathizes with the masses while being opposed to their leaders, both religious and political. So in 10:42ff., for example, a contrast is drawn between those who exercise authority among the nations and those who follow the ideal way of life, seeking to serve, not to be served. However, these generalizations must be qualified if we are to have a valid concept of the total situation. In the first place, despite its prevailing simplicity and directness, the language is sometimes so abrupt that the meaning does not stand out clearly; thus in 1:41 (adopting the D reading) no explicit explanation is offered for why Jesus should be angry when confronted by a leper who pleads for cleansing. In the second place, the evangelist does not object to all forms of established leadership:

---

understands by the *profanity* of the Markan miracle-tales. In his article "Mark 3:7–12 and Mark's Christology" in *J.B.L.*, LXXXIV (1965), 351, L. E. Keck objects to Dibelius' use of the term "profane" in this connection. It would seem, however, that the objection arises from a failure to realize that the outstandingly significant—the *Mysterium Tremendum,* to employ R. Otto's terminology—is differently appreciated in different situations. This is quite obvious in a broad historical sense: for example, the cult of the Earth-Mother and the assimilation of sexual union to the hierogamy Heaven-Earth were conditioned by the discovery of agriculture (cf. M. Eliade, *The Sacred and the Profane,* New York, 1961, pp. 17, 145ff., 168). But the ambivalence of the marvelous also exists on a more restricted, personal level, so that for the same individual in varying circumstances the same kind of epiphany can be sacred or profane, divine or demonic, fatefully serious or merely entertaining. Cf. F. R. Tennant, *Philosophical Theology,* I (Cambridge, 1928), pp. 306ff., where reference is made to a distinction between the numinous and the secular uncanny. For further discussion of Keck's article, see our paper "Mark 3:7–12 and the Alleged Dualism in the Evangelist's Miracle Material" in *J.B.L.*, LXXXVII (1968), 409ff.

apart from the obvious case of Jesus himself, the writer approves of the guidance of John the Baptist in his alleged capacity as Godsent forerunner of the Messiah (1:1ff.; 6:14ff.; 9:11ff.; 11:27ff.); also, while he habitually casts the scribes in a villainous role, the habit can be broken (12:28ff.), and Roman procuratorial authority can be preferred to the Jewish hierarchy (15:1ff.). In the third place, the common people, although usually appearing in a favorable light (as in 12:37), finally act nefariously, even demanding the crucifixion of him who was called King of the Jews (15:13f.); but significantly enough, St. Mark is careful to observe that the chief priests are really to blame for this unprecedented outburst of popular hostility because it was they who stirred up the base passions of the assembled multitude (15:11). Furthermore, in the evangelist's view, since knowledge of the divine Kingdom is imparted exclusively to the Twelve (4:10ff.), the general public is spiritually underprivileged, and must remain so until the time of the Son of Man's resurrection (9:9). But once again qualification is called for. To the end of the gospel the disciples are incapable of grasping the mysterious meaning of what is revealed to them,[42] and on certain occasions representatives of the world at large are allowed to perceive the secret fact which the privileged Twelve fail to understand. Thus at 5:19f. a cured Gerasene apprehends the Lordship of Jesus, and the same seems to hold in the case of the Syrophoenician woman (7:28); at 10:47f. a blind man sees that Jesus is the Son of David, while at 14:3 a woman fittingly anoints the head of Jesus; and at 15:39 a Roman centurion declares that Jesus is the Son of God.[43]

[42] See *M.R.*, pp. 168ff.
[43] The philosophical significance of these five passages is considered above, Chapter 6 (re reason and revelation).

Perhaps the underlying weakness in Trocmé's treatment of St. Mark's antipathies arises from a failure fully to appreciate the complexity of the changing circumstances and evolving motivations that issued in the emergence of the gospels; and this in turn may be partly conditioned by an inclination to interpret the Markan data from the somewhat restricted standpoint of certain sections of the Acts of the Apostles, a document which, while doubtless containing old traditions, reflects a different situation and needs to be used with extreme caution as touching historical matters of fact.[44] In any event, the intensification of anti-Pharisaic feeling discernible in the passage from the earlier to the later gospels scarcely justifies the contention that in St. Mark's presentation the Pharisees act merely as a Galilean syndicate concerned to uphold the purity

[44] Even at the outset of his work the author of Luke-Acts makes several mistakes: (a) Jesus could not have been born during the reign of Herod the Great (Luke 1:5), who died in 4 B.C., *and* at the time of the census conducted by Quirinius (Luke 2:2), which took place 6 or 7 A.D.; (b) taxation censuses were held at different times in different areas of the empire, so there would be no general decree such as is mentioned in Luke 2:1; (c) the census of 6 or 7 A.D. was occasioned by the deposition of Archelaus rather than by an imperial decree that was independently promulgated; (d) people were required to register in their places of residence, not in the regions of their ancestral homes as is implied in Luke 2:4f.; (e) the heads of households had not to be accompanied by their wives when reporting at the census offices (as is suggested in Luke 2:5). See E. Schürer, *Die Geschichte des jüdischen Volkes im Zeitalter Jesu Christi* (Leipzig, 1901–11), I, 508ff. Again, to take an example from the Acts of the Apostles, it is noted in Acts 4:32 that the early church generally was communist, and yet in Acts 4:36f. Barnabas is commended for selling a parcel of land and handing over the proceeds to the church; obviously the writer is here idealizing the situation from reported instances of primitive Christian generosity. See M. Dibelius, *Studies in the Acts of the Apostles* (London, 1956), pp. 123ff.

of individual morality. On two occasions they are associated in a sinister way with the Herodians—that is, presumably, with supporters of the policy of a certain Herodian ruler or with members of his administration: at 3:6, early in the account of the Galilean ministry, they conspire to find ways and means of having Jesus eliminated; and at 12:13, during the brief Jerusalem period, an effort is evidently made to carry the plot a stage further. Also, in 8:15 the disciples are strictly enjoined to beware of the leaven (evil disposition) of the Pharisees and the leaven of Herod, a twofold warning that seems to be addressed by the evangelist to his readers, in which case the Herod concerned cannot be Herod Antipas (4 B.C.– A.D. 39) or Agrippa I (A.D. 41–44). The reference must be to Agrippa II (A.D. 50–100), who, in pursuance of his enduring pro-Roman policy consistently sought to restrain the growth of Jewish messianic groups, whose eschatological fervor was ever liable to express itself in the form of militant revolutionary activity. During the fifties and sixties many of the Pharisees were also prepared to adapt themselves to Roman rule, provided that religious freedom was guaranteed, and hence they tended to exercise a moderating political influence in the restless Jewish world of the time.[45] Thus Mark 3:6; 8:15 and 12:13 are remarkable not so much because they associate stringent moralists (cf. 7:1ff.) with the morally lax,[46] but

---

[45] Cf. above, Chapter 3, n. 11.

[46] Cf. 6:14ff. (the sordid story of John the Baptist's decapitation), which might be compared with the Matthean account of the slaying of the infants at the order of Herod the Great (Matt. 2:16ff.). This latter report may well be a legendary development from the circumstance that in 7 B.C. Herod had two of his own offspring (Alexander and Aristobulus, by his second wife Mariamne I) put to death. In early Christian thought the tendency was to regard all

rather because they are among the very few passages in the canonical gospels that bear witness to the existence of anti-Roman feeling within the sphere of primitive Christianity; and this is a point which Trocmé overlooks.[47]

It is true that, while the plotting of the Pharisaic-Herodian coalition (3:6) is carried forward into the Jerusalem period (12:13), there the matter ends so far as explicit references are concerned, and neither Pharisees nor Herodians find any further mention. At the outset of the Markan passion narrative (14:1) the chief priests and the scribes seek how to arrest Jesus by stealth and have him put to death, and in the subsequent reports the hierarchs are introduced as the principal antagonists of Jesus. Altogether they are mentioned no less than nine times. On six occasions they are named with others: the scribes (14:1), the scribes and the elders (14:43), the elders and the scribes (14:53), the whole sanhedrin (14:55), the elders, the scribes and the whole sanhedrin (15:1), and the scribes (15:31); on three occasions they appear alone (14:10; 15:3, 11). Thus a malicious scheme originally conceived by the Pharisees in concert with the Herodians is apparently taken up and brought to its shameful conclusion by members of the priestly aristocracy. But of course St. Mark's readers are not unprepared for this development since in four passages prior to 14:1 there are indications of the iniquitous role to which the hierarchs will be finally assigned. The first and the third of the three predictions of the passion

the Herods as being equally evil; in fact, of course, this was far from being the case.

[47] Cf. P. Winter, *On the Trial of Jesus* (Berlin, 1961), p. 129, who sees anti-Roman feeling also in the use of the term "legion" (by possessing demons) in Mark 5:9. Luke 13:1 manifestly contains a trace of such political sentiment. Cf. below, n. 64, and above, n. 27.

and resurrection are quite explicit in this regard: in 8:31 it is solemnly declared that the Son of Man must be rejected by the elders and the chief priests and the scribes;[48] and in 10:33f. that he will be delivered to the chief priests and the scribes, who will condemn him to death and deliver him to the Gentiles, and they will mock him, spit upon him, scourge him, and put him to death. The other two indications are not so explicit, but they are possible forecasts nonetheless: at 11:18, an addendum to the report of the so-called cleansing of the temple, it is stated that the chief priests and the scribes sought (or began to seek) how they might destroy Jesus;[49] and a little later in 11:27f., the reference apparently being to the day following the violent action in the temple (see 11:20), it is reported that the chief priests and the scribes and the elders approached Jesus and questioned him concerning the authority by which he acted as he did.

The likelihood is that all four of these indications occur in passages that have traditional connections with the old form of the passion narrative. As for the predictions of 8:31 and 10:33f.,[50] it is not impossible that they are editorial creations based on received information and meant to show that Jesus foresaw the outcome of his mission. Perhaps more probable, however, is the view that behind the predictions lay a tradi-

[48] There are ten Markan passages in which the hierarchs are allied with other hostile elements, namely, 8:31; 10:33; 11:18, 27; 14:1, 43, 53, 55; 15:1, 31; and the first of these is unique in that it is the only one wherein the chief priests do not have pride of place.

[49] The text here *pōs auton apolesōsin*, almost exactly corresponds to the *hopōs auton apolesōsin* of 3:6. The suggestion is that the hierarchs and the scribes take up what the Pharisees and the Herodians were the first to plan.

[50] The second of the three predictions of the passion and resurrection (9:31) speaks simply of the Son of Man's coming delivery into the hands of men, without offering any more specific identification.

tional *logion* which affirmed the mystery of the Messiah's humiliation as the divinely necessary prelude to his exaltation.[51] In any case, the sayings of 8:31 and 10:33f. could not have been composed had it not been for the events recounted in 14:1ff. As for the indications in 11:18 and 11:27f., being involved respectively with the cleansing of the temple and the hostile enquiry about Jesus' authority, they might well have featured in a traditional introduction to the pre-Markan record of the passion.[52] The authority question arises naturally out of the report of the defiant action in the temple, and the latter would provide a concrete explanation of 14:1, where the chief priests and the scribes determine to arrest Jesus by stratagem and kill him.[53]

Accordingly, of the thirteen Markan references to the

[51] For a detailed examination of the redactional history of the predictions, cf. G. Strecker, "Die Leidens- und Auferstehungsvoraussagen im Markusevangelium" in *Z.T.K.*, LXIV (1967), 16ff. Re the general concept of the divine necessity of the passion, see *M.R.*, pp. 218ff.

[52] Possibly in a somewhat modified form Mark 11:1–10 (the triumphal entry) also belonged to such a traditional introduction. The affinity between 11:2–6 and 14:12–16 is certainly remarkable; but both could be due to St. Mark himself. Cf. *M.R.*, p. 259, n. 3; p. 294, n. 19, and above, n. 17.

[53] In his informative article "Temple Cleansing and Temple Bank" in *J.B.L.*, LXXXIII (1964), 365ff., N. Q. Hamilton shows that the temple treasury functioned as a sort of state exchequer, and that Jesus' unauthorized suspension of the official work of the bankers (Mark 11:15f.) could have been construed as a direct claim to royal dignity (*ibid.*, p. 371). To use Hamilton's own words: "An eschatological prophet acting under the obligations of his message came into conflict with civil authorities who also had their obligations" (*ibid.*, p. 372). Thus there are historical or factual reasons for supposing that the temple cleansing was directly connected with the hierarchical decision to have Jesus arrested—on a charge of making claim to kingship (cf. Mark 15:2, 9, 12, 18, 26).

hierarchs nine occur in the passion narrative, and the remaining four in passages connected (directly or indirectly) with the same narrative; and so it may be inferred that in the earliest tradition it was (on the Jewish side) members of the priestly aristocracy who played the decisive role in the events that led to the crucifixion. As Marxsen aptly puts it, the gospel grew backwards, for chapters 14–16 evidently represent the first part of the tradition to be fixed in writing,[54] in which case the first thirteen chapters were designed to prepare the way for the report of the crucifixion. Nevertheless, the account of the Lord's humiliation has a self-sufficiency that distinguishes it sharply from what goes before; and, indeed, it seems likely that the main outline of the passion narrative had long enjoyed an independent existence before St. Mark addressed himself to his task. For the most part this narrative proceeds coherently in genuinely historical time from the plotting of the hierarchs (14:1ff.) to its climax in the story of the empty tomb (16:1ff.); and the notices of time and place (which now occur more frequently than in the earlier chapters) are on occasion so securely woven into the texture of the narrative that they could hardly be regarded as editorial connecting links imposed by the evangelist on what were originally isolated items of traditional material. Admittedly, some of the constituent elements may once have possessed separate existence; and perhaps the story of the anointing (14:3–9), the account of the preparations for the last supper (14:12–16), and the report of the nocturnal trial (14:55–65) were first introduced to their present contexts by the evangelist himself. That the passion narrative under-

---

[54] See W. Marxsen, *Der Evangelist Markus: Studien zur Redaktionsgeschichte des Evangeliums* (Göttingen, 1959), p. 17. Cf. *M.R.*, pp. 219ff.

went expansion in this way is shown by the treatment which the Markan version receives at the hands of the later evangelists: thus St. Matthew adds the story of Judas' suicide (Matt. 27:3–10), the reference to the dream of Pilate's wife (Matt. 27:19), the scene in which Pilate publicly washes his hands (Matt. 27:24f.); St. Luke adds the report of the trial before Herod Antipas (Luke 23:8–12), and so on. But it still remains that a brief account of the principal events (arrest, trial, crucifixion, one or more christophanies) probably existed from a very early date. The main outline of the narrative is the same in all the synoptic gospels; and, what is more significant, even the fourth evangelist, who generally shows much independence with regard to the synoptic tradition, faithfully reproduces the fundamental framework of the passion narrative as it appears in our earliest gospel. Presumably, he is here dealing with a connected tradition which was so old and firmly established in Christian thought and memory that he is unable to treat it with his usual freedom.

Returning to the question of St. Mark's antipathies in the light of the foregoing considerations, we may state that, despite the evidence of the old tradition concerning the passion, the evangelist tends to introduce the Pharisees as the principal adversaries of Jesus, and that he makes such introductions in passages that are not derived from the passion tradition. In all there are eleven or twelve explicit Markan references to Pharisees, and in every instance the attitude is one of hostility. Eight times they are mentioned as allied with others: at 2:18 they are twice coupled with followers of John the Baptist[55]

[55] 2:18 is the only Markan passage in which the Pharisees are mentioned after their allies. Thus it corresponds to 8:31, the only Markan passage in which the chief priests are not mentioned before their several associates; see above, n. 48. Could it be that the controversy story (2:18–20) as St. Mark received it mentioned the Baptists only? Cf. above, Chapter 2.

in a dispute about fasting; as we have seen, in 3:6; 8:15; 12:13 they are associated with the Herodians; at 7:1, 5 they are allied with some of the scribes, the dispute being about ceremonial cleanness; and of course the same topic is involved at 7:2, where they are even conjoined with all the Jews. Three or four times Pharisees appear on their own—in 2:16, where objection is taken to the practice of holding table fellowship with publicans and sinners;[56] in 2:24, where the dispute concerns sabbath observance (as it does in 3:6); in 8:11, where a demand is made for a sign from heaven, presumably, as an unmistakable confirmation of the validity of the church's eschatological proclamation; and in 10:2, where the question is raised as to the legality of a husband's action in divorcing his wife.[57]

Just as the story of the Syrophoenician woman dramatizes an internal ecclesiastical dispute on the vexed matter of integration,[58] so the controversy stories of Mark 2:1ff. and 12:13ff. are for the most part dramatic renderings of early Christian argumentations with outsiders—Pharisees, Baptists and others—who criticized apostolic doctrine and conduct. Such terse and concrete renderings were taken up into the gospel tradition and the controversies were thereby retrojected into the life of Jesus. This was done, not out of a deliberate will to

[56] The reference here is to scribes of the Pharisees, that is, to men learned in the Mosaic law who were of the Pharisaic persuasion. The phrase "the scribes *of* the Pharisees" is unique so far as the synoptics are concerned, and the variant "the scribes *and* the Pharisees" witnessed by certain MSS is doubtless an adaptation to the usual formula (cf. Matt. 23:2; Luke 6:7, *etc.*). But it should be noticed that the *nomikos* ("lawyer" = "scribe") in Matt. 22:35 is a Pharisee (see the preceding verse).

[57] The reference to Pharisees at 10:2 is lacking in D, and perhaps it crept into the Markan text from Matt. 19:3.

[58] That is, the integration of Gentile with Jewish believers; see above, Chapter 5.

deceive (as Reimarus supposed), but issued from the assumption that an essential continuity existed between the life of Jesus and the life of the apostolic church, and this is a point which Trocmé rightly emphasizes. St. Paul could assert that the fellowship of believers constituted the body of Christ (Rom. 12:5; I Cor. 12:12f.), and even that his own ego had been superseded by the Spirit of the indwelling Christ (Gal. 2:20). And it was in accordance with this line of thought that the evangelists and the tradents who preceded them tended to assume that what happened to the communities with which they identified themselves must have happened to the church's Founder; their friends were his friends, and their foes his foes.

In the ecclesiastical tradition, therefore, the representation of the earthly ministry came to be increasingly suffused with reflections of situations that belonged to later decades, preserved memories of a historical past being supplemented through the introduction of elements derived from more recent experience in the continuing life of the church. This largely accounts for the discrepancies and shifting motifs in the canonical gospels—documents which variously crystallize the floating tradition at different stages of its development. More specifically, it helps to explain why St. Mark, in defiance of the well-established data concerning the Lord's sufferings, should be disposed to regard the Pharisees as the paramount opponents of Jesus, even blaming them for the hierarchial[59] plot which issued in the Messiah's destruction (3:6; cf. 11:18, 27; 14:1, 10 etc.). Actually, as we have maintained elsewhere,[60]

[59] It seems likely that the procurator himself was also involved in the proceedings that led to Jesus' arrest; see *M.R.*, p. 299, n. 32.

[60] See above, Chapter 5, n. 12. In agreement with our contention that Jesus was a sort of Pharisee are: P. Winter, *op. cit.*, pp. 111ff., H. F. Weiss, "Der Pharisäismus im Lichte der Überlieferung des Neuen Testaments" (a searching analysis of the relationships among

Jesus himself must have been much more closely associated with certain Pharisaic groups of his time than is commonly supposed; and perhaps a number of his early followers were drawn from their ranks. It is true that Paul of Tarsus in his Pharisaic period violently opposed the Christian movement (Acts 9:1ff.; I Cor. 15:9; Phil. 3:5f.), whereas, according to Acts 5:33ff., Gamaliel, a Pharisaic member of the sanhedrin and a teacher of the law, took a much more sympathetic attitude, and this contrast would imply that Pharisaic reaction to the new faith in its earliest years was not uniform but ambivalent.[61]

However, with the growing threat of revolution in the air, influential Pharisees tended to become increasingly averse to expressions of eschatological enthusiasm, doubtless realizing

---

various Jewish groups in New Testament times), included as an appendix in R. Meyer, *Tradition und Neuschöpfung im antiken Judentum* (Berlin, 1965), and C. K. Barrett, *Jesus and the Gospel Tradition* (London, 1967), pp. 101f. For opposing views, see O. Betz, *What do we know about Jesus?* (London, 1968), pp. 78ff., and D. R. Catchpole's contribution to *The Trial of Jesus*, ed. E. Bammel (London, 1970), pp. 47ff.

[61] It is difficult to determine what precisely the Pauline objections to Christianity originally consisted in. Were they theological or political? They could have been both. In I Cor. 1:22 he states that the proclamation of the doctrine of a crucified Messiah was offensive to Jews. Following this clue one might argue that, prior to his conversion, St. Paul thought it blasphemous (in the sense of the Mosaic law) to assert that anyone who had been cursed of God by crucifixion (Deut. 21:23) was the God-sent Redeemer (Gal. 3:13); and so one might infer that he persecuted the church for theological reasons. However, a political motive also was perhaps entailed, for St. Paul was evidently a Roman citizen (Acts 23:27), and as such he could have reacted violently against the followers of any person who had suffered crucifixion (a mode of punishment usually reserved for revolutionaries or enemies of the state) at the order of a Roman judicial authority (cf. Rom. 13:1ff.).

that such religious fervor, no matter how transcendent in its theoretical form, could only too easily provide the emotional dynamism for militant action against Rome.[62] And among Christians there developed a widespread concern—a concern that would be strengthened through the outbreak of the great insurrection in A.D. 66— to make it clear that they lived under a new dispensation and were not to be confused with the refractory Jews, a thankless people whose suppression was so costly to the empire in men and material.[63] Since the Pharisees assumed the leadership of the stateless Jewish communities after the collapse of the second commonwealth in A.D. 70, they became the butt of the Christian hatred which had only recently been reserved for the Zealotic revolutionaries. Thus the fate of the Pharisees in the thought and estimation of primitive Christianity was far from being an enviable one. During the forties, fifties and sixties of the first century they were blamed

---

[62] The demand for a sign from heaven in Mark 8:11 may well reflect the mid-century intensification of Pharisaic scepticism regarding the value of ardent eschatological expectation. The case of Josephus is relevant in this connection: he was a Pharisee and, after a visit to Rome in his twenty-sixth year, did whatever he could to restrain "tumultuous persons" who advocated revolt against the imperial authority (*Vita*, 2–4). True, no reference is made to the theological affiliations of the "tumultuous persons." But this is characteristic, and is ascribable to Josephus' desire to present Judaism in a favorable light to his Roman readers. Hence allowance has to be made for his tendency to minimize the importance of the religious factor in the Jewish revolutionary movements of his time. Cf. M. Goguel, *The Life of Jesus* (London, 1933), pp. 81f., and in general, see Morton Smith's illuminating paper "Zealots and Sicarii, Their Origins and Relation" in *H.T.R.*, LXIV (1971), 1ff.

[63] Cf. S. G. F. Brandon's article "The Apologetical Factor in the Markan Gospel," *Studia Evangelica*, II (ed. F. L. Cross; Berlin, 1964), 34ff.

for adopting an attitude that was more or less in line with the pro-Roman policies of Agrippa I and Agrippa II; and after the fall of Jerusalem they incurred hostility for having emerged from the disaster as the dominant party of a recalcitrant and trouble-making people.[64]

At this stage the question naturally arises as to why St. Mark fails to adjust the plot of 3:6 to that of 14:1 by adopting the simple procedure of introducing explicit references to the Pharisees at 14:1 itself and elsewhere in the passion story. Trocmé (p. 74) holds that the evangelist still cherished a limited hope of the conversion of the Pharisees, and could this account for St. Mark's reluctance to involve them explicitly in the proceedings which led directly to the crucifixion?[65] Although Christian-Pharisaic relations had considerably deteriorated when the gospel was written, the likelihood

---

[64] Of course this is not to be taken to imply that anti-Roman sentiment disappeared from the church after 70 A.D. In general the Christian attitude remained bipolar: on the one hand, believers despaired of the present order, regarding all political powers as evil (cf. Mark 10:42f.; I Cor. 2:8), and aspiring after a Kingdom not of this world (John 18:36; Phil. 3:20); on the other hand, believers had to adapt themselves to the governing authorities for the sake of the propagation of the gospel, and in Rom. 13:1ff. St. Paul could even go so far as to assert that existing authorities had been divinely instituted to promote good conduct and restrain the forces of evil (cf. II Thess. 2:7). It might further be noted here that the book of Revelation bears witness to the existence of strong anti-Roman feeling in certain Jewish-Christian quarters toward the end of the first century.

[65] Trocmé himself, as we have seen, would explain the discrepancy in terms of his theory of the gospel's redactional history: Mark 1–13 was produced by one person (Philip), Mark 14–16 by another (John Mark). This hypothesis will be discussed in the next section.

is that Jewish believers in the Messiahship of Jesus had not yet been ejected from the synagogues,[66] and so perhaps a ray of hope still lingered in the evangelist's mind. But the existence of such optimism seems somewhat doubtful. In any case, there are other points which should be brought into consideration, one of them being that in several respects our earliest gospel lacks consistency.[67] Conflicting motives evidently competed for dominance as St. Mark proceeded with his writing, and this greatly weakened the formative power of his thought to weld the multifarious traditions he presents into a harmonious pattern of ideas. He even failed to carry out his theory of the messianic secret with anything approaching perfect consistency, as is clear from his manifest concern to blame the Jewish authorities for the Lord's crucifixion, a shameful event which he also considers to be a provision of God's predetermining purpose. Hence it is not altogether surprising that he should have failed to make some adjustment between the Pharisaic conspiracy of 3:6 and the hierarchical machinations of 14:1.

[66] The late Dr. P. Winter pointed out to us (in a private communication) that the ejection (which did not take place everywhere all at once) must have been effected generally by *c.* 85–90 A.D., when the *birkath haminim* was incorporated into the liturgy of the eighteen prayers. This *birkath* contains a curse of the *minim* and *nosrim*, whence it follows that Jewish Christians no longer participated in the worship of the synagogue (for obvious reasons it was withdrawn from the liturgy after Christianity became the official religion of the empire—probably in Justinian's time). The fact of the ejection certainly comes out more clearly in Matt. and John than it does in Mark, a work that was probably written in 70 A.D. or soon afterwards. Cf. J. L. Martyn, *History and Theology in the Fourth Gospel* (New York, 1968), pp. 17ff.

[67] See *M.R.*, pp. 29, 69ff., 122, 128, 155f., 202f., 243; and above, Chapter 6.

It ought also to be observed that St. Mark was relatively less creative from 14:1 onwards. In all probability, before his work was planned, the passion narrative existed as a well-established document that served apologetic and cultic purposes, whereas the thematic materials of chapters 1–13, which are largely without any sense of historical development, stood in need of general organization at the hands of the evangelist. Although we may legitimately hold that he inserted such pericopes as 14:3–9 (the anointing at Bethany) and 14:55–65 (the nocturnal trial before the sanhedrin) into the traditional record of the Messiah's sufferings, he refrained from modifying its framework and was perhaps disinclined to interfere unduly with the received text. Nevertheless, an implicit (if not explicit) connection with earlier Pharisaic hostility is secured in two ways in the course of the passion narrative. Firstly, in the account of the nocturnal trial[68] it is reported that the hierarchs and *all* the sanhedrin sought testimony against the prisoner (14:55; cf. 15:1) and that they *all* condemned him as guilty of a capital crime (14:64; cf. the "all")

---

[68] For a defense of the view that 14:55–65 was first brought into its present context by St. Mark himself, see *M.R.*, pp. 242f., 259, n. 3, 280ff. It is most unlikely that the *Su eipas* ("You said [it]") in Matt. 26:64 was taken from a supposedly original text of Mark 14:62 which lacked the *egō eimi* ("I am"). The Matthean formula is clearly modeled on the *Su legeis* ("You say [it]") of Mark 15:2, a statement that was intended (by St. Mark and the tradents who preceded him) to show that Jesus had not actually made a claim that would have justified (by Roman legal standards) a procuratorial verdict of death by crucifixion. Similarly, the Matthean *Su eipas* must have been meant to make it clear that Jesus had not committed blasphemy, as certain Jewish authorities seem to have contended. In reality, of course, such a contention would not have applied before Jesus had been crucified and thereby divinely cursed; see *M.R.*, pp. 282, 288ff., 314f.

in 14:53b); and the evangelist must have been acquainted with the well-known fact that the sanhedrin included Pharisees as well as Sadducees among its members (cf. Acts 22:6ff.). Secondly, the term *grammateus*, usually rendered "scribe" (secretary), could denote a Pharisaic civil servant who, unlike a "chief priest" or an "elder" (senator), owed his official position in the politico-religious administration, not to his family connections, but to his legal qualifications. This is shown, for example, in 2:16 where reference is made to "the scribes *of* the Pharisees"—an expression which also implies (and rightly) that not all experts in the pentateuchal law were of the Pharisaic persuasion. But, as is indicated by St. Matthew's gospel, there was a tendency to identify the scribes with the Pharisees;[69] and our earliest evangelist may not have been entirely free from such a tendency, for the scribe of 12:28ff., who agrees that the two greatest commandments are those which require love for God and love for one's neighbor, was probably a Pharisee of the school of Hillel; at all events the summing-up of the Torah to which he assents is definitely in line with a significant trend in Pharisaism as we know it from the talmudic evidence.[70] Hence it is not impossible that the evangelist understands the five occurrences of "the scribes" at 14:1, 43, 53; 15:1, 31 (in all instances along with "the chief priests") as references to officials with a Pharisaic affiliation,

[69] Thus "the scribes from Jerusalem" in Mark 3:22 become "the Pharisees" in Matt. 9:34 and 12:24; and "the scribes" in Mark 12:35 become "the Pharisees" in Matt. 22:41.

[70] Cf. S. E. Johnson, *A Commentary on the Gospel according to St. Mark* (New York, 1960), pp. 202ff. Thus Mark 12:28ff. could be cited in support of Trocmé's thesis that the evangelist still cherished a limited hope for the conversion of the Pharisees. On the other hand, might it not be a case of the exception which proves the rule?

in which case the passion narrative exemplifies a second mode
of implicit connection with the Pharisaic hostility made manifest in the earlier chapters.

As we have seen, Trocmé further contends that in his own
way St. Mark evinces both anti-intellectual and anti-racial
sentiments. Regarding the former, it is argued that the passages directed against the scribes betray an oblique attack on
the church's prominent spokesmen, whose legalistic moralism
and naively apocalyptic eschatology deterred them from
addressing the gospel of salvation to the waiting masses. But
can such a thesis be adequately sustained? In his defense
Trocmé relies heavily on the conversation which follows
immediately on the account of the transfiguration. The three
favored disciples (Peter, James and John) question Jesus
about the (Son of Man's) resurrection (9:10), and then
proceed to inquire why the scribes maintain that Elijah must
first appear, presumably as the messianic forerunner (9:11).
Trocmé holds that the three privileged disciples are here ally-
ing themselves with the officially recognized legal experts
against their Master. However, there seems to be no substantial foundation for such a contention since in his reply
(9:12f.) Jesus is represented as actually assenting to the
scribal hermeneutics brought into consideration: he agrees
that Elijah comes first in the eschatological drama and re-
stores all things (cf. Mal. 4:5), differing from them only in
his assertion of the fulfillment of the prophecy—apparently
in the person of John the Baptist.[71]

---

[71] See *M.R.*, pp. 9ff., 182ff. Cf. the interesting paper "Tracht und
Speise Johannes des Täufers" in P. Vielhauer's *Aufsätze zum Neuen
Testament* (Munich, 1965), pp. 47ff., where it is maintained that
the clothing and diet of the Baptist (Mark 1:6) are primarily connected with the desert motif in Jewish eschatological expectation,

Another passage to which Trocmé appeals in this connection is 12:35ff., where Jesus adroitly propounds a puzzling query (based on Ps. 110:1) which implies that the scribes are in error, seemingly because they hold that the Messiah owes his supernatural authority to physical descent from King David.[72] Trocmé here detects an indirect attack on the church's leading apologists at Jerusalem, who, in the evangelist's judgment, are far too preoccupied with defending the new faith before the intellectual elite at the headquarters of Judaism: instead of involving themselves in scholastic disputations with the scribes in efforts to demonstrate the Messiahship of Jesus on the ground of his Davidic descent,[73] they ought to expose the essential falsity of scribal scholarship, thereby following in the footsteps of the earthly Christ. Again, however, Trocmé's contention seems to have no secure basis in the evidence. As we have seen, at 9:12f. Jesus agrees with the scribes on an eschatological matter, and at 12:28ff. a scribe agrees with Jesus apropos of the two greatest commandments. Also, although it is reported that the Messiah's teaching has a certain authority that is absent from scribal instruction (1:22), in a number of passages Jesus supports his pronouncements by citing the scriptures—as in 2:23ff. (sabbath observance), 10:2ff. (divorce) and 12:18ff. (marriage in the post-resurrection life). And this must have been a scribal

---

their association with the concept of Elijah *redivivus* being a secondary development. The relevant idea in the desert typology would be, to use Vielhauer's own words: "Wie Gott sich in der Urzeit des Volkes in der Wüste geoffenbart hat, so wird er sich in der Endzeit ebenfalls in der Wüste offenbaren" (*ibid.*, p. 54).

[72] Cf. *M.R.*, p. 204.

[73] In view of 10:46ff. and 11:10, Trocmé rightly insists that in 12:35ff. St. Mark does not mean to deny the validity of the doctrine of Jesus' Davidic ancestry.

procedure; for it was the professional business of the scribes to supervise compliance with the revealed will of God, a function that demanded competence in the interpretation of the Torah and the skill to apply its rulings in particular cases.

Thus there is little ground for supposing that, according to St. Mark, Jesus questions in principle the soundness of the fundamental presuppositions of scribal learning, and still less for the view that, in the evangelist's representation, the disciples figure as academically minded persons who seek scribal support against their Master. Admittedly, the Markan Jesus is a thaumaturge and a prophetic man of wisdom: on occasion he finds confirmation for his statements in his miraculous deeds (as at 2:1ff., in proof of his capacity to forgive sins), and sometimes, like Ben Sira, he relies simply on the native intelligence of his hearers (as at 3:22ff., in his refutation of the Beelzebul charge). But the fact remains that he is also concerned to demonstrate that his declarations derive from a proper understanding of the written word of God. Indeed, the pericope with which we are dealing (12:35ff.), so far from being anti-intellectualist in tendency, may well have been included in the gospel to illustrate that Jesus was quite at home in the field of scriptural hermeneutics, being more than a match for those scholars whose academic qualifications were officially recognized in the circle of the sanhedrin. And it is noteworthy that elsewhere in St. Mark's work the titles *didaskalos*—"teacher" (5:35; 9:38 *etc.*) and *rabbounei*—*rabbei* (10:51; 11:21) are applied to Jesus, a usage which implies that, in the evangelist's estimation, the man from Nazareth of Galilee (1:9) was neither a layman nor an uncultured peasant.[74]

[74] In his interesting work *The Prophet from Nazareth* (New York, 1961), M. S. Enslin occasionally describes Jesus as a "layman"

As for the evangelist's alleged antiracialism, Trocmé understands the sentiment in an extremely narrow sense, claiming that it applies specifically to the immediate relatives of Jesus, and especially to James the Lord's brother, who at an early date seems (at first along with Peter) to have assumed the leadership of the church at Jerusalem.[75] But can it be justifiably said that in the gospel James stands out as the object of St. Mark's detestation? In 3:20-35, by framing one story within the earlier and later parts of another, the evangelist doubtless means to suggest a significant parallel between the kinsfolk of Jesus, who declare that he is beside himself (v. 21), and the scribes from Jerusalem who attribute his miraculous power to the inspiration of Beelzebul, the prince of the demons (v. 22). Here we have no explicit reference to James, and the antiracialism involved would seem to be of quite general application, Jesus' next of kin (v. 31) symbolizing the Jewish nation as a whole.[76] The Messiah is born of Israel, and yet he is rejected by Israel's competent authorities. Nevertheless, the blindness and hostility of Jesus' own people serves to bring out the true nature of the family he came to establish; its members are those who belong to the community in which the will of God is done (v. 35). The mother and the brothers of Jesus stand outside (v. 31), whereas the multitude are seated in the house with the Lord (vv. 20,32) and represent his genuine relatives (v. 34). Thus the passage dramatically exemplifies two motifs that figured prominently in the thought

---

(pp. 119, 127) and a "peasant" (p. 152). But he fails to notice that such was not the view of our earliest evangelist, though it may have been the opinion of certain learned opponents of Jesus, whose legal qualifications were officially recognized.

[75] Regarding the prominence of James at Jerusalem, cf. Mark 6:3; I Cor. 15:7; Gal. 1:19-2:12; Acts 1:14; 12:17; 15:3.

[76] Cf. above, Chapter 3, n. 18.

of primitive Christianity, namely, the theme of the Messiah's rejection by the Jewish people,[77] and the concept of the church as the New Israel, transcending all racial and sexual distinctions.[78]

In the account of Jesus' rejection in his native place (6:1–6)—the other passage to which Trocmé appeals in this connection—James does receive express mention (v. 3), though only along with the Lord's other brothers (Joses, Judas and Simon) and his sisters (who remain anonymous). But here again the evangelist's antiracialism would seem to be of general rather than of specific application, the evangelist taking the story to foreshadow the Messiah's final rejection by his own nation,[79] an act that resulted in the apostolic mission to

---

[77] This motif comes to succinct and poignant expression in John 1:11: "He came to his own, and his own received him not."

[78] Cf. Rom. 2:28f.; 9:8; Gal. 3:28f. *etc.* It is frequently overlooked that the Pauline opposition between Abraham's physical offspring (the membership of traditional Judaism) and Abraham's spiritual offspring (the membership of the renovated Judaism of Christianity) misrepresents the actual situation, for in principle it was (and is) always possible for a Gentile to become a Jew by submitting to the rites of initiation into the fellowship of the synagogue. Of course proselytes and their near descendants were variously regarded in different circumstances. Thus while Herod the Great (40–4 B.C.) was disliked as a "half-Jew" (Josephus, *Ant.* 14:15:2), his grandson Agrippa I (41–44 A.D.) was widely respected, at any rate in Pharisaic circles, and laudatory stories circulated concerning his signal acts of piety; see E. Schürer, *Die Geschichte des jüdischen Volkes im Zeitalter Jesu Christi* (Leipzig, 1901–11), I, 549ff. Cf. above, Chapter 6, n. 45.

[79] It is probable that 6:1–6 was composed by St. Mark himself to provide the traditional saying reproduced in verse 4 with a dramatic illustration. The phraseology is reminiscent of what we find in 1:21–28 (cf. 6:2 with 1:21–22, 27), and the motif of 6:6b has a parallel in 1:28. The term *patris* in 6:1 is evidently due to its occurrence in the *logion* (6:4). The dramatization is somewhat roughly done and

the world, which is in some measure symbolized by an extension of the field of the ministry (v. 6b) and the sending forth of the Twelve (6:7–13,30). An exegesis of this kind finds corroboration in the story of the Syrophoenician woman (7:24–31), where the unbelief of the Messiah's own people has its counterpart in the intelligence and implicit faith of a Gentile mother, who prostrates herself before Jesus and addresses him as "Lord." Although the Jewish people, being God's chosen, have prior claims on the Messiah's saving grace (v. 27), a Hellenistic woman can nonetheless discern the divine status of Jesus, and the soundness of her insight is

---

is not free from incoherence. Thus, despite the pronouncement of 6:4, Jesus marvels at the unbelief of his compatriots (v. 6a), and, despite his inability to perform miracles among his own folk, he cures a few sick people by laying his hands upon them (v. 5); also, a certain success (v. 2) is abruptly followed by hostility and comparative failure (vv. 3ff.). This last feature is characteristically Markan, the evangelist being inclined to arrange his material thematically in alternate blocks of light and shade, so that the reader gets the impression that periods of success (usually among the masses) are followed by opposition (usually from the side of the politico-religious authorities). For example, the popular success depicted in 1:14–45 is immediately followed by the controversies of 2:1–3:6. It is noteworthy that in 6:2f. *hoi polloi* are duly impressed by Jesus' wisdom and power, and then are scandalized, turning against him of their own accord, without any malicious intervention on the part of the leading citizens (such as we find in 15:11). Clearly this supports the interpretation that the evangelist's anti-racialist sentiment here comes to expression in a general way, no excuse being made for the masses on the ground of faulty leadership. It is also significant that in 6:3 *hoi polloi* tend to identify themselves with the Lord's next of kin: they acknowledge that his close relatives are there in the *patris* with them, thereby suggesting that Jesus' compatriots are collectively opposed to him. However, the observation that a few cures are effected (6:5b) would seem to be a concession to the fact that a small minority of Jews responded with faith to the apostolic proclamation of the gospel.

promptly confirmed by the healing of her daughter from a distance (vv. 29f.).

Thus a careful examination of the pertinent evidence hardly justifies Trocmé's contention that Mark 3:20ff. and 6:1ff. are directed specifically against James "the brother of Jesus the so-called Christ" (to use Josephus' description), who—along with certain others—was put to death at the order of the sanhedrin in A.D. 62 (*Ant.* 20:9:1). The materials are arranged and adapted in such a manner as to suggest that the evangelist is here giving expression to the philosophico-theological doctrine that the promised Messiah had to be rejected by his own nation before God's new offer of salvation through the crucified Christ could be freely proclaimed among the Gentiles.[80] Of course this does not exclude the possibility that 3:20–21, 31–35 and the *logion* of 6:4 took their rise in a conflict which actually occurred between the historical Jesus and his next of kin;[81] nor does it exclude the possibility that these items of the tradition had been utilized by representatives of the new faith who resented the leadership of James at Jerusalem and the dynastic principle his presidency introduced among the Jewish-Christian sectaries of metropolitan Judea.[82] But as they now stand within the framework of St. Mark's gospel, the passages in question are intimately bound up with the evangelist's philosophy of history, according to which the obscurity and blindness, the

[80] Cf. above, Chapter 5.

[81] This *logion*, like those of 2:19 and 7:27, could have been proverbial.

[82] Besides the tensions engendered by Paulinism, there could have been rivalry between the apostle Peter and the Lord's brother. Cf. P. Winter's article on I Cor. 15:5ff. in *Novum Testamentum* II (1957), 142ff., and M. Goguel, *La naissance du christianisme* (Paris, 1946), pp. 130ff.

hostility and suffering, of the Lord's earthly ministry within the confines of Israel constitute an integral part of the necessary prelude to the post-resurrection period of enlightenment, in which the gospel of salvation is openly proclaimed in the world with courage, understanding and confidence.[83] During Jesus' lifetime God's salvific operations are largely restricted to the Jewish people, whereas after the Messiah's rejection at the hands of those to whom he came, Israelite precedence no longer obtains. The vineyard has been given to others (12:9). The spiritually based community of the new dispensation, the Christ's true family, spreads abroad among the nations in the wake of the Son of Man's final intervention with great power and glory, when the vindication of the church's cause will assume cosmic dimensions (8:38—9:1; 13:24–27; 14:62).

Some of the salient results that have emerged in the foregoing discussion might be usefully brought together in a brief consideration of the thesis put forward by S. G. F. Brandon, who also stresses St. Mark's concern to denigrate the family of Jesus (especially James) and the original apostles (especially Peter), but who, unlike Trocmé, rightly brings out the general import of the evangelist's anti-Semitism. However, if Trocmé tends to minimize the extent of St. Mark's antipathy for the Jewish people as such,[84] Brandon errs on the side of exaggeration.[85] That such is the case can now be

---

[83] See *M.R.*, pp. 168ff., 319ff.

[84] This finds incidental illustration in Trocmé's objection to the present writer's use of the term "anti-Semitism" in characterizations of the evangelist's attitude; see above, n. 9.

[85] S. G. F. Brandon, *Jesus and the Zealots* (Manchester, 1967), pp. 274ff. *passim.* Of Mark 3:20–21, 31–35, Brandon writes: "So categorical a repudiation of the blood-relationship and its replacing by a disciple-relationship is truly amazing, when it is recalled what the

shown succinctly by making a few comments on a couple of statements with which Brandon sums up his findings regarding our earliest gospel, a work he designates as an *Apologia ad Christianos Romanos*.[86]

Brandon states: "There can be traced throughout the Markan Gospel a consistent denigration of the Jewish leaders and people, and of the family of Jesus and the original Apostles, which adds up to a damning indictment of the Jews for their treatment of Jesus. . . . The Jewish leaders and people are responsible for his death. . . ."

To which it may be rejoined: (*a*) In general St. Mark is by no means consistent in his thinking, and this is true specifically of his attitude to Israel.[87] (*b*) In the story of the rejection in the *patris* (6:1ff.) it is not the close relatives of Jesus but *hoi polloi* who take the initiative against him—and so it can hardly be maintained that the members of his family are put in the worst possible light. (*c*) Despite their deficiencies, the Twelve (with the exception of Judas) to the end of the

---

prestige of blood-relationship to Jesus meant in the Jerusalem Church. As we have seen, this was the cause of the sudden emergence of James, the brother of Jesus, to leadership of the movement, and, after his death, it ensured the election of Symeon, another close relative, as his successor. . . . This defamation of the family of Jesus is paralleled by a derogatory presentation of his Apostles, who formed the essential nucleus of the Jerusalem Church. . . . Particularly instructive is the presentation of Peter, who is depicted as the leading Apostle. . . . It is significant that Mark chose also to include in his relatively short Gospel the long detailed account of Peter's denial . . . for . . . it completes a very uncomplimentary picture of this leading Apostle, who was possibly associated with the original Jewish-Christian phase of Christianity in Rome" (*ibid.*, pp. 275–277).

[86] *Ibid.*, p. 279.
[87] *M.R.*, pp. 5f., 29, 69ff., 122, 128, 155f., 243.

gospel remain a privileged group charged with great responsibility. It is to them alone that the secret of the Kingdom of God is communicated (4:11), and although they are unable to comprehend the mysterious significance of their master's teaching at the time (9:32), they can preserve it as authentic tradition pending the new situation to come about with the resurrection of the Son of Man (9:9; 16:7). (d) St. Mark's anti-Jewish feeling is tempered through his evident concern to set forth a contrast between the success of Jesus among the masses and the hostility he encountered among Israel's leaders.[88] (e) In the report of the Barabbas episode (15:6ff.) it is the hierarchs who are to blame for so stirring up the multitude that they make vociferous demands for Jesus' crucifixion.

Brandon also states: "In turn, Jesus is shown as rejecting those of his nation who reject him . . . and as vehemently rebuking his chief Apostle's obsession with a nationalistic conception of his own status and mission. Consequently, in Mark . . . Jesus is portrayed as essentially independent of his Jewish origin and relationships."

To which it may be rejoined: (a) Actually, St. Mark engages in a sustained attempt to make it clear to his readers that the Christ's earthly career was entirely worked out in accordance with the divine will as revealed in the Jewish scriptures.[89] (b) In the story of the Syrophoenician woman (7:24ff.) Jesus is permitted to refer to Gentiles as dogs, a mode of linguistic usage that would scarcely have been allowed had the evangelist been thoroughly anti-Semitic. (c) In 8:32 Peter seems to react not against the enunciation of a universalist soteriology but against the prediction of the Son

[88] See above, Chapter 3.
[89] M.R., pp. 117ff., 218ff.

of Man's sufferings (8:31), and this means that in 8:33 he is sharply rebuked for his failure to grasp the mystery of the divine necessity of the passion. (*d*) In 12:28ff. a recognized Jewish legal authority is permitted to express complete agreement with Jesus concerning the primacy of the two pentateuchal commandments of love to God and love to one's neighbor. (*e*) Much like Trocmé, Brandon does not seem fully to appreciate that the Markan depiction of the disciples' lack of understanding is bound up with the evangelist's doctrine of the secret and with his soteriological philosophy of history.[90]

3. *Redactional History.* As previously pointed out, Trocmé argues that the Markan gospel went through two editions which we designated PM ("proto-Mark") and CM ("canonical Mark"): PM consisted substantially of Mark 1–13, and CM was formed by appending to PM what we designated JPN, a passion narrative that first appeared—to meet cultic needs—in the church at Jerusalem. The marriage of PM with JPN took place at Rome toward A.D. 85. The unidentified redactor responsible for this union (whom we designate FR) was allegedly anxious to fix the night of Thursday–Friday for a Christian festival that had hitherto coincided with the Jewish passover, and he furnished the texts of PM and JPN with appropriate chronological notes and a few explanatory observations. Both PM (a Greek document) and JPN (in a Greek version) had been current in Rome for some time, the latter being used liturgically at an annual commemoration of the crucifixion-resurrection, and, since it was attributed to the John Mark mentioned in Acts, his name was eventually

[90] *M.R.*, pp. 168ff.

transferred to CM. Thus in its Greek form JPN served the same kind of cultic purpose as that which, in its original Aramaic form, it had been designed to serve at Jerusalem. John Mark, if not the author of the Aramaic text of JPN, was at least responsible for its translation, amplification and dissemination among the Hellenistic churches, part of his intention being to wean them from a certain aversion to the regular observance of sacred seasons. The translation into Greek was probably carried out at Rome in A.D. 65–70. As for PM, Trocmé contends that it was authored by Philip the Evangelist, one of the seven deacons of the Hellenists, whose activities are dealt with in Acts 6:1ff. Persecuted by the Jewish authorities in the capital, the Seven and their associates took flight, and from their various places of refuge they continued zealously to propagate their ideas which, while not so broad in their scope as those of St. Paul, were less limited than those prevailing among the so called "pillars" of the church (cf. Gal. 2:9). Expelled by these latter from Samaria, the Hellenists—apparently under Philip's leadership—decided on counter-action in Galilee and its neighboring regions, where, as was believed, they went forward in the company of the Risen Lord and treading in the footsteps of the earthly Jesus. Hence, in Trocmé's assessment, the personal antipathies he claims to find in PM become quite understandable, for its author was hostile not only to the official Jewish elite at Jerusalem, but also to the leadership of the mother church there for its hardening sectarianism and for its undue preoccupation with theological debate and the maintenance of the purity of doctrine. One of the Seven, Philip must have been a Palestinian, Greek-speaking, Christian Jew;[91] and after fleeing the

---

[91] Trocmé (p. 199) takes Nicolaus, a proselyte from Antioch, the last-mentioned of the Seven in Acts 6:5, to be the exception that proves the rule.

capital he settled in Caesarea (Acts 8:40; 21:8f.), where around the year A.D. 50 he wrote PM to justify and enlist support for his audacious missionary enterprises across Samaria and northern Palestine. In the production of his work he availed himself of popular Galilean traditions, supplementing what he considered to be the excessively moralistic and academic traditions preserved at Jerusalem, and thereby seeking to bring out the true ecclesiological intentions of the historical Jesus, the *divine man* who, as the Risen Lord, constitutes the sole divine authority for believers.

This brief recapitulation, read in the light of our discussions in the previous sections, would seem to lend force to a suggestion already made, to the effect that Trocmé fails to appreciate the full complexity of the shifting circumstances and evolving motivations which issued in the emergence of the gospels, and that such a failure is partly conditioned by a tendency to consider the relevant data from the somewhat restricted standpoint of the Acts of the Apostles, a work which primarily bears witness to the views of its author and therefore needs to be used with extreme caution as touching the historical matters reported therein. Hence, in view of the fact that what we know of Philip the Hellenist is founded upon mediated information of doubtful significance, the ascription of PM to his authorship can scarcely deepen our understanding of PM, a document which, after all, lies before us and is known directly.[92] The unsureness of Trocmé's ground in this connection finds ample illustration in his treatment of the pertinent reports in Acts. Thus he infers from Acts 8:4ff., 14ff. that the leaders of the mother church reaped

---

[92] It is not uncommon for scholars to presume that a work of unknown authorship is necessarily illuminated by attributing its origin to some relatively obscure individual who happens to appear elsewhere in the literature of the period.

244 New Light on the Earliest Gospel

what Philip had sown in Samaria, and that the deacon resented such action which was really meant to curb his influence. Actually, however, there is no hint of any hostility in
the text as it stands. Again, Trocmé argues that miracle-
working, public appeals and verbal violence figure prominently in the passages concerning the Hellenists just as they
do in PM. But could not the same sort of thing be said of
Pauline Christianity? Signs, wonders and mighty works are
to the fore in II Cor. 12:2; there is an open appeal in I Cor.
10:15, and violent language in Rom. 1:26ff.

On the doctrinal side Trocmé detects as features shared by
PM with the Hellenists: (a) an antipathy against the temple
at Jerusalem and the hierarchs responsible for its administration; (b) an opposition to the laws of ceremonial purity; (c)
a rudimentary christology which betrays a lack of interest in
a subject that was deemed to be too academic; (d) a pneumatology which ran counter to the apostolic doctrine that the
Spirit is bestowed upon all believers who submit to baptism.
Here again, however, Trocmé's arguments are not altogether
satisfactory. An aversion for the chief priests may well have
pervaded all sections of primitive Christianity; it is evident in
the Markan passion narrative, a text which, according to
Trocmé himself, probably originated in the church at Jerusalem,[93] and the extant Pauline epistles certainly evince no
particular love for the Jewish hierarchy. As for the sacrificial
cultus, this had been liable to become a subject for adverse
criticism from the time of the prophet Amos in the eighth
century B.C., and in so far as the concept of the Messiah's
sacrificial or atoning death (cf. Mark 14:25; Rom. 3:25; I Cor.

---

[93] One should bear in mind that James the Lord's brother fell foul
of the high priest in 62 A.D., when he was executed at the order of the
sanhedrin (Josephus, *Ant.* 20:9:1).

5:7) won acceptance among believers, the view that the temple sacrifices had been superseded (cf. Heb. 9:23ff.) would develop as a matter of course in Jerusalem and elsewhere. If anything, Trocmé's ground is still less secure with regard to christology and pneumatology. There are strong reasons for holding that the evangelist was fundamentally concerned with the christological problem,[94] and this is true even if with Trocmé we leave Mark 14–16 out of account. He may not have succeeded in effecting a satisfying synthesis of the various religious valuations of Jesus which he introduces, but the lack of systematic co-ordination does not mean that he took christology to be merely a matter of academic import. Lastly, in one aspect the evangelist may understand the event reported in Mark 1:9–11 as the model or prototype of the Christian rite of initiation, in which case his pneumatology is such that he considers the gift of the Spirit to be the proper concomitant of ecclesiastical baptism with water.[95]

[94] See, for example, P. Vielhauer's paper "Erwägungen zur Christologie des Markusevangeliums" in *Zeit und Geschichte. Dankesgabe an Rudolf Bultmann* (Tübingen, 1964), pp. 155ff., and reprinted in Vielhauer's *Aufsätze zum Neuen Testament* (Munich, 1965), pp. 199ff.

[95] Cf. *M.R.*, pp. 12ff. It may be noted here that in his treatment of the Hellenists of Acts 6–8 *et passim* Trocmé appeals to the work of his colleague at Strasbourg, Marcel Simon, *St. Stephen and the Hellenists in the Primitive Church* (New York, 1958), where three early Christian groups are distinguished: (a) The original apostolic community at Jerusalem; (b) The group represented by the seven deacons; (c) the Paulinists, whose ideas were still broader than those of Stephen and his associates. Simon, like Trocmé, displays much confidence in the reliability of the relevant passages in Acts, taking the speech of 7:2ff., for example, to be an authentic account, based on a written source, of Stephen's defence before the high court. But this view is open to question; see E. Haenchen, *Die Apostelgeschichte* (ed. 3, Göttingen, 1959), pp. 238ff. On the other hand, it must not be

Respecting the passion document (JPN), Trocmé's thesis that it had a cultic origin is no less open to objection, for the narrative has a comprehensiveness which resists explanation in terms of a single type of motivation. Trocmé himself recognizes that certain elements in the story as it now stands are all but devoid of liturgical import, and he cites as examples the note concerning the young man who fled naked at the arrest (Mark 14:51f.) and the reference to the sons of Simon of Cyrene (15:21b). He considers that these details must have been introduced by John Mark, the witness of the arrest who was responsible for presenting JPN to Hellenistic Christianity. But there are other passages in Mark 14–16 that are without any obvious cultic significance—such as the plotting of the hierarchs (14:1f.), the nocturnal trial (14:55–65), Peter's denial (14:54, 66–72), and so on.[96] Thus, while the three pericopes in 14:12–25, which directly concern the last supper, may have developed in close relation to eucharistic celebrations in the *Urgemeinde,* the narrative contains con-

---

thought that Trocmé follows Simon slavishly. Thus, with F. Overbeck (*Kurze Erklärung der Apostelgeschichte,* Leipzig, 1870, p. 111, n. 2) and against Simon (*ibid.,* pp. 50ff.), Trocmé (p. 86, n. 57) contends that Acts 7:42f. is directed not against the temple's sacrificial cultus as such, but rather against the notion of the temple as God's dwelling-place.

[96] Trocmé (p. 194, n. 70) seems to regard the prominence of Peter in the narrative as due to a redactor who worked over JPN before its translation into Greek was undertaken. However, at an earlier stage (p. 49, n. 187) he suggests that certain passages concerning Peter were added when the translation took place, and he cites 14:12–16, 27–31, 37–39, 54, 66–72, holding that all these reports depend on Petrine testimony and that their inclusion would be meant to secure Petrine authority for the ecclesiastical practice implicitly defended in JPN. Cf. above, n. 14.

siderable items which appear to owe their presence to extra-liturgical motives.

As previously indicated, Trocmé is in broad agreement with Schille, who supposes that pertinent reminiscences first crystallized around a yearly celebration of the Christian passover at Jerusalem, a ritual that involved three main commemorations: (a) of Jesus' last evening (Mark 14:18–72); (b) of the crucifixion (15:2–41); and (c) of the first Easter morning (15:42–16:8). However, it seems unlikely that the story of the discovery of the empty tomb formed part of the passion narrative in its earliest form, and the reference to the women's silence in 16:8 could have been originally meant to explain why the story, unlike the reports of the christophanies, did not establish itself in the Christian tradition from the beginning of the church's existence. There is no allusion to the empty tomb in the Pauline epistles, and the story has all the appearance of being a relatively late development based to some extent on the Pharisaic doctrine of the resurrection of the body.[97] In his treatment of the second main constituent of the supposed commemorative liturgy (15:2–41) Schille claims

[97] Cf. *M.R.*, pp. 160, n. 17, 250f., 256f. We still think that Dibelius' hypothesis is as sound as any: (a) the pre-Markan passion narrative contained a report of a resurrection appearance to Peter and the other disciples (cf. I Cor. 15:5); (b) 14:28 originally referred to that appearance; (c) the evangelist decided to end his work with the story of the empty tomb, but he wished to point forward to that christophany (and perhaps others)—hence he retained 14:28 and interpolated 16:7; and (d) since the story of the appearance to Peter would tell of his reconciliation to his (now risen) Lord, the thought of the post-resurrection meeting in Galilee would be associated with the thought of Peter's denial, and this explains why the prediction of 14:28 is immediately followed by the prediction of 14:29–31. See M. Dibelius, *From Tradition to Gospel* (London, 1934), pp. 181, 183, 189ff., and *M.R.*, p. 157, n. 13.

that the division of the duration of the crucifixion into two
three-hour periods is affiliated with the three hours of Jewish
prayer: the execution begins at the third hour (15:25),
darkness covers the whole earth from the sixth hour to the
ninth (15:33), and at the ninth hour Jesus utters his last
articulate cry (15:34) and expires (15:37). But there are
various considerations which militate against the existence of
such a liturgical *liaison* with traditional Jewish practice: (*a*)
precise notices of time and location are characteristic of the
passion narrative (cf. 14:1, 12, 17, 26, 32, 53; 15:1, 40, 42;
16:1f.), and in a general way reveal a sense of *historical* development that is unique in the gospel tradition; (*b*) the
reference to the sixth hour (that is, midday) at 15:33 is
probably meant to emphasize the miraculous nature of the
darkness; (*c*) if the note regarding the third hour (15:25)
had a liturgical significance, the other synoptists were either
unaware of it or considered it unimportant, for there is nothing corresponding to 15:25 in their works; (*d*) the time
references in 15:25, 33, 34 may reflect the evangelist's manifest predilection for groups of three;[98] and (*e*) the New
Testament nowhere contains any allusion to a passiontide
celebration that extended over a single or double three-hour
period. Finally, so far as the first main constituent of the
alleged commemorative liturgy is concerned, while 14:22–25
and perhaps 14:18–21 are doubtless directly subservient to the
exigencies of the primitive eucharistic cultus, the remaining
pericopes of the chapter give primary testimony to the operation of extra-cultic interests. Thus the scriptural quotation of
14:27 shows that the flight of the disciples was provided for
in God's sovereign purpose; 14:30 indicates that Jesus knew

[98] See *M.R.*, pp. 123, 203, 205, 232, 236, 243ff.

in advance what the future held; 14:35 reveals that the son of God was subject to temptation; 14:62 makes it clear that the concept of Christhood needs to be construed in terms of the notion of the transcendent Son of Man; 14:64 demonstrates that, despite the manner of his death, the Messiah was condemned by his own people—and so forth. Accordingly, the passages in question (14:26ff.) exemplify a wide variety of early Christian interests, but it can hardly be said that a cultic or liturgical concern figures prominently among them.[99]

Moreover, if as Trocmé himself acknowledges, such passages as 14:51f. (the young man who fled naked) and 15:21b (the sons of Simon of Cyrene) possess no discernible cultic value and were absent from JPN in its original Aramaic form, why should they have been inserted by a translator whose sole design was to promote a particular ecclesiastical practice by making a liturgical document more widely available? Again, like the attribution of PM to Philip the Hellenist, the identification of the translator of JPN with the John Mark of Acts belongs to the realm of pure speculation and is dangerously liable to engender a feeling of confidence that is in fact destitute of any secure foundation.[100] Our knowledge of the said John Mark is extremely limited, and the pertinent reports we do have in Acts nowhere hint that he was especially interested in liturgical matters. Also, if FR, the final redactor allegedly responsible for the marriage of JPN with PM, aimed

[99] The allusion to the singing of a hymn in 14:26 has a backward, not a forward reference, the meaning being that the prototype of the Christian eucharist concluded with the chanting of a psalm. It should also be borne in mind that the account of the nocturnal trial may well be a Markan interpolation (cf. *M.R.*, pp. 242f., 259, 280ff.), in which case it could not have formed part of a supposed passiontide liturgy in the *Urgemeinde*.

[100] Cf. above, n. 92.

at fixing the night of Thursday-Friday and the morning-afternoon of Friday for a Christian festival that had hitherto coincided with the lunar dating of the Jewish passover, it is hard to understand how he could have allowed the chronological discrepancy between 14:2 and 14:12 to remain in the narrative.[101] The statement of 14:2 implies that Jesus was arrested before the passover began, in which case the last supper could not have been a paschal meal; on the other hand, in 14:12–16 it is assumed that the last supper *was* a passover meal. And, we submit, such an inconsistency would never have been permitted by an editor so deeply concerned about times and seasons as FR is supposed to have been.

But perhaps the most serious weakness of Trocmé's redactional theory lies in his contention that PM was designed and published as an independent document and that its union with JPN to form CM was not effected by FR until around A.D. 85, some thirty-five years after its composition. As we have previously maintained,[102] St. Mark's gospel, despite its ideological inconsistencies and doctrinal antinomies, is a well integrated work in the overall sense that the passion story forms its climax so that in a general way the first thirteen chapters may be described as a preparation for it. The death of Jesus is already hinted at in 2:20, where it is reported that the wedding-guests will fast when the bridegroom is taken away from them, and in 3:6, where it is observed that the Pharisees and the Herodians conspire against Jesus with a view to having him destroyed. But besides foreshadowings of this kind, the first thirteen chapters present certain regulative ideas in the light of which, as the evangelist believes, the reader may be enabled to interpret the passion correctly. Thus the concep-

---

[101] Cf. *M.R.*, pp. 258ff.   [102] See *M.R.*, pp. 218ff.

tion of the supernatural authority of Jesus, which frequently comes to expression, helps to make it possible for the reader to understand the passion as a supreme act of divine condescension: Jesus is endowed with divine power and he uses it not for personal aggrandizement but solely in the interest of human salvation, finally humbling himself even to the extent of sacrificing his earthly life. Again, the stories dealing with controversy contain indications that Jesus always remains faithful to the true meaning of the scriptures; and in this way the ground is prepared for the interpretation of the crucifixion as the outcome of unwarranted hostility on the part of the Jewish authorities. But it is the first main section of the second part of the gospel (beginning at 8:27) which has the most obvious bearing on the passion and its rightful interpretation. For, on the basis of Peter's confession, the Master proceeds to instruct his disciples in the fateful significance of his Christhood, showing that his impending sufferings and death are the divinely appointed prerequisite of his exaltation and glorious return as the triumphant Son of Man. Thus, in the Markan representation, the story of the passion recounts the historical realization of the essential meaning of Jesus' secret status—a meaning which is already made known to the reader before the account of the Jerusalem ministry begins; and, although the disciples cannot understand the passion in this light at the time of its occurrence, they (with the exception of Judas) are destined so to understand it when, as witnesses of the resurrection, they openly proclaim the gospel to the world.

However, while it is most improbable that PM *per se* ever existed, the same cannot be said of the passion story, for this narrative exemplifies a sense of historical development and a striking self-sufficiency which distinguish it sharply from the preceding sections; and it seems likely that the main outline of the narrative enjoyed an independent existence several decades before A.D. 70, when St. Mark—as we are inclined to think—decided to undertake his work. On the whole the story moves forward coherently from the report of the plotting of the hierarchs (14:1f.) to the account of the discovery of the empty tomb (16:1ff.); and the indications of time and place are on occasion so securely woven into the texture of the narrative that they could hardly be regarded as editorial connecting links imposed by the evangelist on what came to him as isolated items of traditional material. It is true, of course, that some of the constituent elements of the narrative may have originally possessed separate existence: thus the story of the anointing (14:3–9), the account of the preparations for the last supper (14:12–16) and the report of the nocturnal trial (14:55–65) are among the pericopes that could owe their present contexts to the evangelist himself. That the passion narrative underwent amplification in this way is shown by a consideration of the treatment which St. Mark's version of it receives at the hands of the later evangelists: St. Matthew, for example, adds the story of Judas' suicide (Matt. 27:3–10), the reference to the dream of Pilate's wife (Matt. 27:19), the report of Pilate's washing his hands in the presence of the public (Matt. 27:24f.), and so on. But it still remains that a brief account of the principal events (arrest, trial, crucifixion, burial, one or more christophanies) existed from a very early date. The main outline of the narrative is the same in all three synoptic gospels; and, what is more significant, even a deviationist like the fourth evangelist faithfully reproduces the fundamental framework of the passion narrative as it appears in the Markan gospel. Presumably, he is here dealing with a concatenated tradition that was so firmly fixed in Christian thought and memory that he refrains from treating it with his usual freedom.

As we have seen, the early establishment of a connected account of the passion cannot be explained in terms of what was an essentially cultic interest on the part of the apostolic communities. Nor can it be explained by reference to a supposed biographical form of motivation, for if such a concern had been operative the relative paucity of the traditions regarding the ministry would become an arch enigma. Indeed, from a purely biographical point of view, an account of the early life of Jesus would have been much more valuable than a detailed description of the circumstances of his death. It would appear, therefore, that the early establishment of a passion narrative in Christian tradition must have been largely due to the special soteriological significance which the apostolic church attributed to the shameful death of the Messiah. As we gather from I Cor. 15:3f. the primitive gospel consisted essentially of three fundamental affirmations: that Christ died for our sins according to the scriptures, that he was buried, and that he was raised on the third day according to the scriptures. It is noteworthy, too, that in all the epistles of the New Testament there is not so much as a passing allusion to the mission of John the Baptist or to the Galilean ministry. Moreover, besides glorying in the cross on the basis of a salvific valorization (I Cor. 1:18ff.; Gal. 6:14), St. Paul seems to construe the Lord's crucifixion and subsequent resurrection eschatologically, as constituting a divine pledge or guarantee of the Christ's expected second coming (I Thess. 4:14; I Cor. 11:26), the resuscitation on the third day being an anticipation of the final resurrection of the elect (I Cor. 15:20). Thus the passion and the resurrection associated with it were events of such profound importance for the apostolic message of salvation that some account of them would be an inevitable accompaniment of the earliest Christian preaching. The protagonists of the new faith would be called upon to show how the paradox of the cross was resolved in the triumph of Easter, and how the death of Jesus in shame and humiliation was brought about through the malevolence of his own folk and yet by the determinate counsel and foreknowledge of God (cf. Acts 2:23), whose sovereign will was believed (among Jews and Christians alike) to be already disclosed in the prophecies of the Old Testament. Hence the Markan passion narrative contains numerous allusions to the scriptures, as well as remarkable illustrations of the precise foreknowledge of Jesus. The historical interpretation is informed and sustained by soteriological and eschatological motives.

But a mode of ethnico-political motivation is also entailed, for the narrator obviously seeks to demonstrate to his readers that it was really through the ill will of the Jewish people, as represented by their official leaders, that the Messiah was rejected and crucified—an idea that finds attestation in the extant Pauline writings (cf. I Thess. 2:14–16). Moreover, as is shown by a comparison of the gospels, St. Mark's successors tend increasingly to emphasize the innocence of Jesus, the unwillingness of Pilate and the guilt of the Jews. Such an anti-Jewish tendency may be fairly described as a natural outcome of the church's developing historical situation. For, whereas the gospel was meeting with wide acceptance in the Gentile world, Jews were increasingly setting themselves in opposition to it. The gulf between Judaism and the sect to which it gave birth became wider and deeper, and feelings of mutual antipathy eventually prevailed. On the other hand, the Roman authorities for a time seem to have adopted an attitude of detached indifference, taking it to be what of course it originally was—a sectarian denomination within Judaism. And since the missionary activities of the apostolic preachers were being conducted within the confines of the Roman empire, it was manifestly of urgent practical importance for the church's survival that its message should be set forth in such a way as to avoid offending the susceptibilities of those who represented the imperial government.[103] So the exponents of the historical content of the gospel were at pains to show that, although the crucifixion followed on a charge of sedition at a procuratorial trial, it was actually due to the unwarranted hostility of the Jewish authorities that the church's Founder was put to death.

It would appear, then, that Trocmé, while exaggerating the part played by cultic motivation, rightly insists on the existence of an integrated form of the passion narrative prior to its incorporation into CM. On the other hand, his hypothesis that PM enjoyed an independent existence from around A.D. 50 to 85 has little to commend it. Moreover, even if, for the sake of argument, we provisionally assume the validity of this unlikely hypothesis, there are good grounds for thinking that FR, the supposed editor who operated about thirty-five years after the appearance of PM, could not have been responsible for the documentary marriage which resulted in the production of CM. For careful scrutiny shows that certain stylistic and doctrinal connections obtain between Mark 14–16 and the preceding chapters; and these connections are so varied and occasionally so subtle as to persuade us that whoever composed Mark 1–13

---

[103] Cf. Rom. 13:1ff., where the writer exhorts his readers to respect the authority of the state as a divine institution which holds evil in check and facilitates the promotion of good.

intended from the outset of his literary enterprise to conclude his work with a somewhat modified version of JPN.[104]
In what follows the connections we have in mind are briefly
considered in turn:

1. A predilection for groups or series of three is reflected
throughout CM. If 2:13f. is not integral to 2:15–17, there
are six pericopes in the largely controversial sequence of
2:1–3:6, the first three being concerned with sins and sinners,
the second three with Jewish religious customs; and there
are six pericopes in the rather simiar sequence of 12:13–44,
the first three demonstrating the facility with which Jesus
answers questions, the second three presenting him as the
assailant of his opponents. Three parables appear in 4:1–34,
three predictions of the passion-resurrection in 8:27–10:52
(the first main section of the second part of the gospel), three
miracle stories in 4:35–5:43 (if 5:21–43 may be taken as a
single unit), after the relatively prolonged teaching of 4:1–34,
and three miracle stories in 7:24–8:10, after the relatively
prolonged teaching of 7:1–23. Only three of the disciples are
privileged to feature in connection with three outstanding
events—the raising of the little girl (5:37, 40), the transfiguration (9:2) and the agony in Gethsemane (14:33). The
eschatological discourse of 13:5ff. is composed of three
principal sections: verses 5–23 deal with the birth pangs of
the new age, verses 24–27 delineate the closing scene of the
eschatological drama, and verses 28–37 bring out the need for
vigilance on the part of believers: also, in the concluding
paragraph of the discourse (13:32–37) the exhortation to
watch is given three times (vv. 33, 35, 37), and it should be

---

[104] We continue to employ this abbreviated expression since we are
of the opinion that, as Trocmé argues, the passion tradition received
by St. Mark may well have originated in the church at Jerusalem.

noticed that in the Gethsemane scene Jesus comes to the three privileged disciples on three occasions, exhorting them to watch in the first two instances (14:34, 38). In 14:12-25 there are three pericopes dealing with the last supper, and in 14:27-31 there are three predictions: in verse 27 Jesus tells the disciples that they will all be caused to stumble, in verse 28 that he will nevertheless go before them into Galilee, and in verses 29-31 that Peter will disown his Master three times—a direful prognostication which prepares the way for the story of Peter's threefold denial which is given in verses 53-54, 66-72 of the same chapter. Moreover, after the report of Jesus' arrest (that is, from 14:53 onwards) the Markan narrative falls into two triads of sections: 14:53-72; 15:1-20 and 15:21-32 set forth the processes leading directly up to the Messiah's death; and 15:33-41; 15:42-47 and 16:1-8 concern the connected historical themes of the apostolic message of salvation—the Lord's death, burial and resurrection (cf. I Cor. 15:3f.). As for the first of these two series of three, all three constituents are introduced by notices of change of place;[105] in all three Jesus is subjected to mockery;[106] and all three are to a greater or less extent designed to bring out a contrast.[107] It should also be borne in mind that the duration of the crucifixion is divided into two three-hour periods in

---

[105] See 14:53 (from Gethsemane to the high priest's residence); 15:1 (from the high priest's residence to Pilate's court); 15:21f. (from Pilate's court to Golgotha).

[106] See 14:65 (mocked as a prophet by certain members of the sanhedrin); 15:16-20 (ridiculed as a king by the soldiers); 15:29-32 (taunted by spectators, by chief priests with scribes, reproached by those crucified with him).

[107] In 14:53ff. the calm courage of Jesus is set over against Peter's cowardice; in 15:6ff. the innocent prisoner is set over against the suspect Barabbas; and in 15:26f. the King of the Jews is set over against the two revolutionaries.

15:25, 33f., that three classes of mockers are distinguished in 15:29–32, and that three women witnesses of the execution are named in 15:40.[108]

2. The report of the agony in Gethsemane (14:32–42) seems to have been worked over by the person who produced the first thirteen chapters of the gospel. For, while the Gethsemane story dramatically illustrates the evangelist's basic conception of Jesus' afflictions as the prelude to his final triumph, it shows a tendency discernible elsewhere in his work to transcend the category of means and end by interpreting the passion directly in terms of its awaited outcome in great power and glory.[109] Thus, in the first place, the form and content of 14:37–42 are reminiscent of the conclusion of the eschatological discourse (13:37–42), where the four[110] disciples are enjoined to watch (the charge being given three times) lest the Lord should come suddenly and find his servants sleeping: in 13:32 the term "hour" is used of the Son of Man's expected manifestation in glory (cf. 13:26), and when this hour has arrived, presumably there will be no further need for vigilance; in 14:41 the term "hour" is used of the Son of Man's passion, and now that this hour has arrived the three disciples may sleep on and take their rest; such parallelism is remarkable enough and suggests that St. Mark is anticipating the Johannine interpretation of the passion as the hour of the Christ's glorification (John

---

[108] The thesis that Mark 1:11; 9:7 and 15:39 constitute a triad, reflecting the high points in an ancient enthronement ritual, has been argued by P. Vielhauer; see below, n. 115.

[109] Cf. *M.R.*, pp. 117ff., 208f.

[110] Andrew is an auditor of the eschatological discourse, along with the three especially privileged disciples; see 13:3. The evangelist evidently holds that Peter and Andrew, James and John have been disciples for the longest time; see 1:14ff.

12:23; 13:1; 17:1). In the second place, the Gethsemane story in certain of its features resembles the account of the transfiguration in 9:2ff., where Jesus fleetingly appears in the glory of his divine nature; in each instance the three privileged disciples are permitted to behold their Master in a new and mysterious aspect, and in each instance they utterly fail to understand the significance of their daunting experience; in 9:6 it is reported that "he [Peter] did not know what to answer," and in 14:40 that "they did not know what to answer him."[111] Accordingly, the hand traceable in 14:32ff. is also traceable in 9:2ff. and 13:37ff.

3. Although in this instance there is no close linguistic parallelism, it may be that the three hours' mourning of nature for the death of the Creator's Son (15:33) refers back to 13:24f. For this cosmic testimony, unlike the testimonies of the temple (15:38) and of the centurion (15:39), is given before Jesus actually expires, and perhaps this is due to the sequence of events in 13:24–27: the darkening of the sun and the moon and the stars precedes the parousia of the Son of Man in glory, and so in 15:33 the darkening of the sun at noonday precedes the manifestation of glory in the Son of Man's death.

[111] In his *Jésus Transfiguré* (Copenhagen, 1947), pp. 283ff., H. Riesenfeld rightly insists that the fear attributed to the disciples in Mark 4:41; 9:6, 32; 10:32, and to the woman in 16:8, is not so much a psychological as a theological phenomenon, being tantamount to a lack of faith or of spiritual insight. He further suggests that the spiritual insensibility in Gethsemane is indicated by sleep (not fear) because in this case (14:33) fear and anguish characterise the Messiah himself (*ibid.*, p. 286, n. 27). But could it be that the sleep motif is introduced into the Gethsemane story through the influence of 13:36? In any case, if the fear at 4:41 *etc.* (including 9:6) has the same technical significance as the fear at 16:8, the unitary thesis we are defending is further strengthened.

4. In Mark 1–13 the story of the triumphal entry (11:1–10) is to the parable of the wicked husbandmen (12:1–12) what in Mark 14–16 the story of the anointing (14:3–9) is to the account of the nocturnal trial (14:55–65). For in 11:1–10, as in 14:3–9, the evangelist's faith in Jesus' Christhood is pressing for a mode of open expression in defiance of the requirements of his doctrine of the messianic secret,[112] and in 12:12, as in 14:62, the pressure (reinforced by a desire to blame the Jewish authorities for the crucifixion) becomes so great that all barriers confining the salvific truth are broken down.

5. In 14:61f. the momentous reply ("I am; and you shall see the Son of Man sitting at the right hand of Power and coming with the clouds of heaven") to the high priest's question ("Are you the Messiah, the Son of the Blessed?") is reminiscent of 13:26 ("And then they shall see the Son of Man coming in clouds with great power and glory"), as well as of 8:38 ("For whoever is ashamed of me and of my words in this adulterous and sinful generation, of him shall the Son of Man also be ashamed when he comes in the glory of his Father with the holy angels"). These are in fact the only Markan passages which refer to the awaited eschatological coming of the Son of Man, and so they constitute yet another illustration of the evangelist's predilection for triads. There is no allusion to clouds (cf. Dan. 7:13) in 8:38, but it is noteworthy that, like 14:62, the pronouncement has a forensic connection:[113] in 8:38 the Son of Man is

[112] It is unfortunate that Trocmé (see esp. pp. 99, n. 97, 123, n. 63) is disinclined to take the theory of the secret with the seriousness it deserves.

[113] Cf. P. Vielhauer, *Aufsätze zum Neuen Testament* (Munich, 1965), pp. 76ff., 101ff., and E. Haenchen, "Die Komposition von Mk.VIII 27—IX 1 und Par." in *Nov.T.*, VI (1963), 81ff.

quite definitely introduced in his capacity as the ultimate judge of mankind, and the declaration of 14:62 is addressed to the judges of the Jewish high court, the implication being that the *eschaton* will bring about a turning of the tables—those who now judge will themselves by judged, and he who is now judged will himself preside over the great assize at the end of the world. Moreover, besides forming a fitting third constituent of a series of three, 14:62 represents a rudimentary christological synthesis, for it confirms the validity of Peter's assertion of Jesus' Messiahship (8:29) and offers further support for the doctrine of his divine Sonship (cf. 1:11; 3:11; 9:7).

6. Though each of the predictions in 8:31; 9:31; 10:33f. has its climax in a reference to the resurrection, almost all the details given concern its prelude in the passion; and this corresponds strikingly to the comparative brevity of the story of the empty tomb (16:1–8) in relation to the detailed passion narrative of the two preceding chapters.

7. The argument that the superscription "The beginning of the gospel of Jesus, Messiah, Son of God" (1:1) requires another ending than 16:1–8), an ending in which Peter acknowledges Jesus as Son of God,[114] is not a strong one, for the Jewish confession at 8:29 has its Gentile counterpart in the centurion's confession of the divine Sonship at 15:39. So it is arguable that the person who wrote 1:1 was also

[114] Cf. C. H. Turner in *A New Commentary on Holy Scripture including the Apocrypha*, ed. C. Gore and others (London, 1929), Pt. 3, p. 124. The omission of the title "Son of God" from the text of Mark 1:1 by certain ancient authorities (including the Codex Sinaiticus and Origen) is regarded by Turner as accidental; he points out that accidental omission would be especially easy in this case since, being a sacred designation, the expression had probably been subjected to abbreviation (*ibid.*, Pt. 3, pp. 50f.).

responsible for inserting 15:39 into the passion narrative as he received it.[115]

[115] In his paper "Erwägungen zur Christologie des Markus-evangeliums," reprinted from the Bultmann *Dankesgabe, Zeit und Geschichte* (Tübingen, 1964), in his *Aufsätze zum Neuen Testament* (Munich, 1965), P. Vielhauer puts the confession of Mark 15:39 in a new light. He argues that the evangelist distinguishes three stages in his portrayal of the divinely regal Sonship of Jesus, and he sees a significant parallel in the triadic scheme of the enthronement ceremonial that existed in ancient Egypt. To translate Vielhauer's own words: "The baptism corresponds to the apotheosis: Jesus receives the divine gift of the Spirit and is adopted as God's Son. The transfiguration corresponds to the presentation; he is set forth and proclaimed as a heavenly and earthly being in his dignity. The crucifixion corresponds to the actual enthronement; world-dominion is handed over to the Crucified One, as is made clear by the cosmic marvels, by the acclamation of the centurion who represents humanity, and then at 16:6 by the word of the angel" (*Aufsätze*, p. 213). Thus the pronouncements of 1:11; 9:7 and 15:39 constitute a dramatic triad, signifying that the baptism is to be understood as adoption, the transfiguration as proclamation, and the crucifixion as acclamation—three events that are made mysteriously impressive through being uniquely accompanied by miraculous cosmic signs (*ibid.*, p. 213, n. 46a). Vielhauer defends his thesis with singular acuteness, but certain points seem to require further consideration: (a) In view of 12:6, 10f., can 1:11 really be construed as a formula of adoption which excludes the Son's pre-existence? See Vielhauer, *loc. cit.*, p. 200; and *M.R.*, pp. 16ff. (b) Is there sufficient evidence for the view that the enthronement ritual is exemplified in such extra-Markan passages as 1 Tim. 3:16 and Heb. 1:5ff.? (See Vielhauer, *loc. cit.*, p. 212). (c) Do not the testimonies of the demons (1:24, 34; 3:11f.; 5:7) and of Jesus himself (14:62) upset the alleged triadic schematism? If the title "Son of God" in 15:39, where it is without the article and where the verb is in the past, has its high christological sense, why should it not have the same kind of significance in 3:11, where there are two articles and where the verb is in the present? The ascription of the messianic title to Jesus (legitimatized at 1:1 and 14:62) is followed by an injunction to silence (8:29f.), and, analogously, ascriptions of the filial title to him (legitimatized at 1:1 and 14:62) are also followed by injunctions to silence (3:11f.). See Vielhauer, pp. 209ff., and *M.R.*,

8. A fondness for the introduction of one story into the body of another is evidenced both in the passion narrative and in the preceding chapters. Such intercalations sometimes simply allow for a lapse of time (see 5:21–43), sometimes they suggest a parallel (see 3:20–35; 11:12–25), and sometimes they set forth a contrast (see 6:7–30; 14:1–11; 14:53–72).

9. The account of the public activity of John the Baptist (1:2–9) is much more sketchy than the story of his death (6:14–29), and similarly the Markan account of Jesus' ministry (1:14–13:36) is much more sketchy than the passion narrative (14:1ff.).

10. If, as Trocmé (p. 54) contends, the ending of the gospel at 16:8 is abrupt, may not the same be said of its opening paragraphs, where John the Baptist and Jesus of Nazareth are introduced without any notifications about the circumstances of their birth and upbringing?

---

pp. 62ff., 96ff. (d) Can the three disciples who witness the transfiguration be authentically likened to the gods who feature at the Presentation, the second high-point in the old enthronement ceremonial? Cf. the "rabbi" in 9:5 and the words "he did not know" in 9:6. (e) The acclamation of 15:39 takes place *before* the resurrection (cf. 16:6), which is the Messiah's exaltation to the right hand of God (see Vielhauer, p. 213, n. 47), and can this order of events be said to harmonise with what occurs in the final phase of the cited Egyptian religious ritual? On the other hand, it has to be conceded that 15:39 (like 14:41) may bear witness to St. Mark's tendency to interpret the passion as the hour of the Christ's miraculous glorification (cf. above, p. 258), in which case, however, the doctrinal import of the passage would run counter to that of the angelic announcement in 16:6, where a time-lag between death and exaltation is implied (cf. *M.R.*, pp. 177ff., *et passim*). (f) If there is a triadic schematism in this general regard, would it not be more satisfactory to connect the three Markan passages 14:62 (self-proclamation), 15:39 (world-recognition) and 16:6 (resurrection as actualization of re-enthronement)?

So we bring to a termination our exposition and critical examination of *La formation de l'évangile selon Marc*, one of the most thorough and highly stimulating studies of the earliest gospel to appear in recent decades. Our main conclusions are: (*a*) that, since a lively sense of the supernatural was a widespread feature of primitive Christianity, the Markan gospel can scarcely reflect a dualism between rustic miracle materials of Galilean provenance and ethico-legalistic traditions of a more academic character that must have been derived from the relatively sophisticated *milieu* of the mother church at Jerusalem; (*b*) that, while the evangelist is averse to the Jewish leadership generally, he betrays a definite tendency to regard the Pharisees as the principal opponents of Jesus; and (*c*) that the Markan gospel did not pass through two editions, but was written in A.D. 70 or soon afterwards by a person who composed the first thirteen chapters to provide what might be termed a propaedeutic to a suitably adapted form of the traditional passion narrative.

Select Bibliography

(The present list is largely confined to books cited in the footnotes. Works marked with an asterisk contain useful pertinent bibliographies.)

Abrahams, I. *Studies in Pharisaism and the Gospels.* 2 vols., Cambridge, 1917–1924.

Ahlström, G. W. *Aspects of Syncretism in Israelite Religion.* Lund, 1963.

Allon, G. *Researches in the History of Israel.* 2 vols., Tel Aviv, 1957.

Bammel, E., ed., *The Trial of Jesus.* London, 1970.

Barrett, C. K. *Jesus and the Gospel Tradition.* London, 1967.

Beare, F. W. *The Earliest Records of Jesus.* Oxford, 1962.

Bertram, G. *Die Leidensgeschichte Jesu und der Christuskult.* Göttingen, 1922.

Best, E. *The Temptation and the Passion: The Markan Soteriology.* Cambridge, 1965.*

Betz, O. *What Do We Know About Jesus?* London, 1968.

Bevan, E. *Hellenism and Christianity.* London, 1921.

Black, M. *An Aramaic Approach to the Gospels and Acts.* 3rd ed., Oxford, 1967.

Brandon, S. G. F. *Jesus and the Zealots.* Manchester, 1967.

Büchler, A. *Der Galiläische 'Am-ha-'Ares.* Vienna, 1906.

Bultmann, R. *Die Geschichte der synoptischen Tradition.* 4th ed.,

Göttingen, 1958. English trans., *The History of the Synoptic Tradition*. Oxford, 1968.

Bultmann, R. *Theology of the New Testament.* 2 vols., London, 1952–1955.

Bundy, W. E. *Jesus and the First Three Gospels.* Cambridge, Mass., 1955.

Burkill, T. A. *God and Reality in Modern Thought.* Englewood Cliffs, N.J., 1963.

———. *Mysterious Revelation: An Examination of the Philosophy of St. Mark's Gospel.* Ithaca, N.Y., 1963.*

Bussmann, W. *Synoptische Studien.* 3 vols. Halle, 1925–1931.

Buttrick, G. A., ed., *The Interpreter's Dictionary of the Bible.* 4 vols. Nashville, Tenn., 1962.

Cadoux, A. T. *The Sources of the Second Gospel.* London, 1935.

Carrington, P. *The Primitive Christian Calendar: A Study in the Making of the Marcan Gospel.* Vol. I: "Introduction and Text." Cambridge, 1952.

———. *According to Mark: A Running Commentary on the Oldest Gospel.* Cambridge, 1960.

Catchpole, D. R. *The Trial of Jesus.* Leiden, 1971.*

Cranfield, C. E. B. *The Gospel according to Saint Mark.* Cambridge, 1959.

Cross, F. L., ed., *Studia Evangelica II.* Berlin, 1964.

———, ed., *Studia Evangelica IV.* Berlin, 1968.

Cullmann, O. *The Christology of the New Testament.* London, 1959.

———. *Salvation in History.* London, 1965.

Dibelius, M. *From Tradition to Gospel.* London, 1934.

———. *Studies in the Acts of the Apostles.* London, 1956.

Dinkler, E., ed., *Zeit und Geschichte: Dankesgabe an Rudolf Bultmann.* Tübingen, 1964.

Dodd, C. H. *New Testament Studies.* Manchester, 1954.

Ebeling, H. J. *Das Messiasgeheimnis und die Botschaft des Marcus-Evangelisten.* Berlin, 1939.

Eliade, M. *The Sacred and the Profane.* New York, 1961.

Elliott-Binns, L. E. *Galilean Christianity*. London, 1956.

Enslin, M. S. *The Prophet from Nazareth*. New York, 1961.

Farmer, W. R. *The Synoptic Problem: A Critical Analysis*. New York, 1964.

Filson, F. V. *A Commentary on the Gospel According to St. Matthew*. New York, 1960.

Finegan, J. *Light from the Ancient Past*. Princeton, 1946.

Fridrichsen, A. *Le problème du miracle dans le Christianisme primitif*. Strasbourg, 1925.

Gerhardsson, B. *Memory and Manuscript*. Uppsala and Lund, 1961.

Glover, T. R. *The Conflict of Religions in the Early Roman Empire*. London, 1918.

Goguel, M. *L'évangile de Marc et ses rapports avec ceux de Mattieu et de Luc*. Paris, 1909.

——. *The Life of Jesus*. London, 1933.

——. *La naissance du christianisme*. Paris, 1946. English trans., *The Birth of Christianity*. London, 1953.

Gore, C., H. L. Goudge, and A. Guillaume, eds., *A New Commentary on Holy Scripture including the Apocrypha*. London, 1929.

Grässer, E. *Das Problem der Parousieverzögerung in den synoptischen Evangelien und in der Apostelgeschichte*. Berlin, 1960.

Haenchen, E. *Die Apostelgeschichte*. 3rd ed., Göttingen, 1959.

——. *Der Weg Jesu: Eine Erklärung des Markus-Evangeliums und der kanonischen Parallelen*. Berlin, 1966.

Hahn, F. *The Titles of Jesus in Christology: Their History in Early Christianity*. London, 1969.

Hare, D. R. A. *The Theme of Jewish Persecution of Christians in the Gospel According to St. Matthew*. Cambridge, 1967.

Hartman, L. *Prophecy Interpreted*. Lund, 1966.

Higgins, A. J. B., ed., *New Testament Essays: Studies in Memory of Thomas Walter Manson 1893–1958*. Manchester, 1959.

——. *Jesus and the Son of Man*. London, 1964.

Horstmann, M. *Studien zur Markinischen Christologie*. Munster, 1969.

Johnson, S. E. *A Commentary on the Gospel according to St. Mark*. London, 1960.

Jüngel, E. *Paulus und Jesus: Eine Untersuchung zur Präzierung der Frage nach dem Ursprung der Christologie*. 2nd ed., Tübingen, 1964.

Keck, L. E., and J. L. Martyn, eds., *Studies in Luke-Acts*. Nashville, Tenn., 1966.

Klausner, J. *Jesus of Nazareth: His Life, Times and Teaching*. London, 1925.

Klostermann, E. *Das Markusevangelium*. Tübingen, 1936.

Kümmel, W. G. *Verheissung und Erfüllung*. Basel, 1945.

Lagrange, M. J. *Evangile selon Saint Marc*. Paris, 1929.

Lambrecht, J. *Die Redaktion der Markus-Apokalypse*. Rome, 1967.

Lightfoot, R. H. *History and Interpretation in the Gospels*. London, 1935.

——. *Locality and Doctrine in the Gospels*. London, 1938.

——. *The Gospel Message of St. Mark*. Oxford, 1950.

Lohmeyer, E. *Galiläa und Jerusalem*. Göttingen, 1936.

——. *Das Evangelium des Markus*. Göttingen, 1951.

Lohse, E. *Märtyrer und Gottesknecht: Untersuchungen zur urchristlichen Verkündigung vom Sühnetod Jesu Christi*. Göttingen, 1955.

Loisy, A. *Les évangiles synoptiques*. 2 vols. Paris, 1907–1908.

——. *L'évangile selon Marc*. Paris, 1912.

Manson, T. W. *The Teaching of Jesus*. Cambridge, 1935.

——. *The Sayings of Jesus*. London, 1949.

Martyn, J. L. *History and Theology in the Fourth Gospel*. New York, 1968.

Marxsen, W. *Der Evangelist Markus: Studien zur Redaktionsgeschichte des Evangeliums*. Göttingen, 1956; 2nd ed., 1959. English trans., *Mark the Evangelist: Studies on the Redaction History of the Gospel*. Nashville, Tenn., 1969.

Meyer, R. *Tradition und Neuschöpfung im antiken Judentum.* Berlin, 1965.

Minette de Tillesse, G. *Le secret messianique dans l'évangile de Marc.* Paris, 1968.*

Montefiore, C. G. *The Synoptic Gospels.* London, 1927.

Overbeck, F. *Kurze Erklärung der Apostelgeschichte.* Leipzig, 1870.

Perrin, N. *Rediscovering the Teaching of Jesus.* London, 1967.

Quesnell, Q. *The Mind of Mark.* Rome, 1969.*

Reploh, K. G. *Markus—Lehrer der Gemeinde.* Stuttgart, 1969.

Riesenfeld, H. *Jésus Transfiguré.* Copenhagen, 1947.

———. *The Gospel Tradition.* Philadelphia, 1970.

Robinson, J. M. *Das Geschichtsverständnis des Markusevangeliums.* Zurich, 1956. English trans., *The Problem of History in Mark.* London, 1957.

Sanders, E. P. *The Tendencies of the Synoptic Tradition.* Cambridge, 1969.

Sandmel, S. *The First Christian Century in Judaism and Christianity.* New York, 1969.

Schmithals, W. *Paulus und Jakobus.* Göttingen, 1963.

Schreiber, J. *Theologie des Vertrauens.* Hamburg, 1967.

Schulz, H. J., ed. *Die Zeit Jesu. Kontexte III.* Stuttgart, 1966.

Schürer, E. *Die Geschichte des jüdischen Volkes im Zeitalter Jesu Christi.* 4 vols. 3rd and 4th ed., Leipzig, 1901–1911.

Schweizer, E. *Das Evangelium nach Markus.* Göttingen, 1968. English trans., *The Good News According to Mark.* London, 1971.

Sharman, H. B. *Son of Man and Kingdom of God.* New York, 1943.

Simon, M. *St. Stephen and the Hellenists in the Primitive Church.* New York, 1958.

Sjöberg, E. *Der verborgene Menschensohn in den Evangelien.* Lund, 1955.

Streeter, B. H. *The Four Gospels: A Study of Origins.* London, 1924.

Suhl, A. *Die Funktion der alttestamentlichen Zitate und Anspielungen im Markusevangelium.* Gütersloh, 1965.

Taylor, V. *The Gospel according to St. Mark.* London, 1952.

Tennant, F. R. *Philosophical Theology.* 2 vols. Cambridge, 1928.

Tödt, H. E. *The Son of Man in the Synoptic Tradition.* London, 1965.

Turner, C. H. *The Gospel According to St. Mark.* London, 1928.

Trocmé, E. *La formation de l'évangile selon Marc.* Paris, 1963.*

Vaganay, L. *Le problème synoptique: une hypothèse de travail.* Tournai, 1954.

Vermes, G. *Scripture and Tradition in Judaism.* Leiden, 1961.

Vielhauer, P., ed., *Festschrift für Günther Dehn.* Neukirchen, 1957.

———. *Aufsätze zum Neuen Testament.* Munich, 1965.

Wellhausen, J. *Das Evangelium Marci.* Berlin, 1903.

———. *Einleitung in die drei ersten Evangelien.* Berlin, 1911.

Wolff, H. W. *Jesaja 53 im Urchristentum.* Berlin, 1952.

Winter, P. *On the Trial of Jesus.* Berlin, 1961.

Wrede, W. *Das Messiasgeheimnis in den Evangelien.* Göttingen, 1901.

Index

*New Light on
the Earliest Gospel*

Designed by R. E. Rosenbaum.
Composed by Kingsport Press, Inc.
in 11 point linotype Janson, 3 points leaded,
with display lines in monotype Janson.
Printed letterpress from type by Kingsport Press
on Warren's 1854 text, 60 pound basis,
with the Cornell University Press watermark.
Bound by Kingsport Press
in Columbia book cloth
and stamped in All Purpose foil.

Library of Congress Cataloging in Publication Data
(For library cataloging purposes only)

Burkill, T   Alec.
   New light on the earliest Gospel.

   Bibliography: p.
   1. Bible. N. T. Mark—Criticism, interpretation, etc.—Addresses,
essays, lectures. I. Title.
BS2585.2.B83   225'.3'066   74-37777
ISBN 0-8014-0706-0